1999

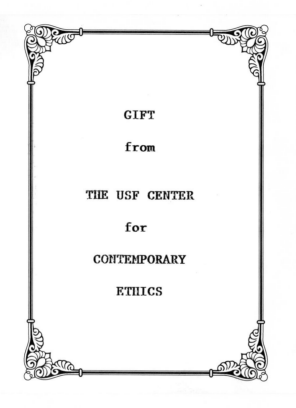

WRONGNESS, WISDOM, AND WILDERNESS

SUNY Series in Social and Political Thought
Kenneth Baynes, Editor

WRONGNESS, WISDOM, AND WILDERNESS

Toward a Libertarian Theory of Ethics and the Environment

TAL SCRIVEN

State University
of New York
Press

Published by
State University of New York Press, Albany

© 1997 State University of New York

Production by Susan Geraghty
Marketing by Bernadette LaManna

Printed in the United States of America

For information, address State University of New York
Press, State University Plaza, Albany, N.Y., 12246

Library of Congress Cataloging-in-Publication Data

Scriven, Tal.
    Wrongness, wisdom, and wilderness : toward a libertarian theory of
ethics and the environment / Tal Scriven.
        p.   cm.
    Includes bibliographical references and index.
    ISBN 0-7914-3371-4 (hardcover : alk. paper). — ISBN 0-7914-3372-2
(pbk. : alk. paper)
    1. Environmental ethics. 2. Utilitarianism. 3. Libertarianism.
4. Human ecology.
    GE42.S37 1997
    179'.1—dc20
                                                                96-26396
                                                                CIP

10 9 8 7 6 5 4 3 2 1

For Jeremy, Casey, and Winter Lee

CONTENTS

PART 3   WILDERNESS

ACKNOWLEDGMENTS

The following individuals have read various parts of this book and made valuable comments: Luc Bovens, Jane Cullen, Peter French, John Hospers, Glenn Irvin, Edward Johnson, Russell Lascola, Joe Lynch, Paul Miklowitz, Laleh Quinn, Shannon Toshach, and several anonymous reviewers. Special thanks are due to Clay Morgan, Susan Geraghty, and everyone else at SUNY Press who laid hands on the manuscript.

Special thanks are also due to Cal Poly, the University of Colorado, and the National Endowment for the Humanities for generous support of the research that went into this project.

INTRODUCTION

At the beginning of this decade, an article in the *New York Times* entitled "Europe Recycles American Liberalism" gave voice to a commonly perceived irony about contemporary political theory: The ideals of Locke, Jefferson, and Mill were (and still are) quite alive and well in Poland, Czechoslovakia, Germany, France, and even Russia and China while, in America, academics have been bogged down for decades in an amorphous muck of neo-Marxism, neofascism, neoclassicism, postmodernism, and, now, postdeconstructionism. By the end of the 1980s, the fascination for anything antiliberal

> had come to dominate American literary and scholarly conversation. . . . The language of American liberalism—in a prosaic dialect of surveys and statistics—was spoken in the 1980s only by social scientists, think-tankers and other policy intellectuals. Of the liberal imagination, spirit and tradition, little was heard.[1]

Although there is some truth in this assessment, the rumors of the death of liberalism among American academics were being greatly exaggerated here. Certainly, attacks from both the left and the right have caused some serious reexamination over the last few years. Leftists have been successful in showing that liberalism carried to the libertarian extremes—as it is in works like Nozick's *Anarchy, State and Utopia*[2]—is, if nothing else, at least descriptively inadequate.[3] Nozick's theory just does not capture and, in fact, rules out as a matter of principle the institutionalization of various social welfare mechanisms that just about everyone in the West has come to view as essential in any civilized society. Other critics, often coming from a neoclassical point of view, have had some success in showing that theories based mainly on macroscopic distributional considerations (like utilitarianism and Rawls's theory of justice) appear to say little of real value about how individuals ought to analyze and conduct their day-to-day lives. As a consequence, there has been considerable interest lately in various theories about individual virtue and wisdom as well as various approaches to applied ethics that are often completely atheoretical.

Nevertheless, American moral and political philosophy has been, and continues to be, dominated by debates within the tradition of Enlightenment liberalism. A list of the major players in the game over the last thirty years would have to include Rawls, Brandt, Dworkin, Feinberg, Gauthier, Gibbard, Nozick, Raz, and Sen. All of these figures (and many others who could be listed) are either themselves liberals or are widely known mostly because of their writings about liberalism. But, even though most of the work going on in the field is within this single tradition, there remains considerable disagreement about the essential issues involved in social and individual morality. Moreover, the basic relationship between social and individual morality remains especially problematic. In addition, things have been further complicated lately by concerns about our relationship, as individuals and as societies, with the natural world. A large chunk of the recent writings on environmental ethics has centered on the assertion that Enlightenment thought generally, and Enlightenment moral theory specifically, is utterly incapable of reckoning with contemporary ecological realities.

A large part of the difficulty with contemporary moral theory is to be found in the fact that a major assumption that runs all through the philosophy of the Enlightenment has been variously misstated, misunderstood, or ignored. The assumption I have in mind is the one that the relationship between the individual, the state, and nature is one of opposition. The job of government is to leave people to pursue their own ends as they see fit and to secure them from the brutishness of the wild without asking for submission to a social tyranny that might be worse than wilderness.

I take this antiholism to be the single most important feature of Enlightenment moral thought. Moreover, the failure to take antiholism seriously is, I think, the single most important cause of a lot of misguided contemporary criticism of Enlightenment theories. On the assumption of antiholism, one should not expect that a normative theory would be able to address different kinds of moral problems under a single unifying principle. What might work as a theory of social ethics cannot be expected to work as a theory about the worth of life to the individual. Similarly, whatever values predominate in a social ethic cannot be expected to be grounded in any ends alleged to exist in the natural world.

One might think that this assumption guarantees the inference of a fairly extreme libertarianism (or, at least, a fairly strong anticommunitarianism), and, indeed, many of the consequences of the theory to be developed here are fairly libertarian (and definitely anticommunitarian). But my theory is not at all rooted in the rights approach of Locke and Nozick. (Nor does it have many of the unappealing consequences of this brand of libertarianism.) Rather, I see it growing out of the utilitarian tradition and, particularly, out of Mill's thought.

The plight of utilitarianism in this century gives us one of the best examples of how the confusion of individual with social ethics has led moral philosophy astray. Although the classical utilitarians did spend some time talking about individual virtues and practical wisdom, they never put forth anything as myopic as what is referred to in the textbooks as "act utilitarianism." They were, as I will argue later, mainly concerned with questions of legislation and other forms of social control. Nevertheless, of the routine criticisms against utilitarianism, the most serious are those that attack the theory because of its failures as an individual ethic. The objections against it as a social ethic are not really compelling at all; most of them were, in fact, convincingly handled by Mill over a century ago.

Making this claim stick will be one of the first orders of business in this work. I will then attempt to formulate a version of utilitarianism that renders it deliberately silent on questions related to the meaning of life for individuals. This silence, I will argue, is not at all ad hoc from an historical perspective; it is, in fact, something that figures like Mill were often struggling to maintain. Moreover, this silence will give my theory a kind of descriptive adequacy that other forms of utilitarianism lack. I then propose a theory that still retains a starkly utilitarian theory of wrongness but is based on the abandonment of all hope of finding a sensible theory of the good. The problem with all theories of the good, be they utilitarian or not, is that they collide viciously with the pluralistic foundations of liberalism.[4] The common moral sense of the liberal West is that one's actions should be liable to social control only upon the demonstration of likely dire consequences in the absence of control. Otherwise, individuals are to decide for themselves (and only for themselves) what is the best and wisest course of a life. This, of course, is exactly Mill's position.[5]

In Part II of the book, I will attempt an outline of some of the theories that might serve as candidates to fill the vacuum left at the individual level. I will be drawing on philosophers as diverse as Plato, Nietzsche, and Mill, not in order to fully elaborate a distinctive theory of individual wisdom but, rather, to give some picture of what such a theory might look like and to show the important respects in which such theories can't be seen as parts of social theories or evaluated from a social point of view. Although there are interesting connections between social theories like utilitarianism and certain theories about how to live one's life, these connections are very roundabout, and it is not philosophically desirable (although it might be logically possible) to reduce the social level of moral concern to the individual level. Social morality and individual wisdom are just about different things; social morality should concern itself with the prevention of harm; individual wisdom should concern itself with the pursuit of the good. To reduce either branch of normative theory to the other is simply to confuse the nature of both.

Finally, in Part III, I will turn to concerns about our relationship with nature. There is a growing literature concerning the suitability of applying so-called anthropocentric theories like utilitarianism to environmental issues. Given the antithesis between individual wisdom and social ethics I will try to establish in the first two parts of the book, it might seem natural that I would favor some sort of "ecocentric" ethic to handle that dimension of moral concerns. However, I will argue that there is something fundamentally confusing about ecocentrism, namely, that its expositors are not being altogether clear about whether their theory is supposed to be a theory about environmental social policy or, rather, a theory of individual wisdom or, perhaps, a theory about both. As a theory about social ethics, I will be arguing that ecocentrism ought to be rejected on the grounds that the position is largely either incoherent or not in sync with the best available accounts of how nature really works. As a theory of wisdom, however, I think there is much about the theory that is clear, right, and interesting.

PART 1

Wrongness

CHAPTER 1

Self and State:
A Historical Perspective

The general Enlightenment project was built on (at least) three basic ideas. First was the faith that only reason and common sensibility could be appealed to in the solution of practical problems. This was held to be true both for technological problems and moral ones. Although this criterion is remarkably vague, and various Enlightenment thinkers tended to place varying degrees of emphasis on either reason or sensibility (sometimes to the near exclusion of the other), the principal aim of this tenet was to rule out of court diverse appeals to authority and tradition in the settlement of practical disputes. To attempt here any respectable clarification of the notions of reason and common sensibility would be to recount huge chunks of the philosophy of the last three or four centuries, and so I will leave the whole matter to the side. Nevertheless, I believe it is reasonable to assert that this assumption (or its clarification) occupies center stage in almost all modern and contemporary philosophical disputes.

The second major faith of the Enlightenment was that nature, as a whole, is devoid of any teleological ends; it is brute mechanism, holding no good clues about what we ought to value, and, furthermore, it is generally hostile to our legitimate goals as individuals and societies. This tenet, of course, has played a huge role in the history and philosophy of science. It also played, and is still playing, a large role as regards our ethical attitudes and policies respecting the natural environment. This consequence of Enlightenment thought will be a central concern in Part III of this book.

The third faith of the Enlightenment was specifically political. It was an explicit premise in the political writings of almost all of the major moralists of the time that, although the establishment of the state is necessary in order for humans to have many real freedoms, once we collectively remove ourselves from the state of nature we will, as individuals, constantly find ourselves at odds with governments that seem to have a tendency to require much more of us than is legitimated by the need to maintain a civil society. The aim of this tenet was to deny a principle about the relationship between the individual and the state that appears to have its origin in Plato's *Republic*.[1] Its effect is evident in most classical and medieval thought, in modern conservatism and monarchism, and in twentieth-century fascism. That principle was the one that claimed an "organic unity" of citizen and state. Just as the value of the individual organs belonging to an organism consists in their contributions to the welfare of the organism, so too does the value of the citizens in the state consist in their contribution to the welfare of the state itself. Of course, the state could not exist without citizens any more than any organism could exist without organs. But, just as organs are useless and without value outside of their functional roles in the organism, so too are citizens who step outside of their functional roles in the state. Moreover, just as a cancerous organ may be sacrificed in order to improve the well-being of the organism, so too a dysfunctional individual's rights must be expendable on behalf of the state.

Despite Hobbes's endorsement of the analogy between organism and state on the first page of the *Leviathan*, and despite the monarchist conservatism of his contractarianism, he usually goes down as one of the first moderns to deny this sort of holism in favor of political "atomism." One need only list the names of a few of Hobbes's heirs in the British and American Enlightenment to make clear the depth of the rejection of organic holism over the next two centuries.

But the rejection of holism is hardly specific to Locke, Jefferson, and Mill. On the first page of *On Liberty*, Mill recognizes his debt to von Humboldt. And, of course, there is another German who is famous for his claim that the state would, in time, "wither away." In the French tradition, the case of Rousseau presents an interesting challenge.

Rousseau's thought is often seen by libertarians as a dangerous prelude to the collectivism that would run amuck in the nineteenth and twentieth centuries. His talk of a "general will" that supersedes "the will of all" and of a need for individuals to be "forced to be free" might even cause a Marxist to pause. But I think there is a way of interpreting Rousseau's ideas so that they are pretty far removed from Marxist collectivism and nowhere near fascist holism.

One ventures interpretations of Rousseau at one's own peril, and I should point out that my intent here is not to give any interpretation that is consistent with the whole of his thought. I am interested simply in drawing out one thread of his work that will place him at least at the edge of Enlightenment libertarianism, and, also, in raising some issues that will be central to remarks that I will make later about more clearly libertarian figures like Mill.

Rousseau's concepts of the "general will," the "will of all," and "forced freedom" must, of course, be understood within the context of his general theory of the social contract. The most useful analysis of the foundation of Rousseau's contract theory is to be found in an old article by W. G. Runciman and A. K. Sen.[2] Their analysis starts from a consideration of the prisoner's dilemma (as have many recent analyses of social contract theory). I will not bother to recount the tale that gives the dilemma its name. Prisoners and confessions aside, the following is a prisoner's dilemma:

		B	
		brutal	*civil*
	brutal	1, 1	3, 0
A			
	civil	0, 3	2, 2

In this situation, A's payoffs appear first and the numbers simply represent ordinal rankings by the two parties involved over the four possible outcomes. The outcome of both parties acting brutally toward one another is meant to represent the state of nature, that is, the state humans find themselves in before the establishment of a social contract. An easy assumption is that this state of affairs (1,1) is worse for both A and B than the one where they cooperate and form an enforceable social contract that constrains them (under threat of punitive sanction) to be civil toward one another (2,2). However, either party would find it most advantageous to be in a situation where he or she could brutally victimize the other. Thus, the (3,0) outcome is best for A while the (0,3) outcome is best for B. But neither party could bring about the desired outcome without causing the war of all against all that leads back to the state of nature.

The dilemma of this situation is that A and B will not be able to enforce a mutually advantageous contract without appeal to an outside authority. Simply promising to be civil rather than brutal will not bring about the desired outcome. Regardless of B's action, it will be advantageous for A to act brutally and, moreover, for A to break any mere promises made to B that A would be civil. The situation is identical for B. So, left to their own devices, A and B will both wind up being brutal (1,1), a state of affairs inferior for both of them to the one where they are both civil (2,2).

There is a straightforward sense in which A and B are being "forced to be free" when they submit to an enforceable contract to be civil. Given a choice between (1,1) and (2,2), either party would freely choose (2,2), and this freedom exists only after the establishment of a contract. Moreover, there is considerable sense in thinking of the postcontractual situation (2,2) as being a manifestation of the "general will" while the precontractual equilibrium point (1,1) is the result of the "will of all" (the will of each acting individually).

All of this points to the fact that Rousseau seemed to be aware of a subtlety in the relation between state and individual that Bentham (among others) was almost completely insensitive to. Bentham claimed that a community could be no more than a matter of the simple "sum" of the interests of the individuals in that community.[3] What the foregoing shows is that the amalgamation of interests in a contractual situation is hardly just a matter of simple summation.

In the first place, the prisoner's dilemma nicely points out that the matter of summation is not simple. There is a clear sense in which the equilibrium outcome (1,1) represents the maximal sum of utility because it is the product of joint action directed under the principle that each individual ought to maximize his or her own expected utility. However, the optimal outcome (2,2) represents the maximal sum of utility *if that outcome can be made available* (and, of course, it can with the establishment of a contract). The identification of the maximal sum, then, depends upon something more than just adding up the numbers; it depends upon the availability of an enforceable contract.

Secondly, we could replace the occurrences of "3" with "5" in the payoff matrix of the previous situation and (under an assumption of cardinality that Bentham would be willing to make) make either the (5,0) or (0,5) payoff the one with a maximal sum, although neither outcome would be an equilibrium one nor would either be practically accessible.

Thirdly, what all of the foregoing ought to make clear is that the manner in which utility is *distributed* over the available outcomes has everything to do with the manner in which the prisoner's dilemma will play out. This consideration is linked to other well-known problems associated with the Benthamian doctrine that the interests of the community can be easily cashed out as the sum of the interests of the individuals in that community. Given three individuals (A, B, and C), two alternatives (x and y), and the following choice situation:

	A	B	C
x	9	9	9
y	0	0	27

a choice principle based on simple summation would yield indifference between x and y. However, all things being equal and all individuals being equally deserving, it would seem that x is clearly better than y. Regardless of the intuitive power that can be generated against Bentham's summation principle by this kind of situation (which isn't much, as we shall see in Chapter 3), the prisoner's dilemma *does* raise some very real distributional concerns that, again, Rousseau seemed to understand in a way that Bentham didn't.

Nevertheless, there is no reason to suspect contract theorists like Rousseau of holding some doctrine of a mystical organic unity that reigns over individuals. The state is ultimately founded on nothing beyond the thoughtful interests of its citizens.But is it possible to derive more than this simple liberalism from Rousseau? Although I have no intention of making Rousseau a libertarian, something far more libertarian than any idea usually attributed to Rousseau does follow from the present analysis of the foundations of his social contract theory.

First, it must be recognized that the enforcement of the contract is not only *a* basis for the establishment of state authority, it is the *only* legitimate basis of that authority. Moreover, individuals need not consent to just any contract. Any number of contractual arrangements (ranging from very libertarian to very authoritarian) will, in principle, be able to insure the establishment of some sort of civility. It would seem that all individuals must commit themselves to, and all that any state has an uncontroversial right to enforce, would be a *minimal* contract, that is, a contract that imposes just enough force to secure civility. The establishment of a regime that would do more than this would seem to go beyond the bounds of what can be secured by the kind of unanimous consent essential to the establishment of a genuine and genuinely justifiable contract.[4] This does not imply that each specific piece of legislation must meet with anything approaching unanimity. However, the general regime under which legislation is derived must be based on unanimity and, thus, any piece of legislation that could not be argued to be essential to the preservation of civility would be unjustifiable to the degree that it was inessential. That a specific regulation would be approved by a majority or be productive of increased welfare for most would not serve as sufficient grounds for the regulation. Even though unanimity need not be guaranteed for each piece of regulation, it is the basis of the contract itself.

Second, a major complication sets in when we begin to wonder about the specifics of the options and outcomes laid out in the preceding table. What, precisely, does "civil" denote? What does "brutal" mean? What do the numbers really represent? Let's start with the numbers. The standard explanation is that the numbers simply represent the raw preference orderings of the individuals involved. In other words, an outcome will be assigned a two for A and another outcome will be assigned a one for A simply because A prefers the former outcome to the latter.

But suppose A likes pain more than pleasure, and, moreover, he likes the suffering of B even more than he likes his own pain. Suppose, in addition, that B is normal, that is, she likes pleasure more than pain and prefers A's suffering to her own. Under these suppositions, how could we reach any optimal bargaining point upon which a contract could be based? The point here is that there must already be some common agreement about ultimate goods and evils before we even enter into a situation where a contract would be mutually beneficial. On the assumption that the basic values of A and B are as radically diverse as supposed above, no motivation for a contract exists. B would be best off simply by getting as far away from A as possible and, if A ever showed up in her vicinity, to be as brutal as possible toward him.

In the jargon of game theory, this situation is a zero-sum game in which an equilibrium is reached by virtue of mutual individual threat. No prisoner's dilemma arises and, as a consequence, no contract is at all beneficial to anyone; it's just dog-eat-dog.[5] Likewise if the basic values of A and B are disjoint, that is, A wants apples and B wants oranges, then we have a one-sum game in which, again, no contract is fortuitous for anyone.[6] It is only when A and B want to maximize their possession of the same sort of good (or minimize the occurrence of a common evil) and, moreover, the bargaining equilibrium is suboptimal that a contract makes sense.

In other words, unanimity is not only a criterion of a valid social contract, it is, at a deeper level (that of basic values), a precondition of even thinking about a contract in the first place. This is not a surprising conclusion, given the history of social contract theory. In Hobbes, Locke, and Rousseau, it is generally made quite clear that there are certain fundamental and universal goods (e.g., happiness and a tranquil state of affairs in which to pursue it) and evils (e.g., pain and violent death) that are to be achieved and avoided by the enforcement of a social contract.[7]

The following, then, opens up as an obvious line of reasoning: If the contract is to be the only basis of *legitimate* social control over the individual, and the only basis of the contract can be found in unanimously shared values then, to the degree that the state acts to restrain the individual for any reason other than that necessary for the optimization of unanimously shared values, its actions are less justifiable. Individuals who can wrangle a better deal for themselves under some other contractual arrangement will, of course, find it rational to work toward the establishment of a contract that guarantees the delivery of their favored benefits (presumably at the expense of others who will not share in those benefits). But this has nothing to do with the *justifiability* of the *regimes* under which various benefits are delivered or not. Anyone can (and probably does) desire special treatment; they just can't *justify* it honestly.

The interesting question now is: How many values can be counted on to be unanimously shared by humans? If the number of such values is small, then the domain of legitimate social regulation is small as well. If, moreover, we place the burden of proving that the number of unanimously shared fundamental values is large on those who wish to extend the domain of social regulation, then we begin to approach libertarianism; a substantial private sphere will be created by the lack of good proof that certain individuals' actions are seriously injurious to the maintenance of the social contract. In other words, substantial individual rights will be created negatively rather than positively.[8]

Locke and Jefferson are good examples of theorists who just specified certain "inalienable" rights and thereby delimited, in a positive way, the range of legitimate social regulation. Under the previous analysis of Rousseau, he is viewed as a successor in the Hobbesian tradition of limiting social control by negative means and, thereby, granting individual rights negatively.[9] In the third chapter I will argue that this sort of attempt to limit social power by granting rights negatively, rather than positively, is central to an understanding of Mill's utilitarianism and his theory of individual liberty.

CHAPTER 2

Self and State:
A Theoretical Perspective

In the previous chapter I mentioned three basic faiths of the Enlightenment. The first two (namely, the ones that all practical wisdom rests on common sensibility and reason and that nature, as a whole, is non-teleological) are, for the most part, prospering in twentieth-century philosophy.

However, the axiom that the interests of the state and the individual are largely incompatible once the state has been established has, generally, been left behind. Although the voices of vested interests have been keen on recalling libertarianism's protection of property rights and low taxes for the rich, moral philosophy has, generally, proceeded to construct and criticize theories on the assumption that a good ethical theory will make prescriptions that extend nicely to all levels of ethical decision. A good moral theory will be composed of the smallest possible set of basic principles that will tell us how to act as individuals as well as how to construct social policy, international policy, and perhaps even environmental policy.

This assumption is not, of course, original to the twentieth century. It can be seen as a natural corollary of Occam's razor, a canon that plays an obvious and central role in modern science. Moreover, even if we look at just the utilitarian tradition, we find the classical utilitarians themselves apparently wholeheartedly engaged in the pursuit of a principle that, to use Bentham's words, will apply to "every action whatsoever; and therefore not only of every action of a private individual, but of every measure of government."[1]

Bentham, of course, is notorious for often missing the forest because he was too busy counting the trees. And so it is not too surprising that he didn't seem to see much of a theoretical problem in figuring aggregate utility as a straightforward function of individual utilities. Perhaps he should not be expected to shoulder too much blame, for, by his own admission in the preface of the *Principles*, he never thought of himself to be offering a systematic account of things like "emotion, passion, appetite, virtue, vice, and some others." Of the one work where Bentham did try to systematize his views about individual ethics (the *Deon-*

tology), Mill offers the dry comment, "We did not expect from Bentham correct systematic views of ethics . . ."[2]

It is in the writings of Mill where we do see both a reasonable understanding of the problems involving the relationship between social and individual ethics and a painful intellectual effort to alternately integrate and then separate the two levels of concern. The analytic crunch comes in the first chapter (pars. 10 and 11) of *On Liberty* when Mill states that the principle of liberty (now generally referred to as the harm principle) is neither self-evident nor absolute but, rather, based on the principle of utility. The problems with this claim are obvious, and Mill himself recognizes two of them in the fourth chapter (pars. 8 and 9) of *On Liberty*.

First, the antipaternalism so forcefully stated in the first chapter as being a consequence of the harm principle seems, in principle at any rate, to be in direct conflict with the principle of utility. Because harm is unconditionally bad, why shouldn't the state act paternalistically in cases where it can without causing more problems than it is solving? Secondly, and more generally, from a utilitarian point of view, the whole intuitive distinction between self-regarding action and social action is specious. All actions can be viewed as social and, thus, evaluated from an aggregate point of view; there simply is no private sphere of actions into which the felicific calculus cannot reach. Not only is it the case that the harm principle cannot be derived from the principle of utility, the two principles are incompatible.

The disturbing depth of this incompatibility between utility and liberty is made clear in a piece of contemporary social choice theory known as the liberal paradox. The original formal statement of the paradox is due to A. K. Sen.[3] A social decision rule is to be understood as a social welfare function (SWF) whose domain is the complete set of individual preferences relevant to an array of social alternatives and whose range is a social ordering over those alternatives.

The proof of the paradox is based on an assumption of three conditions. First is a condition common to most theorems in social choice theory known as the requirement of unrestricted domain (condition U). What this condition requires is that the SWF must work on all logically coherent configurations of individual preferences. So, if a SWF rules out, as a matter of principle, the possibility of a person A preferring alternative x to alternative y and y to a third alternative z, then it violates this condition. A SWF can, however, rule out incoherent preferences as would be the case if A preferred x to y, y to z, and z to x.

The second condition is known as the Pareto principle (condition P). It states that if everyone prefers x to y then x should be ranked above y by the SWF. Sen called the third principle "minimal liberalism" (condition L), which requires that there must be at least two individuals, A and B, each of whose personal choice is to be decisive, respectively, over two pairs of alternatives: x and y for A, and z and w for B. In other words, L is requiring that at least two people have complete personal freedom to make at least one choice each.

At first glance, compliance with P seems to be a remarkably minimal expectation of any remotely democratic SWF and L seems to be a condition that any remotely liberal SWF would meet. Thus, the problem caused by the following combination of individual preference orderings would seem to be that the weakest social guarantee of personal freedom is incompatible with the weakest form of democratic rule:

A	B
w	y
x	z
y	w
z	x

By L, we stipulate that A's personal choice concerns x and y, and B's personal choice concerns z and w. So, because A prefers x to y and B prefers z to w, the SWF must rank x over y and z over w. But, by P, the SWF must rank y over z and w over x since both A and B have these preferences. So, the SWF must rank x over y, y over z, z over w, and w over x, which is incoherent because of a failure of transitivity. Once again, it seems that there simply is no private sphere of action into which an aggregate decision principle cannot reach.

A less abstract rendition of the liberal paradox involves Sen's tale of the lewd and the prude. Here we are to imagine two high-minded proselytizers who each have a serious, nosy interest in what others read. One of them, Prude, would rather that no one read what he holds to be obscene material. (Sen's example of such material is *Lady Chatterly's Lover*.) However, if someone must read such filth, then Prude prefers that he be the one who has to read it rather than someone as corrupt and impressionable as Lewd. Prude's third choice is that Lewd reads the material while Prude is spared from exposure to it. The worst outcome for Prude would be the one where both he and Lewd are exposed to degeneracy.

Lewd, on the other hand would prefer that everyone be more enlightened as to the ways of lust and satisfaction. So her first choice is that both her and Prude read the book. If only one person is to read the book then, Lewd figures, it is better that that one person be Prude since he is in such desperate need of libidinous liberation. Lewd's third choice is for her to read the book while Prude does not. The worst outcome for Lewd is the one where neither she nor Prude are elevated by the book.

The preference orderings of Lewd and Prude, then, can be summarized as follows:

Lewd	Prude
Both read	Neither read
Only Prude reads	Only Prude reads
Only Lewd reads	Only Lewd reads
Neither read	Both read

What the Pareto Principle would require here is a social choice of the state of affairs where only Prude reads the book over the state of affairs where only Lewd reads the book, since both Lewd and Prude have these preferences. In other words, what is Pareto-optimal is that Prude read a book that he does not want to read while Lewd does not read a book that she does want to read. The minimally liberal intuition would be that each should read or not read whatever each wanted to and, moreover, that the preferences of the other have nothing to do with the situation.

Another way of viewing the Lewd-Prude problem is to see it as yet another instance of the prisoner's dilemma:

		Prude	
		reads	doesn't
Lewd	reads	3, 0	1, 1
	doesn't	2, 2	0, 3

As we saw last chapter, the problem with prisoner's dilemmas is that the equilibrium outcome in such cases is not optimal. But, in the above case, the suboptimal equilibrium outcome (1,1) seems to be the right one from a minimally liberal perspective.

What might seem to be an obvious problem with the argument for the liberal paradox is noted by Brian Barry[4] who argues that the fault with the proof lies in the initial assumption that liberalism (or libertarianism), even in a minimal form, says anything at all about what is "socially better." It simply states that, for example, A has a right to control the choice over x and y regardless of the fact that A's choice may result in less social welfare than would be the case if the decision were taken out of A's hands. To use one of Barry's examples, I have a right to paint my walls bright red if I choose even though more social utility might result for myself and for others who have occasion to see the walls if I am forced to paint them white. In the Lewd-Prude case, both Lewd and Prude have a right to read or not read whatever they want, and the social utility derived from the nosiness of others is irrelevant.

Ultimately, however, I must confess that I am as uncompelled by Barry's reasoning as is Sen, who responds that to leave the control of choice to the individual in this sort of case, indeed, *is* to have a *socially* enforced rule that gives the individual this right. Barry seems to have confused a solution to the problem with the problem itself. It is precisely the problem of marking off any private sphere that the liberal paradox is demonstrating. For Barry to insist that we must have an antecedent and socially accepted understanding of where, exactly, the limits of the private sphere are is for him to beg the main question.

And there is more to convince the skeptic of the reality of a fundamental conflict between minimal liberty and minimal concern for aggregate welfare. The obvious fact is that granting any individual any absolute liberty is bound, by definition, to lead to suboptimal outcomes any time that liberty is exercised in a meaningful way (i.e., in a way that conflicts with what conforms to aggregate welfare). I don't need any rights to guarantee my ability to do what everyone else wants me to do. But, as Aanund Hylland points out,[5] things are even more complicated than this in the usual case. Usually, having a right to do something also means that you cannot bargain away that right. For example, I cannot offer, and you cannot accept, a deal where I would give up my right to free speech or due process for ten years in exchange for, say, $20,000. If I really wanted to make such a deal then the presence of the right actually takes something away from me, namely, an opportunity to get $20,000 in return for some right I value less than that. Moreover, the person offering the $20,000 is also losing out since she obviously finds my silence worth the bucks. So, the right is, in this case, doubly nonoptimal.

All of this leads to yet a deeper level of perplexity. Throughout the literature of economics, there runs a line of reasoning that the ultimate justification for allowing maximal liberty is that such allows for the freest possible bargaining. With each bargain we reach a state of affairs that will be Pareto superior to the prebargain state of affairs, that is, everyone will be at least as well off as they were before and at least one person will be better off. If this is not the case, then the bargain will simply not be struck. If, for example, I don't value $20,000 more than my freedom of speech or if the other bargainer doesn't value my silence more than her $20,000, then there would not be a deal.

There is, of course, a rather quaint optimism in this line of thinking, namely, that all such deals occur without attendant negative externalities and that no questions will arise regarding the fact that various dealers may be in prebargain situations so miserable that to deal with them is to exploit them. Nevertheless, it needs to be noted that the reasoning here is exactly parallel to Mill's; a principle of liberty is implied by a principle of utility. The liberal paradox and all of its consequences confirm again the suspicion that Mill simply had no right to make this connection.

CHAPTER 3

Utility and Social Ethics

So, there is, at the level of principle anyhow, a real conflict between the very ideas of liberty and utility. This, of course, does not mean that there is bound to be a pervasive *practical* collision between actual social structures that maximize utility and those that maximize liberty. As we are about to see, the usual arguments to the effect that a utilitarian legislator would have to wipe out liberty after liberty in hypothetical case after hypothetical case are not compelling. Nevertheless, matters of principle are important (at least to philosophers), and the analytic tendency of the principle of utility to obliterate the possibility of a private realm is philosophically disturbing.

In Chapter 5, I will attempt to develop a version of utilitarianism that does, as a matter of principle, leave room for a private sphere of action. This theory will be based on two major claims. The first, which will be the focus of this chapter, is that the usual objections against utilitarianism as a practical social ethic are not good enough to abandon the theory. I do not intend to argue that the theory is unrefutable, let alone that it is the only unrefutable theory of social ethics available. I only intend to show that it is extremely durable. The second major claim, which will be the focus of Chapter 4, is that utilitarianism is neither rich enough nor fine-grained enough to provide a satisfactory view of the value of life for the individual.

What would seem to follow from the latter claim is that utilitarianism fails as any kind of ethical theory because it bases social decisions directly on the effects of those decisions for the well-being of individuals. However, this conclusion follows only if one assumes that utilitarian social prescriptions must be based on *all* of the elements of individual well-being, that is, if one assumes that all of the coherent and remotely relevant desires of the individual must be reflected in every social decision.

My theory is based on the denial of this assumption. In Chapter 5, I will argue that utilitarian social decisions should only be derivable from the most basic and commonly agreed upon individual values, namely, those associated with the desire to avoid simple pain (as well as death and severe psychological suffering) and the serious threat of pain, death, or suffering. On the further assumption that there is a lot more to life than the avoidance of pain, death, and suffering, we will arrive at a theory that poses a very narrow range of actions that are even initially open to legitimate social control, and that, thereby, leaves a broad range of actions in the domain of private control.

The concern of this chapter, however, is the suitability of utilitarianism *as a social ethic*. Again, what I intend to do here is nothing like a general defense of the proposition that utilitarianism is the *only* good theory of social ethics (for that would entail an attack on all other available theories of social ethics). Rather, I intend to show that utilitarianism should be viewed as *one* of the good theories; at least, it should be viewed more charitably than it has been of late.

Of the usual objections against utilitarianism at the social level, I am prepared to argue that none of them are compelling. Actually, I don't have to do much of that sort of argument, for most of the problems still being mentioned in the textbooks were adequately answered by Mill over a century ago. Nevertheless, it might be useful to point out the basic kinds of maneuvers open to utilitarians.[1]

A broad class of objections concerns the apparent incompatibility of utilitarianism with our commonsense intuitions about justice. Mill responded to this complaint in the fifth chapter of *Utilitarianism*. The first stage of his argument was to show that these commonsense intuitions were nowhere near as firm as typically supposed. Mill lists several intuitions normally associated with justice (equality, impartiality, desert, and others) and argues, first, that these intuitions are often inconsistent with one another and, second, that a sensible application of any of them requires the use of the principle of utility.

To take impartiality as an example, certainly we expect this property to obtain in the dealings and deliberations of judges and juries but, just as certainly, we do not expect it to obtain in the dealings of lovers and parents. Clearly, I should be partial toward my wife or children with respect to a wide range of sentiments and actions. I should not distribute Christmas gifts impartially amongst all of the children in the neighborhood nor lust equally after all of their mothers. The reason for ruling out impartiality in this case is most easily explained in a utilitarian way. A system where special bonds and responsibilities are shared between members of small groups who are intimately aware of each other's likes and dislikes just makes more utilitarian sense than one where such intimacy would be replaced by impersonal distributions made from a distance and from ignorance of the relevant personal tastes.

As for principles of equality, even when taken in their milder form as implying mere equality of opportunity rather than of welfare or resources, they are routinely denied because their application would have bad consequences. For example, we do not allow children the same opportunities (like voting and driving) as adults. Similarly, students are not usually allowed to determine grades the way teachers are, and defendants cannot find someone in contempt of court the way a judge can.

If the issue changes from equality of opportunity to equality of resources or welfare, then utilitarians have recourse to the standard considerations about marginal utility. In other words, they can appeal to the fact that any bundle of resources or of goods otherwise associated with welfare will mean less to someone well-off than they will to someone less well-off; a dollar means less to a millionaire than it does to someone who is penniless. So, there will always be, prima facie, a good utilitarian reason to take from the rich and give to the poor. This prima facie consideration is, of course, constrained by the familiar concerns about the effect of redistribution on incentives to produce wealth, but, nonetheless, utilitarianism does have a built-in tendency toward greater equalization of resources and welfare so long as the consequences of such redistribution do not lower aggregate utility.[2]

Closely related to these objections are ones that assert that utilitarianism might require the sacrifice of individual rights for the greater good. For example, if the framing of an innocent individual for a crime she did not commit would optimize aggregate utility, then, the objection goes, not only would utilitarianism *allow* the framing but it would *require* it. Suppose, for example, that one evening the president has a hankering for some Italian food at a favorite restaurant of his in a seedy part of Washington. In the interests of security, plans are made to clear the restaurant of everyone but the chef who will prepare and serve the president's favorite dish. Accordingly, the chef, the president, and five secret service agents will be the only people in this restaurant in a rather deserted part of the city. Indeed, every imaginable precaution has been taken to insure that the outing is secret.

As the meal progresses, the president gets progressively wasted on chianti. At a certain point he charges into the kitchen in an incoherent drunken rage and starts yelling at the chef for being an agent of some obscure foreign despot. A brawl erupts, the president and the chef wind up fighting in the alley behind the restaurant, a gun materializes and the president shoots the chef. But, across the alley from the president and the dead chef slumps a barely conscious alcoholic bag lady. Our five utilitarian secret service agents, we are to believe, all come to the same strategy at the same time, namely, that of sticking the murder weapon (which is not traceable to any of the secret service agents or to the President) into the hand of the bag lady and getting the President back to the White House as secretly as possible.

Why would they settle on this strategy? First, because the consequences of the president's arrest for the crime would be disastrous. Secondly, from the point of view of the bag lady, she might be better off, in the long run, with a few years of jail time in which she could be dried out and given a respectable trade.

As with all hypothetical examples of this sort, the utilitarian will have the following two-level response: First, these sorts of cases always put forward sets of facts that are too neat to be real or, at least, too neat to be believed real by any thoughtful moral agent. For example, there might be some benefit in not having the president brought up on a murder charge but, surely, the consequences of covering the incident up and then having the charge stick after the coverup collapses would be far worse. And the probability of the coverup collapsing is, as a matter of common sense, extremely high. How are the secret service agents to be sure that the crime and the framing activity were not seen? How can they be sure that none of them, or the president himself, will not eventually crack under the weight of guilt and confess all? Who wants a president who gets drunk and kills chefs, anyhow? How would this person act if drunk in the middle of an international crisis?

When we turn to real life cases we can see even more clearly how the utilitarian's attention to facts, in all their grimy complexity, generally points the theory in the direction of guaranteeing, rather than overriding, individual rights. Consider two closely related cases in fairly recent history. One concerns an article in which *Progressive* magazine published plans for the construction of a hydrogen bomb.[3] The other concerns the books of Philip Agee that listed the identities and locations of CIA operatives.[4]

Either of these cases would cause even rights theorists to pause and wonder whether or not the right to freedom of publication was being abused. However, attention to the peripheral details in these cases would, on utilitarian grounds, lead to a position in favor of protecting the freedom. The fact of the matter is that *Progressive* was hardly trying to aid and abet terrorism. Quite to the contrary, the magazine was trying to make a point about the disturbing availability of nuclear weapons technology. All of the information used in the magazine's bomb blueprints was obtained from public places (like city libraries). To suppress the publication would simply have been to perpetuate the myth that such information is all safely locked away in the basements of the Pentagon. And a utilitarian could well argue (as Mill did) that such myths are, in the long run, most dangerous if believed.

As for the other publication, any utilitarian (or nonutilitarian) ought to wonder (once again) about the extent to which anyone can feel secure about the operations of the CIA if someone could compile and publish detailed information about large numbers of CIA operatives and agents. Given that Agee and several of his associates had this information, then how many other people probably had the same information?

Nevertheless, any utilitarian will have to admit that, under some imaginable conditions, rights will have to yield to utility. This is where the second line of argument enters. In cases where the balance of utility is only marginally in favor of suppressing rights (whose observance is generally productive of much good), the two cases just mentioned provide reason enough to think that a utilitarian would (or, at least, could) be in favor of protecting whatever right is in question. But what about when substantial immediate and long-term harm would be avoided by the particular suppression of a particular right? Suppose, for example, that by framing an innocent individual we really could save ten innocent lives. It must be understood that the framing is only in this particular case and that its occurrence here will not lead to further framings. If this case was going to turn out to be the thin end of a wedge, then even a utilitarian would object on the grounds that the general suspension of due process would have consequences far worse than any temporary gains to be achieved by widespread framing of innocent individuals.

So, suppose that no bad consequences would follow from the framing. Suppose, as I did before, that even the person framed would ultimately benefit from being framed. Suppose that no future framings are made any more likely because this one is going to take place. Suppose that there is no chance that this framing will be found out. Now, is it right to frame the bag lady in order to save ten innocent lives? Suppose that, of the ten to be saved, one would eventually discover a cure for cancer, another would discover a cure for AIDS, and yet another would discover a method by which we could travel at 90 percent of the speed of light. Is it right to frame her yet? Suppose we make it ten thousand innocent lives that will be saved? Suppose the fate of the entire planet depends upon her being framed?

The simple point I am trying to make here is that, in a situation where rights collide with utility, utility will always win at a certain point. Make the stakes high enough, and everyone with any sense becomes a utilitarian. One could, I suppose, object that this is true only under the conditions of outrageous hypothetical cases. *But then it is with outrageous hypothetical cases that the alleged antithesis between utility and rights is usually established in the first place.*

Still more objections center specifically on the notion of moral desert. These objections are closely related to the framing cases just discussed. The problem is that the bag lady doesn't *deserve* to be imprisoned. The flip side of the desert problem (specifically, the problem of handing out rewards rather than punishments) does, however, raise slightly different problems and different methods of response for the utilitarian.

The objections usually begin by pointing out that, from a utilitarian point of view, the desirable final state of affairs is one where utility is maximized (or optimized) even though that state of affairs might be one in which the individuals winding up with the utility don't deserve to have it while others may deserve more than they have. The easy response to this gross statement of the problem is that any arrangement of institutions and practices that systematically rewards people who don't deserve reward while underrewarding those who do deserve it will, in the long run, not produce an optimal level of utility. For example, we can imagine that, under a system where laziness is rewarded and productivity is under-rewarded, eventually people will become less productive, and almost everyone will be worse off.

But there are other well-known problems associated with just trying to understand how, exactly, desert is to be determined. We appeal to quite different standards under different conditions in order to figure out who deserves what. If, for example, five people (through equal effort and no prior capitalization by any one of them) discover some fortune upon which no one else has any claim then we might make a straightfor-ward appeal to the principle of equality. We do not appeal to the princi-ple of equality when assigning academic grades, however. There, achieve-ment is the criterion of choice in determining who deserves what grade. Achievement, however, is not the criterion of choice in determining who deserves what amount of welfare benefit. There the criterion of choice is need.

The question now is: How are we to determine which of the above criteria (equality, achievement, need) are to be chosen in various situa-tions? The utilitarian, of course has a ready answer: We appeal to the principle of utility. In some cases a system that uses the achievement cri-terion will maximize utility. In other cases the need criterion will maxi-mize utility, and, in others, the equality criterion will maximize utility. What other principle can be used any more sensibly than the principle of utility in selecting lower-level evaluative criteria? This, as mentioned above, was precisely the line of argument taken by Mill in the fifth chap-ter of *Utilitarianism*.

More disturbing problems come up with respect to distributional concerns. (It was already noted in Chapter 1 that these sorts of concerns cause problems for certain versions of utilitarianism.) The original prob-lem was raised a long time ago by Nicholas Rescher.[5] More recently, things have been made much more troublesome by Derek Parfit.[6] The initial problem is set up by the following question: Which is better, a state of affairs (A) where, say, ten billion people live lives that are (because of strained resources) barely worth living (give each life a numeric value of one) or a state of affairs (B) where ten million people live lives that are (because of plentiful resources) well worth living (give each life a numeric value of one hundred)? Under a utilitarian theory that judges between states of affairs on the basis of sum totals, A would have to be judged morally superior (by a factor of ten) to B even though no one in his or her right mind would choose to live in A rather than B.

The easy way out of the initial quandary is to move from the idea that sum total utility should be maximized and to the idea that *average* utility ought to be maximized. This move does not solve the problem though, for now we can think about a situation where the choice is between B and another state of affairs (C) where there are only two people whose lives have a value of 101 each. Is C supposed to be better than B? Or we can wonder about a comparison between B and another state of affairs that is comprised of the people who make up B plus another group of ten billion people who live on a different continent, who have no contact at all with the people who make up B, and whose lives are worth ninety-nine each. Is B better than this state of affairs?

At this point, a utilitarian might try to reject all of the problematic scenarios as ridiculously hypothetical, but it is not clear that this move will work here. Would the real world be better off if all of the starving Eretreans and Somolians just vanished tomorrow in some relatively painless way? What if their standard of living could be brought close (but not equal) to ours? Should they just vanish anyhow?

A parallel paradox can be applied to individuals. As Parfit puts it, what's better, a "century of ecstacy" or a "drab eternity" of "muzak and potatoes"? Parfit mentions that one way out of the individual version of the problem (which leads to a possible resolution of the social versions of it) is to introduce Mill's notorious idea that some kinds of pleasures are *qualitatively*, not just *quantitatively*, better than others. As we shall see later (in Chapter 10), there is much to be said in defense of this maneuver. However, my path to this discussion and my suggestion about how to get out of the social version of the problem are linked to an intuition quite different from those of Parfit or any utilitarian of whom I am aware.

The most direct way out of Parfit's paradoxes is simply to give up the idea that the way things ought to be should be determined on the basis of the sum or distributional pattern of the good. As I have already indicated, I intend to abandon all theories of the good in lieu of a theory of the wrong that will leave room for a genuinely private sphere of action. Under such a view, none of the social states of affairs that Rescher and Parfit conjure up are to be presumed right or wrong simply on the basis of sums and distributional patterns of good. Moreover, as will be made clear as we go along, I will not be positing a simple mirror image of standard utilitarianism (which would have it that the wrong is always determined by the sums or distributional patterns of badness).[7] Calculations of badness and (with a lot of qualifications) goodness will have much to do with the determination of the wrong, but things will not render down to simple sums and distributions of either goodness or badness.

Even more objections to utilitarianism center on the alleged inability of utilitarianism to give due weight to questions of individual virtue. The shallowness of utilitarian thinking about virtue is something that was mentioned previously with respect to Mill's condescension to Bentham's *Deontology*. Moreover, in spite of Mill's arguments in the second chapter of *Utilitarianism* to the effect that virtue is something to be prized on utilitarian grounds, the precise nature of virtue and its importance *to the individual* are topics that (as I will argue later) really do cause problems for utilitarianism that are, as are the distributional problems mentioned earlier, unsolvable from a direct utilitarian perspective. However, as regards the importance of virtue with respect to *social* ethics, I believe Mill's response is enough: virtue will be praised and rewarded under any good utilitarian arrangement of social practices.

Finally, there is another line of objection that, ultimately, does expose a real problem with utilitarianism at the level of individual ethics but not at the social level. Stated one way, the objection is that utilitarian calculations can be used to deliver whatever result one wishes. In other words, the theory is a great mechanism for generating after-the-fact rationalizations but not for generating specific prescriptions for the future. Mill's reply to this form of the objection was that this charge could be made against any moral theory. Any theory, even the sternest divine command theory, can be misused so as to justify whatever disgusting actions have already been performed for various ulterior reasons. But this is a problem with the people who apply moral theories, not one with the theories themselves.

A slightly varied statement of the objection opens up different, and more serious, questions, though. There is a real problem in getting any prescription that is at all specific when the theory is applied to particular individuals in particular situations. This problem will be a main concern of the next chapter. But, before turning to it, I would like to mention what I think to be a major point of confusion underlying this problem.

The confusion I have in mind concerns the very definition of utilitarianism. Typically, utilitarianism is introduced into discussions of ethics as a theory that claims, first of all, that acts (rather than character or virtue) are the ultimate basis of moral judgement and, secondly, that acts are to be evaluated on the basis of their consequences and their tendency to maximize or optimize aggregate utility. Stated more succinctly, utilitarianism is the theory that holds that any act is right if and only if it maximizes or optimizes aggregate utility.

The problems with this sort of act utilitarianism are usually thought to center on the notions of "maximizing" or "utility." However, I am inclined to think that much more perplexing problems center on the notion of an "act." Our ordinary usage of the term establishes absolutely no bounds on what might count as an act. An act could last for a few seconds, a few days, or a few years (as was the case in the American "police action" in Korea). It could be brought about by the agency of one person, a small group, a nation, or several nations (as was the case in the United Nation's actions taken against Iraq).

The natural sloppiness of the term "act" is, to a large degree, what lies behind the limitless capacity of utilitarianism's detractors to generate counterexamples to the theory and also that of utilitarians to respond to those counterexamples. Typically, the detractor will carve out a small imaginary act with limited consequences (e.g., framing a bag lady), and the utilitarian will respond by weaving that small act into a larger act (e.g., the act of training secret service agents to automatically come up with coverup schemes that they feel good about concocting). Conversely, detractors will present actions that are of a type that, usually, are seen as laudable from the point of view of almost any ethical theory (e.g., honesty), and the utilitarian will respond by carving out a small imaginary act (e.g., a lie that saves a million lives).

All of this carving and weaving may be good for the business of generating pithy objections and defenses in the textbooks, but it renders utilitarianism practically useless in a way that would have nauseated the great utilitarian social reformers of the nineteenth century. Furthermore, it should be clear that switching from act utilitarianism to rule utilitarianism will not overcome this practical impotence. That the rule utilitarian will perform calculations over rules before evaluating the relevant act does nothing to alleviate the problem of the ultimate sloppiness of the acts to which the rules are to be applied. This, of course, is getting us close to an old objection against rule utilitarianism, namely, that before any rule is applied, we must specify both the act we are evaluating and also the rule that we are appealing to in the process of evaluation. By the time we are done with all of the "relevant specifications"[8] at *both* ends of the evaluation (i.e., specification of the rule and also of the *act*), we will wind up with a theory so fluid that it says nothing practically helpful at all because it can say anything depending on the manner of the specifications entered into the decision problem.[9]

I think it has been a mistake to view utilitarianism as a theory about the morality of *actions*. The notion of an "act" is simply too flimsy a target to hit for a theory based on the sort of exhaustive calculation that utilitarianism requires. The theory originated as a theory about *social policy* and about the institutions, practices, and attitudes necessary to maintain social arrangements.[10] And, as a theory of social ethics, I have been attempting to show that it has much to recommend it and little or nothing that counts as a decisive and unremovable refutation of it. However, as a theory about how I ought to conduct my day-to-day life and loves, the theory is a cripple.

CHAPTER 4

Utility and Individual Ethics

Aside from the sloppiness of the notion of an "act," there are problems with the other key terms used in the standard definition of act utilitarianism. And, generally, when combining, into a single formula one vague notion with two others as vague as "utility" and "maximizing," people should not expect clarity to result. (Rule utilitarianism will have an additional problem with "rule.")

Between the terms "maximizing" and "utility," the former is, by far, the least vague. This is due to the enormous literature that has grown up in the twentieth century in economics, game theory, and social decision theory. Generally, as welfarist interpretations of the notion of "utility" have taken precedence over the allegedly primitive interpretations of the classical utilitarians of the nineteenth century, the notion of "maximizing" has been exchanged for that of "optimizing." Rather than postulating some absolute, intrinsically valuable, and interpersonally comparable mental state like pleasure, happiness, or lack of pain, formal modeling has turned to measures of welfare in terms of revealed preferences.

The early "preference utilitarians" disavowed, on positivistic grounds, any notions related to interpersonal comparability or cardinality and stuck closely to ordinal considerations. And as a consequence, the old notion of maximizing by simple summation of individual utils went out the window in favor of Pareto optimization. As this century has progressed and the influence of stern positivism has abated, interpersonal comparability and cardinality have become more respectable from a formal point of view.[1]

However, in spite of the awesome formal precision that may be used to cash out either the notion of optimization or that of maximization, these concepts are obviously tied to the more problematic concept of utility. It is, after all, precisely utility that is to be optimized or maximized, and no amount of formal rigor is worth much if the basic good to be optimized or maximized is, from a normative point of view, unrespectable. And I believe that simple revealed preference is, indeed, an unrespectable basis for social decision theory.

To begin with, nobody thinks that *all* individual preferences are equal and equally important in the determination of social choices. Preferences that are, at a time, rationally incoherent must be disregarded. For example, individual preference orderings that are intransitive must be ignored when they are submitted to any rational social welfare function.

Moreover, there are individual preference orderings that must be disregarded not because they are irrational at any specific time but because they emerge from an individual who is irrational over time. Surely, no theory of individual rationality would require that rational individuals never change their minds about various alternatives available to them but, just as surely, an individual who reorganizes her fundamental desires and all of her consequent specific desires every five seconds could hardly be considered sane, let alone fully rational. This is a problem of individual rationality that is as old as Plato's discussion of the "democratic man" in the eighth book of the *Republic*. Elsewhere, I have argued that this problem with preference utilitarianism is beyond any formal remedy.[2]

Still more problems arise when we realize that certain preference orderings are to be rejected because of the simple ignorance of the individuals who have them. No one is omniscient, and many individual preferences are quite obviously founded on simple mistakes about facts. Someone who thinks that laetrile is a more effective cure for cancer than can be provided by orthodox medicine is simply wrong, and his view that laetrile ought to be made available and its use encouraged is equally wrong no matter how many medically ignorant people he can get to agree with him.[3]

Finally, even in a system of preference utilitarianism as cautiously constructed and as formally forbidding as John Harsanyi's, some provision must be made for the exclusion of preferences that may be rational at the relevant time, rational over time, factually fully informed, but that are also malicious. Harsanyi refers to these, bluntly enough, as "antisocial" preferences, which are quite beyond the protection of the principle of consumer sovereignty.[4] I agree that such preferences must be excluded but to exclude them simply on the grounds that they are "antisocial" is clearly question begging. "Antisocial" can only mean "socially immoral," and social morality is supposed to be defined by a social welfare function that has already excluded all of the "socially immoral" individual preferences. If we know, in advance of the results of the social welfare function, what exactly is socially immoral, then what do we need Harsanyi's social welfare function for?

There are other, and deeper, reasons for my rejection of preference utilitarianism. These will be discussed in the next chapter, where I will argue for a return to primitivism, that is, where I will argue for a return to a form of hedonism even more crude than Bentham's. However, returning to this sort of primitivism will not help utilitarianism at the level of individual ethics. In fact, the more primitive the basic theory of value becomes, the more crippled utilitarianism becomes as an individual ethic.

Two insurmountable problems arise for utilitarianism at the individual level, even if (in fact, especially if) we return to a more primitive conception of utility. The first is a contemporary line of argument belonging to (among others) Jon Elster.[5] The second is a problem that was, in part, the cause of an emotional breakdown for John Stuart Mill.

Amongst many antiutilitarian arguments offered by Elster is one that ties in closely with an argument I was running at the end of the previous chapter, namely, that utilitarianism is simply not fine-grained enough to give me much helpful practical advice in the running of my ordinary affairs. Given the consequential vagueness of real life, any number of actions might or might not maximize utility, and almost any action I might perform can be rationalized as optimally felicific.[6]

To start with trivial concerns, from the point of view of aggregate utility, that is, from the point of view of the collective striving and suffering of all present and future sentient beings everywhere in the universe, it matters not one bit whether I choose to wear a red shirt or a blue one. To suggest that, under ordinary conditions, the choice could make a real difference in terms of aggregate utility is just to be pesky. To argue that I or someone else might have experienced some small, but in principle discernable, thrill if I had chosen otherwise is like arguing that, for me, there is a real difference between a cup of coffee with no sugar in it and one with one grain of sugar in it. Perhaps there *really* is a difference between the two cups of coffee that is, as a matter of minute physiology, discernable. It doesn't matter. I could not *perceive* any difference and, in a like manner, I would assert that the aggregate utility of all sentient beings is not *perceptibly* altered by my choice of shirts.

The point I am making here is that point of view counts. From the point of view of some minuscule neurons, the difference between a cup of coffee with no sugar and one with a single grain of sugar might be real. But from *my* point of view, the difference is not real. Likewise, from *my* point of view, my choice of a shirt might be of some small consequence. But, from the point of view of the collective pains and pleasures of the universe, the difference is not real. And the point of view of utilitarianism involves, precisely, the collective pains and pleasures of the universe.

One might object here that I have gone way too far toward the cosmic perspective. From this perspective, it might be asked, would it make any "real" difference if I machine-gunned my neighbor and left her family without a wife and mother? I suppose I would have to answer: "No." However, it *would* make a difference if the society I lived in did not have an enforceable law against machine-gunning innocent civilians. Can anyone argue that the enforcement of laws against murder, rape, and robbery is without clear consequences no matter how cosmic the moral point of view is?

This brings us back to my main thesis, namely, that, at the level of social policy, utilitarianism applies. At the individual level, it doesn't, except to the degree that the individual is subject to the enforcement of social policy.

To assume that a principle that applies at the social level must also apply straightforwardly to the individual is to commit a simple fallacy of division. Similarly, to think that differences at the individual level must be straightforwardly reflected in social policy is to commit a fallacy of composition. For any individual to think that his or her actions are going to have any real effect on the aggregate good of the world or that his or her special interests deserve to have a direct and substantial impact on social policy is, in almost all cases, sheer narcissism.

This is why Elster's criticisms of utilitarianism are correct. Essentially, his argument is that principles of rationality are of little help when individuals are making choices about what they ought to do. There will, in most individual cases, be a very large array of alternatives that are all equally optimal, that is, equally rational. Given that utilitarianism is capable of figuring rationality from the cosmic point of view and, moreover, that utilitarianism encourages the adoption of the cosmic point of view rather than a narrow egoistic point of view, it will, indeed, follow that most of our individual choices are equally rational and good.[7]

It is precisely the contemplation of the chasm between the cosmic point of view and the individual point of view that drove Mill to depression. As Elster comes to the conclusion that judging individual actions in terms of their specific consequences is a hopeless method of trying to figure out what the individual ought to do, Mill, at a young age, had come to the depressing conclusion that unqualified moral perfection at the cosmic level might mean little to the individual who seeks such collective perfection. No words speak more eloquently to the cause of his dejection than his own:

> It was in the autumn of 1826. I was in a dull state of nerves, such as everybody is occasionally liable to; unsusceptible to enjoyment or pleasurable excitement; one of those moods when what is pleasure at other times becomes insipid or indifferent; the state, I should think, in which converts to Methodism usually are, when smitten by their first "conviction of sin." In this frame of mind it occurred to me to put the question directly to myself: "Suppose that all your objects in life were realized; that all the changes in institutions and opinions which you are looking forward to, could be completely effected at this very instant: would this be a great joy and happiness to you?" And an irrepressible self-consciousness distinctly answered, "No!" At this my heart sank within me: the whole foundation on which my life was constructed fell

down. All my happiness was to have been found in the continual pursuit of this end. The end had ceased to charm, and how could there ever again be any interest in the means? I seemed to have nothing left to live for.[8]

As Mill tells it, the only thing that brought him out of his depression was his love of romantic poetry and of Harriet Taylor. This is, perhaps, enough to make the point that utilitarianism is not only too coarse-grained to provide a theory of individual ethics but also too shallow. The sort of richness that should be present in a life worth living is not to be produced by any aggregate felicific calculus.

Mill was to struggle with the reconciliation of individual ethics and social ethics at length in both *Utilitarianism* and *On Liberty*. In both places, however, one can only be led to the conclusion that he was progressively abandoning any uniform theory that would neatly bridge the gap. The problems associated with Mill's attempt to establish a private sphere by an application of the harm principle have already been mentioned here. Two other infamous passages testify to a particularly troublesome strategy Mill seems to have adopted.

The first of these occurs in the second chapter (pars. 4 and 5) of *Utilitarianism*, where Mill draws a distinction between "higher," distinctly human pleasures and "lower" pleasures that humans share, for the most part, with other animals. The former, he claims, are not just quantitatively but also qualitatively better than the latter. The obvious problem is that this claim seems to amount to an abandonment of hedonism. If pleasure is to be the measure of all things, then how can it be that there is a qualitative rank ordering of different types of pleasure? As Richard Taylor has pointed out,[9] it seems as though Mill must be appealing to some standard higher than pleasure that could form a normative basis for the ranking.

The second passage occurs in the third chapter (par. 2) of *On Liberty*, where Mill argues that individuality is not just instrumentally valuable but also intrinsically valuable. Again, Mill seems to be retreating from any straightforward hedonism in order to come up with a richer theory of value. That he qualifies his claim by arguing that individuality is a *part* of happiness for humans doesn't change things much. All this qualification manages to do is make it clear that Mill is backing away from hedonism by expanding the range of mental states denoted by the words "pleasure" and "happiness." That he still calls his theory hedonism has little to do with whether or not it really still is a form of hedonism.

Aside from any quibble about labels, though, there is a deeper reason for my thinking that Mill's strategy is troublesome and, eventually, wrong-headed. Mill is, I believe, arguing at cross purposes. On the one hand, he wants to move away from Bentham's narrow hedonism in order to arrive at a theory of value that pays proper due to the richness of individual life. On the other hand, he wants to create a private sphere in which the pursuit of the richness of life can proceed as free as possible of social restraint. But, to the extent that the notions of "utility," " pleasure," and "happiness" are broadened and enriched, so too is the notion of "harm." And, to the extent that the notion of harm is broadened, the range of actions that the government may (but is not obliged to) interfere with is broadened.

In other words, to the extent that Mill defends and embellishes individualism, he threatens the normative basis of political liberty. This consideration, along with the fact that complicating the notion of utility the way either Mill or Harsanyi do[10] leads to problems of clarity and mere coherence, leads me to conclude that it is better just to admit that utilitarianism is a failure as an individual ethic. Moreover, constraining the denotation of the terms "utility" and, thereby, "harm" does raise the likelihood that a version of utilitarianism can be constructed that will clearly guarantee substantial liberty.

CHAPTER 5

Utility, Harm, and Liberty

From its beginnings, utilitarianism was based on an extreme suspicion about any attempt to found social policy on anything as dogmatic and variable between individuals, cultures, and times as "divine command," "intuition," or "natural rights." Generally, in the eighteenth and nineteenth centuries these three modes of moral reasoning never got very far away from each other.

For example, we can see in Jefferson's defense of the "right to life, liberty and the pursuit of happiness," an appeal to natural rights theory that, in turn, appeals to intuitionism; these rights are "self-evident." If we look for the origin of Jefferson's claim, we find it in Locke, who argued at length that the natural right to "life, liberty and property" was guaranteed biblically. Needless to say, many passages from the New Testament could lead to substantial doubt about the legitimacy of capitalism and property rights, which could, in turn, lead to the suspicion that Locke first had the intuition that such rights were legitimate and then found the appropriate pieces of scripture to support his prior feelings. In the twentieth century, rights theorists have deliberately tried to avoid the appearance of groundlessness and sectarian piety. Nevertheless, one of the theses that ties most utilitarians together is an extreme suspicion of any theory that makes rights foundational.

Utilitarians, generally, have quarreled not with the rights arrived at by these methods but, rather, with the methods themselves. Rights as important as those guaranteed by the American Constitution must be founded on firmer stuff than a mere feeling that they are legitimate. To this end, the early utilitarians fixed on what appears to be the most widely held values amongst humans. In fact, the values they settled upon were so widely held that they seem to be values for lots of animals. Whatever else humans may value or disvalue in life, there is as wide agreement about this as anything: pain is bad and pleasure is good.[1] Moreover, there appears to be a general squeamishness in people (and lots of other animals) that—given a choice between having a substantial pleasure and avoiding an equally substantial pain—would lead to the selection of the avoidance of pain rather than the pursuit of pleasure. Further still, pain appears to be a more commonly understood mental state than pleasure.

This is because the various means to pleasure are considerably variable from person to person, whereas the causes of simple pain appear to be more constant (e.g., being hit with a hard object, having a dentist drill into a nerve, having cancer, etc.).[2]

Indeed, a great number of specific goods would appear to be pretty clearly linked to pleasure and pain in various ways by various people. For most people, the maintenance of good health is obviously instrumental to the pursuit of pleasure and the avoidance of pain. For most people, the possession of certain material comforts like food, shelter, and clothing are primitive hedonic necessities. For almost anyone in a society with money, its possession will be desirable for the ability it brings to avoid pain and pursue pleasure.

Nevertheless, the slight asymmetry in the relationship between pleasure and pain is clearly reflected in some of the basic working assumptions of any liberal society. The variability of pleasure is reflected in pluralism, that is, in the belief that the kinds and causes of legitimate ends are beyond any paternalistic enumeration. The relative specificity of pain is reflected in the fact that the kinds of damages for which one can be held either criminally or civilly responsible are generally pretty clearly enumerated in the law. There are other reasons for holding to the view that pain is more specific than pleasure as will become clear shortly.

To the degree that social policy is based on the universal guarantee of specific goods and opportunities that are less universal than the desire for some universal pleasure and, especially, the aversion to pain, it must, under my view, be seen as increasingly suspect. One might think that this line of thinking would eventuate in social policy that is far too restrictive to guarantee much liberty. If each proposed liberty depends upon a demonstration that that liberty is clearly productive of widespread pleasure or necessary to avoid widespread pain, then, it would seem, very few significant liberties could be guaranteed.

However, I think this way of looking at things is backward and out of sync with the mainstream of utilitarian social thought. Under the view I am developing, rights are guaranteed not by the postulation of certain "natural," "self-evident," "God-given," or "inalienable" rights but rather by the restraint of government. More succinctly, under my view rights are, for the most part, guaranteed *negatively* rather than *positively*.

What I am suggesting is that utilitarianism serves better as a mechanism for restraining the government than it does as a mechanism for simply fine-tuning the direction of social engineering and government interference in the lives of private citizens. This boils down to a matter of shifting the burden of proof from the individual to the state. In any case where the state seeks to move against the individual, it should not be up to the individual to prove that she or he has a positive right to act in a certain way. Rather, the state should be expected to produce good utilitarian reasons for proscribing or requiring the activity in question.

The insight that liberty is intimately connected to this issue of burden of proof is, I think, the central insight behind Mill's harm principle.[3] Moreover, what Mill's principle requires is not just a good utilitarian argument but a certain kind of utilitarian argument, namely, one that establishes the serious threat of *harm* with respect to whatever activity is to be proscribed or required. And this is even harder to show than that the balance of pleasure over pain would be increased by a certain regulation. Many policies could be justified on the grounds that they would bring about more pleasure than would be the case if they were not enforced, even though the activity being regulated could not be shown to be directly related to any specific harm. For example, many supererogatory acts could be required even though their nonperformance could not sensibly be viewed as a cause of harm. I might be compelled to give Christmas gifts not only to my children but to my neighbor's children as well, even though it makes little sense to charge me with harming my neighbor's children last Christmas when I gave them no gifts.

Given what I said before about the variability of pleasure when compared to the constancy of pain, I think it makes sense to side with Mill in asserting that the causation of harm (as well as the failure to prevent it under certain conditions) should be the necessary condition of government action. Regulations requiring the provision of pleasure to others require too much that is too vague. Although I am reasonably sure about what will cause or prevent pain to a stranger, I may know extremely little about what would or would not cause him pleasure. Thus, obliging me not to cause him pain is reasonable while obliging me to bring him pleasure is not.

A troublesome class of cases arise around what have become known as "bad Samaritan" scenarios. In the bad Samaritan case, one does not directly cause harm to another but, rather, fails to enact an "easy rescue" of someone from a harmful situation. Feinberg has written extensively on this subject, and I am inclined to agree with his position.[4] He argues that performing an easy rescue (e.g., reaching out of one's poolside lounge chair to save a drowning child) can hardly be viewed as simply failing to provide a supererogatory benefit. There is a distinction, he argues, between failing to provide "active aid" and failing to provide "gratuitous benefit." I agree and suggest that the distinction is underwritten by what I have been saying about pain and pleasure. Generally, except where special relationships exist, failing to provide pleasure cannot be required, but such a failure cannot be confused with a failure to prevent pain. And in cases where the pain can be prevented "easily," I see no reason (other than that generated by a fallacious application of the slippery slope) for thinking that such prevention could not be required morally and legally. Moreover, it should be pointed out that Feinberg is not alone in suggesting that individuals should be compelled to prevent harm. Mill made the same suggestion in the first chapter (par. 10) of *On Liberty*. More will be said about bad Samaritan cases in Chapter 7.

Pain is the one thing amongst the wide class of goods and evils that have been suggested and analyzed over the last three thousand years that every reasonable person can understand and, *ceteris paribus*, be expected to avoid. Moreover, it is the one thing that we can all agree about as a basis for legislation and social regulation generally. No veils of ignorance or original positions are necessary in order to establish that any rational individual wishes to avoid pain except (as often is the case) when the pain is instrumental to the pursuit of some more valuable end. It must be understood that I have nowhere suggested that the avoidance of pain is the most important thing in anyone's life. I am simply claiming that it is the only thing that is universally held to be intrinsically evil.

The dropping of Rawlsian jargon in the last paragraph is not incidental to the main line of my argument. I think that the view of utilitarianism I am developing here is based on the same sort of intuition that motivates contractualism. The basis of a legitimate social contract must be some universally shared goods or evils that will be either provided or avoided only by the establishment of a social contract. Rawls constructs his list of basic goods from the consensus of fully rational agents in an original position. I am suspicious, as are most utilitarians, about this device for insuring some idealized consent. I prefer, rather, to ground things in a simpler soil. Needless to say, much of the liberal egalitarianism that appears to follow from Rawlsian theory will not find much nourishment in this bed of libertarian weeds.

But just how libertarian are the consequences of the theory I am suggesting? In order to answer this question and also in order to give a little substance to my theory, I will turn to an analysis of Mill's reformulation of the harm principle in the fourth chapter of *On Liberty*. This analysis is, admittedly, going to be done from the point of view of the primitivism I have outlined above. As such, I am making no pretense about being very faithful to Mill's actual words. I am certainly not presuming to explain what Mill really meant.

The reformulation of the harm principle that comes in the fourth chapter (par. 10) of *On Liberty* has struck many as really being a new formulation of an independent principle that is utterly different from the "simple principle" asserted in the first chapter. Certainly, on the surface, it sounds like a completely new idea. The "simple principle" asserted at the beginning of the work simply requires the demonstration of harm to others as a necessary condition of legitimate social coercion. The second version of the principle is couched in entirely different terminology and requires the demonstration of an individual's violation of a "distinct and assignable obligation to others" as a necessary condition of legitimate social coercion.

I believe that the effect of this reformulation is simply to make precise the original formulation and, moreover, to more closely tie the harm principle to the principle of utility. That is to say, I think it can be argued that Mill had a right to think of the second formulation as a genuine *re*formulation of the "simple principle" and, moreover, that he had a right to think that this reformulation resolved the antitheses between the principle of liberty and the principle of utility that he brings up in the fourth chapter (and that I discussed in the second chapter of this work). But, obviously, everything turns on the meaning of the phrase "distinct and assignable."

By "distinct" Mill apparently just means "reasonably clear." Clarity can be the cause of considerable disagreement when regulations are actually applied in the real world. Lack of such clarity has bred endless debate when laws have hinged on concepts like "obscene," "negligent," "willful," and many others. To avoid any amateurish adventure in jurisprudence at this point, I will simply point out that neither Mill nor anyone else could ever expect *perfect* clarity in the delineation of social obligations. What is expected is simply *reasonable* precision. Following my general line of interpretation, it can also be expected that the burden of establishing reasonable clarity is on the agencies of social coercion, not on the individual.

If this is all the distinctness criterion amounts to, then most of the moral work of the reformulation is being done by the assignability criterion. Mill mentions two components of assignability. First, any regulation must be made reasonably public. This might seem to be a trivial requirement, but it is not. In order for a regulation to be public, obviously, it must be the case that the regulation *could* be made public. Here Mill is, in fact, enforcing a principle that is exactly like one put forward by, of all people, Kant in *Perpetual Peace*.[5] And it obviates a standard line of criticism against utilitarianism, namely, that utilitarianism may entail courses of action that maximize utility only if the actions remain secret. To return to a previous example, the framing of the bag lady has good consequences only if the utilitarian intrigue leading up to the framing remains secret. At another level, even J. J. C. Smart has argued that the best way to bring about maximal utility may be to encourage people to act in nonutilitarian ways, since most people are either not bright enough or too easily inclined to calculate egoistically to properly assess the consequences of their actions. What has happened to make this line of argument useless against the version of utilitarianism I am defending is that we are now concerning ourselves with laws and regulations, not individual actions. And laws and regulations, by their very nature, require public promulgation. There are certainly private actions, and there may be nothing inherently contradictory about a private moral principle (Kant to the contrary), but there is certainly no such thing as a piece of private social legislation.

The second component of the assignability criterion that Mill mentions requires that any assignable obligation be based on utility. By the lights of the kind of utilitarianism I have been developing, this amounts to a requirement of a demonstration of harm, that is, of substantial pain that would result if the obligation were not enforced. That the enforcement of the obligation would bring about pleasure under someone's understanding of pleasure is too flimsy a reason for coercion. This constraint on coercive regulation would seem to be libertarian enough in its consequences, but there is more.

Mill clearly intended the danger of harm to be a necessary but not a sufficient condition for social coercion. What counted for sufficiency (in addition to distinctness, publicity, and demonstrable danger of harm) was that the type of activity in question was not associated with a long-term utility that outweighed the disutility associated with the activity. To be more specific, running people out of business in a free market system poses a serious threat of harm to them and to their associates (since it poses the threat of poverty and all of the painful contingencies attendant thereto). Nevertheless, we allow such harm to occur because of the long-term utility associated with the operation of the free market. Likewise, substantial harm may result from flunking out students who can't compete with their peers, but we allow such harm because of the utility associated with a competitive educational system.

What should be noticed here is that the vagueness of pleasure and the relative specificity of pain is being used doubly in favor of individual liberty and against the justification of social coercion. The state must demonstrate the legitimacy of coercion by appealing to the more demanding and precise standard of proof of pain, while the individual can appeal to the looser standard of proof of pleasure associated with the type of act in question. (The notion of a *type* of act is in need of clarification, and this will come later.)

However, at this point we may formulate the harm principle in terms of the following conditions, which are individually necessary and jointly sufficient to justify the enforcement of a social proscription:

1. The proscription must be made reasonably clear.
2. The proscription must be capable of universal promulgation within the jurisdiction of the proscription. Moreover, it must be reasonably well promulgated within that jurisdiction.

3. The type of action (or inaction) proscribed must be shown to pose a serious danger of harm.

4. The harm associated with the type of action (or inaction) proscribed must not be outweighed by the pleasures associated with that type of action (or inaction) and the harms associated with proscribing it.

Again, the burden of proving that all of these conditions obtain is on the *state*, not the individual.

Aside from the problems associated with the term "type," there are, of course, problems with "harm" and "pleasure" as well. All of these will be taken up in the next chapter. In the chapter after that, I will attempt to draw out some applications of this version of the harm principle. But, at this point, some preliminary observations about the application of this principle are in order.

It should be obvious that this principle poses a test that is far more demanding than those routinely suggested by legislators' arguments even in fairly libertarian countries like the United States. We often hear it argued that "if this law will save just one life, then it is worth it." Obviously, this "one life" principle would allow all sorts of laws that could not meet the standard of the harm principle. It would, for example, warrant a law banning travel by automobile, airplane, train, or boat regardless of any pleasures derived from such travel.

Likewise, we often hear that certain legislation is necessary in order to preserve the "moral fabric" of the society. The vagueness of this sort of legal moralism generally speaks for itself; but, clearly, something more than rhetoric about ethical upholstery is called for by the harm principle. Similar considerations apply to appeals made on behalf of an undefined "general good," "compassion," or "will of God."

Perhaps such appeals could be cashed out in a manner acceptable under the harm principle, but, usually, there is not even the *pretense* of such an attempt. The closest that legislatures usually come to any sort of demonstration of harms and benefits is when they appeal to public opinion polls or to direct plebiscites, and these are a far cry from any appeal to real (as opposed to publicly perceived) harms and benefits. In many cases, there is, after all, nothing going on with most individual citizens that could count as a serious and enlightened assessment of information about the actual costs and benefits of various pieces of legislation that might be voted on. More often than not, what is really going on is that individuals are simply acting on the same vague notions of "moral fabric," "God's will," or "compassion" that determine the rhetoric of legislatures.

So, to return to the principal theoretical thesis of this chapter, I have been attempting to lay out an understanding of the harm principle that, first of all, clearly creates a substantial private sphere and, secondly, lends some kind of substance to Mill's claim that the harm principle is based on the principle of utility. Actually, what follows from my analysis is not only the claim that the harm principle is based on utilitarian calculations of harm and benefit but, moreover, that the application of utilitarianism to questions of social policy is based on the harm principle. The harm principle establishes the conditions under which harms and benefits become relevant to the determination of social regulations; harms are relevant to the extent that the state can prove that they will follow from certain types of action, and benefits are relevant to the extent that the state can show that they will *not* follow from the types of actions it seeks to prohibit.

In other words, the harm principle and the principle of utility are, for all practical moral purposes, interdependent. To talk about either independently of the other is to misconstrue the proper context of application for both, as well as to muddle the historically conditioned motivations behind utilitarianism. It was really not the case that the classical utilitarians first stumbled upon the principle of utility and then discovered that it had libertarian consequences. They settled upon the principle of utility precisely because it would, when cautiously applied, have libertarian consequences.

Understanding this matter of motivational ordering, we can attribute considerable sense to a little-mentioned criticism of utilitarianism that occurs in Marx's *German Ideology*.[6] Marx asserted that any pretense to show that the greatest good for the greatest number required the establishment of a capitalist economy was simply an exercise in question begging. The fact of the matter, he contended, was that the notion of good or utility was, from the outset, an utterly economic notion that had nothing fundamentally to do with any basic idea of happiness or pleasure. Utility was, by definition, to be maximized by allowing the greatest number of "free" trades (most of which, for Marx, were really just instances of exploitative blackmail against workers) in a "free" market such that each would increase the utility of the parties involved in the trades by virtue of the mere fact that the trades occurred at all.

Marx's criticism is, I think, wrong-headed regarding the issue of what the terms "good" and "utility" *must* mean, but correct in two important respects. First, his criticism certainly applies to most versions of preference utilitarianism. Second, even if we reject preference utilitarianism (as I do) there is still something right about his claim that the classical utilitarians were determined to make utilitarianism have certain libertarian consequences, like the defense of capitalism. If utilitarianism could not guarantee a free market, then Bentham and the Mills, quite likely, would have turned to a different moral theory that *would* have had the desired consequences.

Historical motivations aside, understanding the harm principle as a mechanism for applying the principle of utility has a direct bearing on the formal perplexities raised in Chapter 2. If the proof of Sen's liberal paradox is valid (and it is), then at least one of the three conditions required in its proof must be abandoned. The fact of the matter is that my combination of the harm principle and the principle of utility will violate *both* of the controversial conditions in the proof.

The condition of minimal liberalism is violated because my theory will not guarantee that there is one single purely individual choice. In the real world, the negative approach I have taken will, as a matter of *contingent* fact, secure substantial liberty. But, as a matter of principle, there will be no *necessarily* individual choices.

The Pareto principle will be violated because the fact that everyone wants or would, in fact, benefit from a law is not sufficient to justify the existence of the law; the prevention of harm must be demonstrated to be a consequence of the law. Again, as a matter of practice, I doubt that any law which is universally beneficial could not also be argued to be necessary to prevent some kind of real harm. Still, the apparent theoretical implausibility of denying the Pareto principle is something that needs to be addressed.

In the first place, it must be pointed out that the Pareto principle can only be used as a principle for determining legislation under extremely unlikely circumstances. Strong Pareto superiority (which exists when everyone prefers one alternative to another) is certainly not, by itself, a necessary condition for legislation since hardly any law could be argued to be universally beneficial or harm-averting. But it is not, by itself, even a sufficient condition either because, in principle, several incompatible laws could all be universally beneficial relative to the status quo even though they could not all be legislated. The Pareto principle is something we can appeal to in order to rank-order various possible pieces of legislation, but it cannot be used as a justification for actually choosing any state of affairs except under the extremely unlikely circumstance that it establishes a complete ordering over all of the relevant alternatives.

To make the point more clearly, consider the following possible social arrangements:

	x	y	z
A	1	6	500
B	5	600	500

Here x, y, and z are possible social states of affairs, and A and B are the only parties affected by the choice over these alternatives. For convenience, we can assume that A and B each represent half of the entire population of a nation. What follows from the Pareto principle is that y is preferable to x (i.e., it should be ranked above x by any rational social decision procedure) and that z is preferable to x. But neither y nor z is preferable to the other and, moreover, if either y or z was the status quo, then the Pareto principle would not warrant any movement to the other. If x is the status quo, then the principle still does not warrant any choice between y and z, although it says that either is preferable (though not equally preferable) to x. In other words, the Pareto principle is an incomplete mechanism for determining choice sets, and it will not determine a choice set at all unless there is some alternative that everyone prefers not just to the status quo but to all other available alternatives.

All of this leads to the second independent reason for rejecting the Pareto principle. Alternatives become available over time. For example, with respect to the above figure, we might suppose that, at some time, x and y were the only available alternatives and, thus, the Pareto principle really could have been used to justify a choice of y over x. But then alternative z became available at some later time. At that later time (if we suppose that z had become the only other available alternative), the Pareto principle would not warrant any movement to z. This does not mean, of course, that the principle would not *allow* any movement to z, because it generates no ranking between y and z at all. But still, it is not hard to see the economic and political difficulty of moving from y to z given that B has a vested interest in maintaining y and, under y, probably has the power to maintain y as the status quo.

I am dealing here in a reasonably sterile way with a very real political problem. The fact of the matter is that when political systems begin to determine legislation on the basis of whom it will positively benefit rather than on the basis of whom it will save from real harm, the benefits bestowed will have an effect into the future. People will be trapped by those previously granted benefits in strange and unforeseen ways. This will be a major concern of Chapter 7.

CHAPTER 6

Refinements

So far, the statement of my version of utilitarianism has been deliberately stark and oversimplified. It is now time to deal with the sorts of vagueness about key terms that force consideration of the kinds of complications that all moral theories face. When such complications are honestly faced, the usual result is a theory that is less clear in its specific applications than would appear to be the case at first glance. This is certainly the case with my theory. What I will be arguing here is that, although my version of utilitarianism does seem to have definitely libertarian consequences, the precise amount of libertarianism entailed is open to considerable debate. The manner in which we define terms such as "harm," "type," and the like will have a direct bearing on the practical consequences of the theory.

The most troublesome term to contend with here is "harm." So far, I have appealed to what I have called "primitivism," by which I intend to denote the position that "harm" is to be stipulated[1] as simple physical pain. One might be tempted to suggest that the denotation of "harm" should be even narrower than that, for not all pain is harmful, just that which is not productive of some greater good for the individual. For example, anyone who is serious about weight lifting expects to encounter the proverbial pain without which there is no gain. Such pain, it might be argued, is not harmful unless it is connected with an injury that causes an impairment of the weight lifter's performance.

But I am inclined to reject this suggestion. There is, indeed, a bit of masochism in most of us that leads us to the conclusion that some pains are desirable. But all that follows from this is that certain pains are *instrumentally* valuable. It does not follow that any pains are *intrinsically* valuable, nor does it follow that any pains are not intrinsically bad. All things being equal, wouldn't the weight lifter prefer to have the same results without pain if that was possible? What value can the pain itself have aside from the instrumental value practically and psychologically associated with it? So, I am inclined to assert that pain is always harmful and, *in and of itself*, undesirable. Obviously, however, it may be instrumental to the achievement of goods that outweigh the harm and, thus, seen as instrumentally desirable for the individual suffering it or for others.

But is pain the only thing that is to be counted as harmful? This is, clearly, the more troublesome question. At the opposite end of the spectrum of things that might be called harms would be the simple frustration of desire. Given what I have said before about preference utilitarianism, one should be able to infer my antipathy to this idea.

First of all, people's desires are often incoherent, and by frustrating these desires I might, in many cases, actually be helping people rather than harming them. For example, when I frustrate my daughter's desire to stick a paper clip into an electrical outlet, I can hardly be accused of harming her. Secondly, given that desires often amount to reaching for the moon, to define harm as the frustration of a desire is to broaden the class of potential harms beyond all sensible limits. My son may have an intense desire for a $20,000 toy, and I cannot reasonably be accused of harming him because I am not willing to go $20,000 in debt to buy it for him. Finally, to define harm as the frustration of any desire is to make the range of actions to which social regulation might apply too large. In other words, I am inclined to openly beg the question against this definition by rejecting it precisely because it has consequences I don't want.

I want to make it clear that I am not, at this point, committing myself to the denial of the proposition that anything that satisfies any desire is intrinsically good. Although I don't subscribe to this proposition myself, I suspect that one could build enough rationality constraints into a notion of "rational desire," "real wants," or "genuine interests" to make it reasonable and to save it from the objections just listed. My claim is only that the frustration of desire should not be defined as harm.[2] It might well be that the satisfaction of "real" or "rational" desires can be viewed as beneficial. Although I am not harming my son by buying him the $20,000 toy, it makes sense to think that the purchase would benefit him in many direct ways.

In between the definition of harm as pain and the definition of harm as the frustration of any desire, there is a broad continuum of alternate definitions that have been suggested by a number of philosophers from Mill on. The territory has been exhaustively staked out by Feinberg, and I will not pretend to add anything of real substance to his analyses. I should point out, however, that I will be carrying out my discussion of this territory in a substantially different manner than Feinberg does. Whereas he gives a fairly narrow definition of harm (which is heavily qualified by constraints derived from legal considerations); carefully separates harms from the likes of "hurts," "offenses," and "moral harms"; and then proceeds to analyze various alternatives to the harm principle, I have stuck myself with the harm principle. As such, I will proceed by trying to figure out whether offensiveness, for example, should be considered harmful (and, thus, liable to social control) rather than whether the harm principle needs to be supplemented by a distinct "offense principle." The difference between my way of talking about the basic problems and Feinberg's is, I think, mostly verbal.[3]

There is another, and more important, way in which my approach is different from Feinberg's. Feinberg makes it clear from the outset of his enterprise that he is concerned with a narrower project than was Mill. Whereas Mill was concerned with the establishment of a principle that would protect the liberty of individuals from *all* forms of social coercion (moral, legal, and that established by custom), Feinberg is only concerned with the domain of coercion associated with criminal law.[4] This, in part, explains why I am interested in a more primitive definition of harm than Feinberg is. He can start with a broad definition of harm as any "setback to an interest"[5] and then later make it clear that such interests will have to pass through a filter of *legal* constraints connected with justifiability, excusability, and basic legal rights.[6] Thus, he puts considerable distance between his view and anything like preference utilitarianism. Moreover, because of these constraints, the broadness of his basic definition of harm will not result in an excessive expansion of the domain of activity that is prima facie open to social control.

Unlike Feinberg, I *am* concerned with the wider range of social control and, being a utilitarian, I cannot just jump out of the system and appeal to a set of basic rights without making the whole enterprise seem hopelessly ad hoc. As such, I must be more worried about the broadness of the definition of harm because moral claims (whose enforcement is carried out through extremely varied and subtle social mechanisms) do not have to withstand the same kinds of scrutiny on a case-by-case basis that legal claims do. A person does not have to convince a judge and jury that she or he has been *really* harmed in order to assert and gather enough public support for some informal (but nonetheless severe) moral sanction on the basis that someone else has harmed her or him and, thus, ought to face that sanction. Thus I am much more insistent than Feinberg must be on the point that a simple setback to any interest does not, even initially, constitute a real harm. Some interests deserve initial respect, and many others don't. On his view, the difference is, eventually, to be sorted out in a court of law. On my view, the difference between the two is that a respectable interest is one fairly directly connected to the existence of some kind of pain, and this must be sorted out in a context far less orderly than that which exists in a courtroom.

The identification of harm with pain when coupled with the claim that the harm principle will, eventually, be shown to exhaust the realm of truly moral concerns[7] gives rise to a series of obvious objections. What objection could there be to the painless killing of someone? Under my view, it appears, this would not constitute a harm to this person. Likewise, what would be wrong about forcibly putting people under an anesthetic and leaving them in this state until they die?

One small objection to these kinds of cases ought to be mentioned before going further, namely, that, even if death and incapacitation cannot be argued under my view to be harms to the individual who dies or is incapacitated, it is hard to believe that such would not result in harms (or failures to prevent harms) to others. The death of a breadwinner is certain to expose his or her dependents to harmful contingencies. Some person or agency anesthetizing people for no particularly good reason (other than to present philosophical counterexamples) would assuredly be seen as posing a threat of harm to others. Nevertheless, there would certainly be something odd about being forced into the position that death and terminal incapacitation are not really harms *to those who die or are incapacitated*. So something must be said directly in answer to these objections.

The first one is easily handled by just counting death as a harm.[8] Once again, this would not imply that death would, under all circumstances be considered bad or undesirable. Under certain conditions (e.g., the terminal stages of a painful disease), death might be preferable to painful life. Also, death might really be better than some forms of dishonor. As was the case with pain, the claim here must be qualified to assert only that death is *intrinsically* bad, not that it is always *instrumentally* bad.

The second objection is trickier. The common intuition about the prospect of facing terminal anesthesia is that it should count as a harm precisely because it would entail the frustration of desires and life plans, and it is precisely this conception of harm that I am intent upon resisting here. Initially, I could respond that terminal anesthesia is, for all intents and purposes, death (and, therefore, harm). Subjectively, what difference should it make to me whether I will die tomorrow or go under anesthesia and die a year later? My life is over today either way.

However, the objection could be modified so as to avoid this response. For example, let's suppose that tomorrow's anesthesia will not be terminal but, rather, will only last for a few years, then I will be revived and allowed to go on my way. In this case, I would claim that considerable pain would be a necessary consequence. One does not (even with the best physical therapy imaginable) just get out of a bed after several years of immobility and walk away without going through a long period of painful recovery. Moreover, the effect of having lost several years of my life would likely bring about a state of rather severe depression and, as we shall see a little later on, I think it does make sense to broaden the notion of harm to include not just physical pain but also severe mental suffering.

But the objection could be modified and pushed again. Suppose that, rather than anesthesia, I am to be given some drug that would make me a happy (but barely functional) idiot. I would be capable of little more than drooling and playing with rubber toys, but I would experience no more pain than I would have without the drug. Here I am prepared to merely deny the plausibility of the counterexample. I don't know what sort of creature can suffer significant brain damage without also suffering severe pain, but it wouldn't be a person. Every person I have ever seen who has suffered from some sort of mental impairment (whether it was congenital or induced by some injury, overdose, or whatever) was also really suffering from other conditions clearly related to that impairment. Without an extremely compelling real life example (and I doubt that anyone can produce one—after all, who can know what is actually going on in the mind of a hopeless idiot?), I would maintain that the hypothesis that anyone could be turned into a genuinely happy idiot is just that—a hypothesis with no practical (or even theoretical) import.

A more troublesome problem in the same vein comes from Parfit's example of the misconceived child.[9] Here we are to suppose that a woman knows that any child she might conceive now will be substantially disabled (but not so impaired as to face a life not worth living at all). She is prescribed a medication that will eliminate the possibility of conceiving a disabled child within one month. Still, she carelessly allows the conception to occur now, and the child is born with the disability. There is no sense in which she has harmed the child since it would not have existed without the conception, and it is better off being disabled than would be the case if it were never born. Still, our intuitions tell us, things would have been better if she had waited for the medicine to do its work and conceived one month later. Feinberg is prepared to admit this kind of case as a rare (but ultimately untroublesome) exception to the harm principle; it is a "harmless wrongdoing." I am not prepared to go this far. If there is no harm at all that results from the birth, neither to the child nor to the parents nor to the recipients of government aid who might now receive less aid because the child needs it more (and these are all very dubious assumptions), then I am not sure I have the intuition that Feinberg does that there is anything *wrong* about the conception. I don't see why anyone here should have any civil or criminal recourse or, moreover, any reason to even ostracize the mother (except on the grounds that she may have acted *imprudently* in that her life might have turned out better, by her own lights, without the hardship of raising the disabled child). To admit that there is anything *morally wrong* in this particular case is to open up a really dangerous line of thinking. If this mother's conception is wrong because she should have had a normal child rather than a disabled one, then is the conception of a normal child wrong because its place in the world could have been filled with someone else's superior child?

In short, I find none of these cases compelling enough to give up the primitive notion of harm or the claim that what is not harmful is not wrong. The only modifications that seem to be necessary are the small ones I have conceded to, namely, that harm should include not only physical pain but also death and severe psychological suffering.

Mill himself, of course, never confined the meaning of "harm" to anything as restrictive as this. He apparently intended "harm" to cover property damage and, also, being victimized by breeches of "decency" (i.e., being offended). It is not entirely clear whether Mill thinks that "indecency" (at least when it occurs in public) poses some indirect threat of harm or, rather, that indecency should be subject to social restraint regardless of its harmful consequences. Indeed, the text[10] seems to indicate that he believed the latter.

At any rate, the issues of property damage and indecency give us somewhere to start in the examination of other, and broader, conceptions of harm. Given what I have said before about the historical libertarian motivation for utilitarianism, it would make sense to suggest that Mill could have been expected to just beg the question in favor of property rights by counting any violation of those rights as a harm. Indeed, Mill may have been doing precisely that. However, I am inclined to deny the idea that property damage should be counted as harm. I have no doubt that property losses can be every bit as undesirable as physical pain and, in fact, considerably more so.[11] Moreover I have no doubt that private property must be, in some general sense, legally protected. But I don't see why the protection of these rights should hinge on a matter of definition.

There is more than enough reason to believe that substantial strife and physical suffering would result if private property was not protected by the enforcement of laws against theft, vandalism, and the like. Without such laws it would fall to each individual to protect his or her property with whatever violence and guile he or she could muster. The result would surely be mayhem. This is why all societies (including socialist ones) that produce anything worth stealing or smashing have such laws. They are easily justified by even the most stringent application of the harm principle.[12]

Moving farther down the continuum we come to the other kind of activity that Mill, apparently, considered harmful, namely, that concerning "indecency," or, to use Feinberg's terminology, "offensiveness." It is easy to come up with examples of the kinds of activity that almost everyone will think offensive enough to be prohibited regardless of the tendency of the activity to damage anyone in any material way. Likewise, it is easy to come up with examples of activities that were, in some distant time, or are, in some distant land, considered grossly offensive but that are, for the vast majority of late-twentieth-century Westerners, accepted as commonplace. Moreover, many regulations once thought necessary to prevent widespread offense (e.g., those requiring the segregation of races or the subordination of women) now strike most of *us* as offensive.

But whether or not offensiveness is a legitimate warrant for social control is beside the point of my present concerns. The only relevant question here is the one about whether or not offensiveness can be seen as harm. And, pretty clearly, it cannot be seen as harm. It might be seen as leading to the possibility of harm, but it cannot be seen as harmful in and of itself. A grossly indecent demonstration may reasonably count as an incitement to riot, but it is the riot that has likely harmful consequences, not the indecency itself. Someone defecating in public on a camp toilet under a banner that reads "This is what I think of the Kikes" while a recording of vile noises blares in the background[13] may be seen as engaging in behavior so odd that we should wonder what other (and probably harmful) action he is prone to, but it is the threat posed by his likely psychosis that is of ultimate moral concern, not the indecency of his current action.[14] Even in cases where the offensiveness does not portend any mental instability on the part of the offender, there is likely to be a reasonable concern about harm down the road. Here one thinks of cases where neighbors pile junk in their yards or play their stereos late at night and so forth. In these cases some harms (due to children playing in the junk or health problems related to loss of sleep and so on) can be directly attributable to the nuisances, and others can be attributed to the threat of violence breaking out because of understandably frayed nerves.

Similar considerations apply to other examples presented by Feinberg.[15] For example, the activities of a Peeping Tom can be viewed not just as offensive but also potentially dangerous. Anyone prepared to go that far in the invasion of others' privacy is quite likely to go beyond the peeping to actual breaking and entering and, quite possibly, rape. There is, at least, a good reason for the law to act on the basis of this anticipation. Related anticipations would appear to be the motivation behind many recent "stalking laws." Many states have prohibited "stalking" because it has, in many disturbing real cases, preceded actual assaults.

Another example of Feinberg's concerns someone taking a hammer to the face of a human corpse in public. Here, again, I (and, I think, most others) would look upon such an activity as indicative of a kind of psychosis that could wind up motivating violence against the living. How far away is the person who would take a hammer to the head of human corpse (for whatever reason) from taking a hammer to the head of a live human? Not far enough, I would say, to leave the hammerer unmolested by the law (let alone moral censure). Here I am bordering on a line of argument advanced by Kant concerning brutality toward animals. What should concern us, from a moral point of view, about the dog beater is, according to Kant, not the welfare of the dog (for, Kant thought that, in itself, morally inconsiderable) but rather the malicious nature of the beater. Such considerations allow us to separate the dog beater from the butcher. The behavior of the butcher (although every bit as bad for the cow as is the behavior of the dog beater for the dog) can be seen as less of a threat to the rest of us because it is not fueled by an underlying cruel personal motive. Similarly, the behavior of a coroner performing an autopsy (although every bit as destructive to the corpse as is the behavior of the hammerer) can be seen as less of a threat to the rest of us. The same might apply in the case where someone has donated his body to art (in much the same way as one might donate his body to science) for the purpose of being hammered as an artistic statement about something. The artist-hammerer might then (with an awful lot of explanation) be able to make the case that the hammering should go on not just in the name of art for art's sake but, also, in order to comply with the wishes of the demised. Whatever reasons there might be for prohibiting or condemning such an excursion to the fringes of artistic expression would have to be couched in terms of the potential harmfulness of such displays (which, I think, could be pretty easily done). If no one could muster such reasons, then it is just not clear why the "art" should not occur.

Feinberg also confronts us with the prospect of being trapped on a bus with some vile, farting, nose-picking wretch who eats her own vomit. If the wretch is engaging in these behaviors just to annoy her audience, then we have reason to suspect that she might eventually tire of such practices (because her audience becomes numb to it, as many city dwellers today have become numb to all sorts of vile eccentricities they witness in public) and escalate to other forms of behavior that, eventually, might well cross over the line that separates nuisance from harm. Taken in and of itself, though, it is not clear to me that any of the distractions Feinberg subjects us to on his "ride on the bus" are any more disgusting or viscerally repulsive than those brought about by people who exhibit gross deformities, smells, or noises that are related to organic conditions over which they have no control. Are we to return to the days when the handicapped were confined to dungeons so that we "normal" folks wouldn't have to be "offended" by them?[16]

In all such cases I am prepared to claim, without further argument (which could go on as long as someone can continue to conjure up ingenious new examples of depravity), that any example of offensiveness either (1) can be reasonably connected to harmful contingencies or (2) should be tolerated or (3) should be dismissed as unhelpfully hypothetical.

It is often argued that allowing certain types of offensive behavior might lead not to the sort of harm I have been considering but rather to some kind of "moral harm." Moral harm can arise either at the individual or the social level. One can complain that certain acts of indecency can lead either to the moral harming of the person or to long-term "social decay." As for social decay, it is enough here to simply point out the absolute vagueness of this claim.[17] In many cases, this vagueness turns on a simple piece of circularity. A certain allegedly indecent activity is argued as conducive to social decay and then social decay is defined as the state of affairs where such acts of indecency are allowed to occur. For example, people might complain that a certain piece of music or a certain movie are responsible for social decay, and then when they are asked how we identify the existence of social decay, they will claim that it exists whenever this kind of music or movie is tolerated. Moreover, social decay, taken literally as the process whereby a political regime actually approaches collapse, cannot be seen as necessarily bad; some regimes ought to decay.

Moral harm to individuals takes us in a more serious direction. The literature on such harm goes back to Plato, and, even if we reject Plato's claim that immorality always harms the immoral agent, we can agree that there are certain types of activity that can have such damaging consequences to a person's moral and psychological well-being that the activity ought to be considered harmful. For example, holding someone in solitary confinement except for frequent periods of intense (but completely nonviolent) brainwashing can easily been seen as harming the individual, even if not a single bruise results. Such treatment could turn an otherwise intelligent and thoughtful person into a squeamish drone.

Special problems arise concerning the treatment of children. Without laying a hand on a child, a parent can malign, corrupt, and retard that child in ways that any adult could resist (but hardly any son or daughter could). An adult who always shows video tapes depicting violent rapes when adult company comes will probably just be avoided by his victims who were only momentarily offended by his choice of entertainment. However, a father who raises his son on rape videos with an occasional live demonstration on the child's sister or mother is, pretty clearly, going way beyond the bounds of mere indecency. Under such an ugly scenario the son is clearly going to be harmed (not to mention the direct physical harm to the sister and mother). The actual depth of the misery and psychological distress of such abuse is a subject of a considerable literature in clinical psychology, and there is no need for me to pretend any elaboration of it here.

In all of this, however, it must be pointed out that there is good reason for thinking that the misery must be really severe and, moreover, intricately connected to some sort of physical suffering before it should be counted as harm. What separates harmful psychological distress from nonharmful psychological stress is not entirely clear, but there is surely a distinction between the two. People will, after all, que up and pay money for the privilege of being caused terror, pity, and discomfort in a movie theater. Such emotions cannot, therefore, be seen as intrinsically bad; they are, after all, the precise and desired end of the people paying to have them. People do not go to see a horror film to learn about life, become better people, or anything else. Nor do they go because they are deranged or confused about the content of the movie. They go precisely to feel the sensation of horror, and they would feel disappointed if the movie didn't supply them with that sensation. The sensation would, of course, be entirely different—and entirely undesirable—if it was connected with the real possibility of pain; it is one thing to watch someone being chased by a chain-saw murderer on a movie screen and quite another to be chased by a real murderer. And this, the perceived potentiality of real physical suffering, may be exactly what it is that separates harmful psychological distress from nonharmful distress.

At any rate, what I have been attempting here is the staking out of a continuum of phenomena that have been alleged to be harmful or, at least, a fit target of social control. The continuum runs from simple physical pain and death to severe psychological and moral damage to property damage to mere offensiveness (where no harm can be even potentially connected to the activity) to vague social "moral harms." I am inclined to think that severe psychological and moral damage should be counted along with pain and death as types of harm (in large part because these kinds of damage are usually connected with pain and death). Property damage can be handled by virtue of its instrumental connections with pain and suffering. Mere offensiveness and conduciveness to "moral decay" are too vague and subject to too much disagreement to count as harms. Cases of extreme offensiveness can, generally, be handled as cases of potential pain and suffering.

This splitting of the continuum will result in a pretty libertarian outcome when the harm principle is applied. Of course, the continuum could be split in other places with different attendant consequences. It is important to see here not whether my intuitions about where the line ought to be drawn are correct but, rather, that the drawing of the line will determine how libertarian the harm principle will be. Moreover, the drawing of the line will be determined by how libertarian the line drawer is. A libertarian will tend to draw the line near where I have and then assert that the onus for showing that the domain of real harm ought to be larger is on those who believe that such things are real harms. And to the degree that there is far more disagreement about the undesirability of these "new" harms than there is about the undesirability of pain, any regulation based on their assignment as harms will be less justifiable as a matter of rhetorical fact and as a matter of moral principle.

For example, I take it that the arguments for the belief that various forms of distress caused by child neglect and abuse constitute harms as serious and as unquestionable as physical pain have been so compelling that our laws (and the manner of their enforcement) as well as our personal opinions concerning the degree to which parents are free to raise their children as they see fit have been substantially changed in favor of the welfare of children.

As an example on the other side, certain feminist and religious organizations have been largely unsuccessful in convincing many legislatures that pornography causes real harm either to women or to "the moral fabric" of the nation. And, as a result, regulations concerning the sale, distribution, and public display of pornography have been spotty, irregularly enforced, and regularly overturned in the courts; pornography is now much more widely available than it has ever been before, and the general disapprobation of it is less than it has ever been before.

"Harm" is not the only concept that needs refinement in order to even begin to apply the harm principle. Before we can determine whether or not a certain type of activity is harmful and, additionally, whether or not the benefits associated with that type of activity outweigh the demonstrable harms associated with it, we must grapple with the manner in which we are going to single out the relevant *type* of activity for consideration.

To illustrate the problem, consider the history of drinking-age laws in the United States over the past few years. During the Vietnam War, the voting age was reduced from twenty-one to eighteen. The argument that young men who were being compelled to serve in an unpopular war deserved to have some voice in the election of the politicians who were voting to continue the adventure was overwhelming. Shortly thereafter, many states reduced the drinking age from twenty-one to eighteen. Again, the argument that anyone old enough to drink and face death in Vietnam ought to be able to buy a beer in-country seemed to make sense. For all intents and purposes, the age of full adulthood had been reduced to eighteen.

Within a decade of the American withdrawal from Vietnam, the push was on to raise the drinking age to twenty-one and, eventually, the federal government compelled all states to do so (under the threat of removing federal highway funding if they didn't). The argument for the change to the status quo ante bellum was based on at least a good pretense of a demonstration of the real harms caused by teenage drinking and driving. Admittedly, anything like a drinking age is, to a large degree, arbitrary; such are the necessities of social enforcement. Maturity and ability to responsibly use alcohol are much harder to check before a sale than is a driver's license. But once an arbitrary age of adulthood is established, there should be a very clear demonstration that a whole class of those adults should be deprived of a liberty still granted to the others before the liberty is actually deprived.

In the case of teenage drinking, the public perception of the numbers was that, indeed, this class of adults posed a special threat on the highways. Granted, for the sake of argument, that the numbers did show that eighteen- to twenty-one-year-olds were responsible for more deaths and injuries per capita than any other three-year age group, it is still hard to see why such a sweeping prohibition was in order. It is, I would guess, true that twenty-one- to twenty-four-year-olds are the cause of more drunken automotive mayhem than forty-one- to forty-four-year-olds, but no one (at least no one who was being seriously listened to) was suggesting raising the drinking age to twenty-four or twenty-seven or thirty. Moreover, the pleasures derived from drinking by eighteen- to twenty-one-year-olds cannot plausibly be argued to be less than those derived by other age groups.

At any rate, I am not interested at this point in arguing that the change in drinking age laws was unjustifiable. My intent here is to point out that this legislation was aimed at a broad type of activity. The target was not just teenage drunk driving; drunk driving was already illegal for everyone. Nor was the target just teenagers who had some sort of history of irresponsible drinking; that could have been handled by some procedure like marking the driver's licenses of eighteen- to twenty-one-year-olds (or anyone else, for that matter) who had alcohol-related convictions and then prosecuting anyone who served alcohol to someone with a marked driver's license. The target was *all* teenage drinking, regardless of the fact that the vast majority of teenagers who drink, like the vast majority of other adults who drink, do so without any criminal incident.

Once again, we are faced with a question about where to split a continuum. To the extent that the types of activities to be proscribed are targeted in a broad way, the consequences of the harm principle will be less libertarian. Thus, a libertarian could be expected to take the general position that the types of actions to be prohibited should be drawn as narrowly as possible so that the laws are targeted only at the specific types of actions that can be clearly demonstrated as harmful and as without redeeming social benefit.

Needless to say, splitting this continuum poses questions about jurisprudence and law enforcement that are far less theoretical than the matter of defining harm. I will not presume to be able to delve into such complications with the intent of framing some simple-minded algorithm for determining how relevant types of acts ought to be determined. Obviously, targeted types of action can be so narrowly focused that enforcement is made virtually impossible. Nevertheless, the prejudice of the libertarian would be in favor of narrowness, and more importantly, it would be in favor of placing the burden of proving the real necessity of broad targeting on those who favor such broadness.

Closely related to questions about the broadness of legislation are those connected with how far the state should go not just in order to react to violations of the law but in order to prevent violations. It is one thing to arrest a drunk driver who has already killed someone, another to arrest a drunk driver even though she hasn't killed anyone yet, another to revoke her driving privileges because she once drove drunk, and quite another to deny her either driving or drinking privileges because she belongs to an age group (or gender or ethnic group or religion) that, as a matter of statistics, poses a special threat on the highways. Again, all I am prepared to claim is that the consequences of the harm principle will be less libertarian to the extent that legislation is targeted at threatened crimes rather than actual ones. But even the most radical libertarian is going to admit that substantial effort must be made to prevent crimes as opposed to just retaliating against them. Mill certainly never thought that authorities had to wait until a harm had actually occurred before they intervened.

So far I have not been entirely clear in my use of phrases such as "social regulation," "social coercion," and the like. Most of the issues dealt with thus far have been discussed in terms of legal control with, admittedly, only a partial indication of the complications (which Mill was especially concerned about) involved in social control *generally* (be it by a law, custom, or moral criticism that is presumed to carry legitimate force). In connection with this, I need to bring up one more continuum that must be split in order to apply the harm principle, and that concerns the nonlegal mechanisms of social control.

A society is more than citizens, police, courts, and jails. If any society hopes to survive very long, it must develop a complicated system of institutions and customs that, in turn, can be counted on to inculcate a general sentiment of nonmaleficence and a respect for the specific laws, mores, and institutions that really maintain social order. No society can afford enough cops to police a nation of individuals who are all psychologically predisposed to violate the law whenever such seems prudent, and no society can afford to take care of generation after generation of children raised under conditions that would predispose them to break the law (or, at least, the law as it ought to be) whenever such would serve one's self-interest.

The continuum that arises here concerns the degree to which social institutions are to encourage obedience to laws and customs and, also, the degree to which individuals are to be encouraged to ostracize their peers for breeches of the ideal law that the state, acting through its established offices cannot, or will not, enforce. Mill, of course, devoted considerable attention to this issue. In fact, he thought it the most important of the considerations addressed in *On Liberty*. Mill's position, as articulated in the third chapter of *On Liberty*, stakes out the libertarian end of the continuum.

There is a tendency, Mill notes, of individuals not just to conform to necessary regulation but to go beyond simple necessary conformism to a point where conformism is worshipped for its own sake. There is a dangerous tendency on the part of the bland middle class to prize anything that contributes to blandness and inoffensiveness of character and, thus, to prize the indoctrination of a similar boring nature in others and to relish the opportunity to lambast anyone who is not as boring as the average person. Although he was one of the ablest defenders of democratic ideals, the real danger of modern democracy that Mill was speaking to in *On Liberty* was that, under democratic regimes, the average has a tendency to take on a moral authority it does not deserve. The way things are ordinarily done by ordinary people in ordinary situations becomes the *right* way to do things regardless of the fact that certain unordinary ways of doing things are in no way really harmful and, thus, are in no way really *wrong* (though, they may be *imprudent*).

As a consequence, Mill thought it best to structure institutions in a manner so that the push to pointless conformism would be thwarted and, thereby, the tendency of citizens to criticize their peers just for being different would be abated. Mill's discussion of education in the fifth chapter of *On Liberty* is typical of his general point of view. Although he thought that education ought to be mandatory, he opposed the establishment of a state-run school system.

The misgivings he had about such a system have turned out to be genuinely prophetic. His fear was that the general curriculum of any state system would, over time, be completely standardized and, since choices made for any student would now be choices made for all students, every piece of the curriculum would have to run through a gauntlet of special interest groups each of which could argue that their children should not be compelled to be subjected to ideas that parents felt wrong or offensive. As a consequence, only the blandest of intellectual pablum would be served up, and the product would be generation after generation of thoughtless robots raised to believe that the recitation of homey platitudes constitutes knowledge and wisdom.

One need only look at the educational systems in most parts of the United States to see that Mill had a point. The Bible cannot be seriously discussed because to do so would offend non-Christians. The theory of evolution and the big bang theory cannot be seriously discussed because to do so offends Christians. Mark Twain offends blacks, James Joyce offends women, Plato offends homophobes, and so it goes. Censorship beyond the belief of Plato has resulted in students being "educated" in science and the arts in such a manner that they that can't even begin to fathom the understanding of science and art that Plato got from Socrates on the streets. It should come as no surprise, then, that many American students find the information they get on the streets more valuable than that which they get in school.

The point of Mill's argument is twofold. First, the nature of the attitudes and underlying character of the individuals in a society will be determined not just by the openly professed aims of the institutions in question but also by the structure of the institutions themselves. Secondly, whether one is concerned with the structure of the institutions or the various gospels they attempt to inculcate, one should lean towards a state of affairs where individuality and respect for individual differences of opinion and temperament are tolerated and respected. Certainly, respect for just and necessary law, benevolence, and, especially, nonmaleficence are to be ingrained as much as is necessary to preserve a just regime. But conformism for its own sake is unnecessary for the survival of any free state and, from the point of view of the Millian liberal, undesirable as a character trait of free individuals.

The other end of the continuum is marked by a position that would have it that tradition and conformity to the preconditions of a maximally secure state are of utmost importance. The common wisdom of common people is all the average citizen needs to know. Whatever confuses the average citizen confounds the need for stability. Under such a system, central coordination of the mechanisms of indoctrination and homogeneity of the institutional gospel will seem reasonable. Moreover, individual citizens will be encouraged not only to be obedient to all authority but also, whenever possible, to go beyond mere compliance and harass anyone who does not feel the need to go above and beyond the duty to obey and conform. (A defender of this position would, of course, find some far more charitable way of stating things, but I will leave such conservatives to fend for themselves.)

The issue of pointless conformism has a troublesome corollary in the form of the problem of partial compliance. The partial compliance problem is closely related to the foundational issues surrounding the prisoner's dilemma and the formation of social contracts. Given that a sufficient level of enforced cooperation is needed to get individuals around suboptimal equilibrium points, what does one do when there is not a level of cooperative sentiment present to bring about an optimal outcome? To state matters less abstractly, given that a certain amount of conformity to a law is needed in order for that law to have any good effect, what should one do when there are not enough people in compliance with the law to get the good effect? Should one go ahead and obey the law anyhow (perhaps with the hope that one's good example will encourage others to follow, but perhaps not), or should one just view things as being like the state of nature where the only rational choice is to act in one's own best interests and without regard to the welfare of others.

Partial compliance cases can also arise in situations where social morality dictates not conformity with a law but rather disobedience of it. For example, segregation laws seem to be clearly immoral given almost any theory of social morality, but their removal required conspicuous disobedience of them. What should one do if one believes that a certain law should be disobeyed but not enough other people are going to be disobedient to result in anything other than one's own pointless imprisonment, torture, or death? Should a person even voice opposition to an unjust state of affairs and, thereby, face even mere ostracism if the gesture will only succeed in making that person an outcast?

Partial compliance cases mark the edge of the boundary between social ethics and individual ethics. I believe that the reason they have caused so much trouble for various forms of utilitarianism and for theories like Rawls's is that such theories have been based upon the premise that there must be some uniform decision principle that applies neatly to all levels of ethical decision. Moreover, I believe that a genuine understanding of partial compliance problems can only be accomplished by a recognition that they are unresolvable within the context of a purely social ethic. The question of whether or not one ought to obey a just but unenforced law or disobey an unjust but enforced law is a question concerning individuality, integrity, and nobility of character. A central thesis of this book is that such questions are not reducible to social concerns and, in fact, the values that attach to the lives of individuals may be largely antithetical to perceived social needs.

CHAPTER 7

Applications

The point of this chapter is not to make a bunch of recommendations about concrete social policy based on the foregoing theoretical considerations. In the first place, although the view being developed here is an indirect form of utilitarianism, it is still a form of utilitarianism. Any utilitarian ought to think that it is really stupid to pretend any kind of useful analysis of concrete issues without marshaling much more empirical data than I intend to here. In the second place, such an exercise would not be of any interest without an assumption that the theory antecedent to the concrete consequents was reasonable, and I am not presuming yet that this should be believed of my theory.

The point here is, rather, to add to the believability of the theory by pointing out that its consequences are, at least, not necessarily and wildly counterintuitive. Specifically, I want to give good reason to believe that, although the theory is basically libertarian, it is not ridiculously libertarian. To put things in terms used earlier, I want to show that my view is not prima facie descriptively inadequate.

The toughest problems for any remotely libertarian theory concern the charge that such theories are utterly insensitive to the kinds of undeserved impoverishment that modern welfare systems are designed to address. Unimaginative optimism about benefits "trickling down" to starving children will hardly do as a solution to the problems made obvious by the gross inequities of the contemporary world.

I have mentioned before that a straightforward application of utilitarianism will have a tendency to move social arrangements in the direction of egalitarian results. But this fact will not help my theory, for I have rejected the idea that utilitarianism ought to be applied in a straightforward way even to social problems. Given the manner in which I have suggested that the harm principle ought to be used as the mechanism by which the principle of utility is applied, I am stuck with having to show that, somehow, a reasonable set of welfare institutions can be justified on the basis of their necessity in preventing harm.

The issue of harm prevention brings us back to a topic introduced two chapters back, namely, that of bad Samaritan laws. Previously, I indicated my support of Feinberg's position that there is no good reason standing in the way of requiring, morally *and legally*, that individuals perform "easy rescues" of others in situations where serious harm is threatened. We are now in a position to add a little more argumentative substance to this claim.

Consider again the case of the poolside lounger who fails to enact an obviously easy rescue of a drowning child, but, this time, in light of the conditions of distinctness and assignability laid out two chapters ago. Could a law proscribing the lounger's inaction pass those tests? As for the first assignability condition, namely, the requirement of reasonable promulgation, the fact that several European nations and a couple of American states, in fact, have and enforce bad Samaritan laws seems to settle the issue.

As for the other assignability conditions, the harm caused by the bad Samaritan's inaction is clearly serious and, also, not counterbalanced by any reasonable assessment of the pleasures gained by him. Moreover, the harms associated with the enforcement of bad Samaritan laws seem to be no greater than those associated with most other laws. Indeed, witnesses may be hard to find in such cases but, when they are available, the enforcement of this kind of law seems to pose no special threat of the government being overly intrusive or overly restrictive of individuals' ordinary activities.

The main line of argument against bad Samaritan laws seems to center on the condition of clarity. The fear, from Macaulay on, has been that such laws are the thin end of a dangerous wedge.[1] If I am to be required to take one step in order to save a child's life, then why not two? If two, then why not three? If three, why not three thousand? If I am required to save one child then why not three thousand? This line of argument is plagued by a general problem shared by all slippery slope arguments. By dropping black paint one drop at a time into a vat of white paint there is, clearly, no special drop that turns the paint in the vat from white to black. But, just because there is a broad array of grays in between white and black, we should not infer that there is no perceptible difference between black and white.

Likewise, constructing laws to get at the poolside lounger do not seem, as a matter of logical or legal principle, to entail the imprisonment of people who don't give enough money to starving beggars in the streets. The problems associated with the enforcement of bad Samaritan laws seem to pose little more problem than the enforcement of mundane traffic laws. That we want to get at people who drive through school zones at 140 miles an hour doesn't imply that we are committed to ticket every one who goes as much as one mile an hour over the speed limit on a freeway.

Nevertheless, one must admit that there is, indeed, no sharp break between "easy" and "hard" rescues. Moreover, the class of genuinely easy rescues need not be confined to just the sort of grossly insensitive neglect shown by the poolside lounger. Indeed, if one can save the life of a beggar whom one passes in the street by simply dispensing some small change, then isn't the rescue there just as easy as it is in the case of the lounger? The answer, I think, must be "Yes."

But there are two problems, which Feinberg calls "coordination problems,"[2] with any legal or moral requirement that one dispense this sort of easy rescue. In the first place, the mechanism of aiding beggars does not insure that aid is distributed on the basis of genuine need; very effective beggars could receive much more than they really need to avoid harm while other, less effective ones starve. In the second place, distributions in this free market charity system may not be remotely based on the ability of the givers to give. Moreover, the dispensation of relief might not occur at any appreciable level at all if the population of potential givers is an especially uncaring lot.

It is because of these coordination problems that the duty to give charity is viewed as imperfect. What is really lurking behind the distinction between perfect and imperfect duties in this kind of case is that the duty can only be assigned collectively and, furthermore, can only be satisfied through collective and coordinated effort. Those in a position to help have a collective duty to help those who face the threat of serious harm without such help, but none of those in a position to do so have any perfect duties toward any specific needy person. In response to this need for collective coordination, we have, almost everywhere in the West, turned the imperfect duty to give charity into the perfect duty to pay taxes so that the government can then effectively dispense aid to those who need it most and, ideally, those who need it at all in order to avoid the threat of harm.

So, turning again to the specific conditions of distinctness and assignability, certainly, laws and institutions set up to collect taxes and dispense welfare benefits can be arranged so as to meet the clearness condition. Just as certainly, the regulations requiring the payment of taxes and those requiring government agencies to effectively distribute aid in noncorrupt ways can be publicized. The harm to be prevented is demonstrable and substantial. Finally, the harms that would arise if various welfare agencies did not move to prevent them can (no doubt with considerable controversy about a lot of grimy facts) be argued to outweigh any benefits that might have been derived without the welfare systems and any harms caused by their operation. Of use in making this last claim stick against extreme libertarian factual assessments to the contrary will be those considerations about diminishing marginal utility that I previously dismissed. The fact that goods and services mean more to people to the degree that those people are without them cannot be used as a direct argument for redistribution of resources. However, it can be used to support the claim that obligations to provide welfare benefits are assignable, since the harms prevented by aid to the poor will have a tendency to be greater than the harms brought about by taxing the nonpoor.

This line of reasoning goes a long way in the defense of what I have, somewhat misleadingly, called welfare "benefits." Under my theory, the only benefits that are legitimate are those necessary for the prevention of harm where "harm" is rather narrowly defined. The provision of mere "benefits," strictly speaking, is not warranted under my theory. Those in a position to give have a collective obligation to fund programs that, to use Feinberg's phrases, dispense "active aid" but none that dispense "gratuitous benefit."[3]

Thus, institutions dedicated to feeding, housing, and curing those who would otherwise suffer in obvious ways can be easily justified. Institutions dedicated to the provision of free education for those who need it are less justifiable (since it is not clear that a formal education necessarily or even regularly avoids harm), but, I am inclined to think, justifiable enough to warrant at least something like the voucher system apparently advocated by Mill.[4] A centralized state educational system is far less justifiable and, perhaps, not justifiable at all. Subsidization of medical research, improvement of agricultural techniques, and so on are likely to be justifiable. Subsidization of agricultural nonproduction and of the writing of philosophy books is less justifiable and, probably, not justifiable at all. There is no clear sense in which a huge subsidy to a large agricultural conglomerate or a grant to a philosophy professor are necessary in order to prevent any real harm to anyone.

In the case of agricultural subsidies, I suppose one could provide a case on their behalf by pointing to the consequences of widespread economic collapse of the agricultural industry if parity programs were suspended. I will leave such disputes to the economists. In the case of funding for research in the humanities, the arts, and many of the social sciences, though, the line of defense is likely to border on a weird sort of legal moralism. Someone might argue that, although not a single life, not a single moment of pain, might be saved by the funding of research in philosophy and history or of projects in music and photography, the possibility of cultural decay without such funding is obvious. Once again, we are back to talk about various kinds of erosion of the spiritual seatcovers of the land that must, on my analysis, not be taken seriously when we are talking about social coercion (which, indeed, we are when we are talking about taxation).

Returning to the kinds of programs about which I have confessed a faith of justifiability, it is only fair that I point out that there are grave practical concerns that might be voiced in opposition. In the first place, even if we consider programs like the American Medicare system, almost any American worker need only look at his or her pay stub to be brought to the point of wondering whether the rescue of those receiving Medicare benefits is, any longer, "easy." Secondly, there are the well-worn arguments that any time even crucial needs are provided by the government, there is less incentive for individuals to even try to take care of those needs by themselves. Furthermore, there is a new incentive for people who used to take care of those needs themselves to stop doing so.

There is no point in rehashing these debates about incentive and taxation here. I am only intent on pointing out where the problems are with respect to the important moral principles involved, and I would not pretend to have detailed solutions to all of these complex social and psychological quandaries.

There is a third, and trickier, problem that Mill showed some sensitivity to in the fifth chapter (par. 22) of *On Liberty*. It is one that primarily concerns public rhetoric on issues affecting individual liberty. The problem is that, once some social program is in place to take care of some basic need, the presence of that program can be used as a reason to infringe upon apparently unrelated liberties. To use a contemporary example, arguments are often made to the effect that people must be compelled to wear motorcycle helmets or seat belts not so much because of the threat of harm to themselves if they do not but, rather, because of the threat of harm to others who will have to pick up the tab for the care of the injured driver or rider.

The harm to others talked about here could not, on my analysis anyhow, be construed simply as economic harm. Although I have argued before that laws protecting property rights could be justified under my principles, I rejected the idea that taking someone's money away was, in and of itself, an instance of harming her. Nevertheless, when we are dealing with the distribution of public funds, if those funds have to be spent in one place, then they are not being spent somewhere else where they may be needed to alleviate harm. So, the unhelmetted motorcyclist could be held as an indirect cause of a failure to prevent harm elsewhere. At any rate, what is important to see is that a liberty as initially unrelated to public funding of health care programs as motorcycling without a helmet can be opened to infringement because of the prior commitment to such public programs. All sorts of activities could be limited even though (absent the existence of the public programs) they pose no clear threat of harm for anyone but the people engaging in those activities. I am not, of course, arguing that such concerns should count as decisive arguments against public health care programs; the potential of such programs to prevent harms not otherwise preventable is, after all, enormous. Moreover, the American experience with a mostly private health care system gives us every reason to believe that the harms involved are, indeed, not preventable without a public health care system. (This consideration alone may well give the advocate of public health care all he or she needs to win the argument here.) However, the danger that, under a system filled with publicly financed programs, almost every activity that poses any kind of danger to the individual engaged in that activity would become a legitimate state concern is a serious one, which should be weighed in against whatever merits can be claimed for the establishment of the programs.[5]

This brings us to the second major consequence of my theory, which, to some degree, separates it from other libertarian theories and, in particular, from the version of libertarianism suggested by the "simple principle" in the first chapter of *On Liberty*. In that chapter, Mill is more than clear in pointing out that it is only harm *to others* that is to serve as a necessary condition of social coercion. Harm to oneself is definitely *not* a good reason to stop someone from doing something. The way I have laid out the conditions of the harm principle, it doesn't matter whether the harm to be used by the state as a defense of coercive intrusion is to self or others.

This is not, I think, out of line with the fourth chapter reformulation of the harm principle with which I have been most concerned. In the fourth chapter (pars. 8 and 9), Mill clearly recognizes the problem of ruling out social concern about self-harm *as a matter of principle*. It seems as though he eventually (Chapter IV, par. 11) comes to the view that social coercion in cases of self-harm is better argued against on the basis of the bad *instrumental* consequences of such legislation rather than on the basis of fiat. Whatever he had in mind, it is the generally bad instrumental consequences of paternalistic legislation that cause me to doubt the legitimacy of much of it, although I must admit that there is nothing *necessarily* wrong about paternalism so long as the paternalism is directed at the prevention of harm rather than the promotion of some notion of the good life which is being foisted upon people.

The instrumental difficulties involved even in the prevention of self-harm (even when those harms are freely admitted to be harms by the individual who is to be protected from the consequences of her or his own actions) are pretty obvious. First, the amount of surveillance and intrusion required to keep people from harming themselves is usually much greater than that necessary to keep people from harming others. Second, even in cases where paternalistic legislation could be enforced with little intrusion, as would be the case with laws requiring the use of motorcycle helmets, the argument must be mounted that the harms avoided by enforcement of the legislation outweigh the pleasures enjoyed by the individuals engaging in the activity in question. The problem here is that if bareheaded motorcyclists, hang gliders, and mountain bikers insist that the pleasures derived from their activities are felt by them to outweigh the risks of harm associated with their pursuits (even when they are fully informed about those risks), then it's not clear that the rest of the population is in much of a position to argue that the risk takers are wrong. This would have a tendency to make the kinds of calculations required under my version of the harm principle marginal at best and, as such, would tend to settle things against the state because of the overarching burden of proof that falls in its direction. But, again, the existence of public health care programs that are independently justifiable under the harm principle will tend to skew the argument in favor of some forms of paternalistic intervention (especially when the activity in question is very risky and fairly easy to police).

Another set of especially annoying problems for libertarians revolve around cases where the liberty of individuals is threatened not by the state but, rather, by private organizations with which the individuals are, ostensibly, voluntarily associated. As an example of such a problem, consider the issue of drug testing done by corporations. The problem here is that, on the face of things, corporations are not obligated the meet the conditions of the harm principle in order to impose severe limitations on the liberties of employees. And it must be pointed out that drug tests are only the tip of the iceberg. Corporations have been known to resort to all sorts of personality tests, honesty tests, and other more direct means of prying into aspects of employees' private lives that may have no real connection at all with job performance.

In order to get at the problems caused by corporate drug testing, I will begin with some predictable libertarian lemmas about drug regulation generally. From Mill on up to Milton Friedman, libertarians have argued that blanket prohibitions of the use of various intoxicants are unwarranted. Applying the harm principle as I have formulated it seems to me to support this conclusion. There is little problem with clarification or promulgation of drug regulations. However, on the remaining conditions, there is enough doubt to conclude that the state's burden of proof is probably not going to be met.

In the first place, the harms of drug use that can be prevented by prohibition are not as massive as is usually thought and, more importantly, a serious calculation of these harms is rarely even pretended by the advocates of drug regulation. There is much talk about the destruction of life associated with drug use when, in fact, the number of "cocaine-related" and "heroin-related" deaths annually (2,952 in 1986)[6] is less than half that for deaths due to routine use of household consumer products (6,092 in 1981 to 1982).[7] The number of emergency room treatments caused by household products (10,787,052 in 1981 to 1982)[8] is roughly three hundred times greater than those related to cocaine and heroin use (37,576 in 1987).[9] Of course, these sorts of statistics seriously understate the full extent of the damage due to drug use. There are all sorts of harms to the users, battered spouses and children, victims of intoxicated drivers, and so on that are obviously not being tallied here. No one can deny that these harms are substantial. Nevertheless, it must be kept in mind that the relevant concern is not the amount of harm that can be attributed to drug and alcohol use but, rather, the amount of harm that can be prevented by trying to stop the use of these substances through criminal prosecution. The damage caused right now by drug use is, after all, resulting in spite of the prohibition of drugs and a highly concerted effort involving a broad range of local, state, federal, and even military branches of government to enforce the prohibition. All too often, it is forgotten that prohibition of an activity does not entail the disappearance of that activity. In any reasonably liberal society laws will never be capable of the sort of draconian enforcement that would, perhaps, insure near total compliance.

In the second place, the harms associated with the enforcement of drug laws are, indeed, grave. Most of the deaths and injuries claimed to be a result of drug use are really a result of drug prohibition, just as the cause of gangland violence in Chicago in the 1930s was a direct result not of alcohol use but of the criminal activity organized in response to prohibition.

In the third place, the pleasures derived from drug use are substantial. At least a partial indication of the pleasures derived from drug use is the amount of money paid out at street level for drugs. To assert by fiat that such massive expenditures are all, or even largely, a simple function of unchosen addictive behavior is to be as completely out of touch with the realities of casual drug use as the WCTU was about casual alcohol use in the 1930s.

The failure to appreciate the fact that a major problem with prohibitions of intoxicants is simply lost pleasure still informs a lot of bad thinking about the fate of the prohibitions of sixty years ago. To hear the usual tales about why prohibition failed one would believe that what really happened was the unfortunate practical failure of a good idea. But the fact of the matter is that prohibition failed largely because Americans like to drink, and telling them that they couldn't was a bad idea not just in practice but in principle. The pleasures experienced by drinkers were excluded as illegitimate as a matter of principle whereas, under the harm principle, such pleasures should have been given an initial accounting and then, perhaps, later found to be illegitimate because they were associated with a type of activity whose benefits were outweighed by its harms.

However, wherever government prohibitions may fail, corporate enforcement may succeed with scary efficiency. The government, under current laws, can arrest only on the basis of either sale or demonstrated possession or present intoxication. But the sorts of drug tests administered by employers can test for drug use quite removed in space and time from the testing and, moreover, come up with positive results even if the testee never sold, paid for, or was appreciably intoxicated by the drugs used. Additionally, while the criminal penalties for possession of small amounts of some drugs has been reduced below that of a speeding ticket in some states, the penalty for a positive drug test result in some corporate programs can be dismissal, virtual blacklisting within one's profession, or submission to some lengthy drug treatment program at the employee's expense. In other words, one may lose one's career, be imprisoned for several weeks in a hospital, or face tens of thousands of dollars in fines exacted in the form of lost wages and treatment fees for an addiction that doesn't even exist.

But on what basis should the state move against corporate infringement of employees' liberties? Certainly, the operations of a large organization like a corporation should, prima facie, warrant more scrutiny than the actions of an individual (since the wrongdoings of a corporation are likely to be of more consequence than those of an individual). Nonetheless, any move the government makes against any nongovernment organization must, under my theory, be argued for in terms of its necessity to prevent unjustified harm. It is not at all clear that firing people is harming them at all (let alone harming them in an unjustifiable manner) under the stringent notion of harm to which I have committed myself. The fact that corporations are acting in ways that infringe upon civil liberties that their employees ought to have does not, in itself, constitute any harm that is remediable by legitimate state intervention.

If corporations move over the line that separates nonviolent punitive threats (like the threat to fire) from violent ones, then the state would have warrant to move. When an employer threatens violence rather than firing then, really, the employer is no longer an employer but a slavemaster, and the employee is really a slave. It hardly needs to be mentioned that many workers in many parts of the world are really slaves in this sense. But a typical worker in the more advanced nations of the world could only be speaking metaphorically if she refers to herself as a "wage slave." Wages don't enslave; threats of violence do.

So, under my analysis, any coercion of employees by employers, no matter how exploitative it may appear, is immune from government sanction unless that coercion entails a threat of real harm. It should be kept in mind at this point that I have already argued for the justifiability of various welfare programs, and these curb the exploitative power of business considerably, for no employee could be counted on to endure conditions of employment more miserable than going on welfare. Nevertheless, there must be something more than the comfort of welfare for workers who face poor wages, generally rotten working conditions, and specific annoyances like drug testing. And, short of government interference in the conduct of business, there are a number of factors that, indeed, ought to constrain employers.

In the first place, few employers can secure an exceptional work force by engaging in practices that aggravate employees. To the extent that management attempts to control workers in ways the workers find intolerable, they will quit or organize and threaten to strike (which, of course, they are free to do under my theory). Simple prudence dictates that employers be careful about intruding too far into the private lives of employees.

In the second place, there is an argument made famous by Milton Friedman[10] that appeals to a more general set of prudential considerations. In arguing that the only legitimate social responsibility of corporations is to maximize profit, Friedman held that when corporations seek to do socially good things that do not ultimately benefit the company they are, in effect, passing illegitimate taxes onto the three main groups of corporate beneficiaries. The costs of these "socially responsible" endeavors will, in reality, be borne either by employees in the form of lower wages, by stockholders in the form of lower dividends, or by consumers in the form of higher prices. In any of these cases (and usually the costs of "social responsibility" fall on all three groups) the corporate officers have taken it upon themselves to induce an opportunity cost to people who did not elect those officers to act as tax agents and spend these funds on programs that, apparently, could not find genuine public support with the government officials who really are elected to tax and spend on social programs.

Now, on the assumption that drug testing cannot be justified on the basis of serious calculations of harms and benefits associated with it, corporations that engage in such testing are doing exactly what Friedman encourages them not to. Unless serious calculations of profits lost because of off-the-job drug use can be produced and, additionally, it can be shown that those lost profits are greater than the costs to corporations associated with the tests, then corporations must be engaging in the testing for some other reason. That other reason is, to judge by the public rhetoric on the subject, to help build "a drug-free America." When we ask why a drug-free America would be a good thing we are, of course, back to the issue of drug regulation generally, and if the argument at this level rests on nothing better than the arguments of people like Richard Thornburgh (the former attorney general) and William Bennett (the former "drug czar"), then corporations are taxing their workers, stockholders, and consumers in order to help save the moral fabric of America.

If there are serious statistics to appeal to about casual off-the-job drug use, then corporations could, barring further objections (of which there are many, as we are about to see), justify their activities. But it would seem that, with respect to drug testing and other forms of intrusion into the private lives of employees, the burden of proving that the costs of such intrusions are outweighed by higher profits should fall upon the corporate officers who want to conduct the intrusion. Although corporations don't have to face anything as stringent as the harm principle when regulating employees, they cannot, in principle or in practice, just do anything they want even though the government can do little to regulate them unless their activities pose a threat of unjustified harm to their employees.

A third kind of restraining influence on corporate control of employees is more general and less a matter of straightforward prudence. In the last chapter, I mentioned the importance of inculcating certain attitudes and character traits and the connection between these attitudes and the institutions that will be counted on to instill them. Under an ideal libertarian arrangement, individualism and a respect for privacy will be fostered as much as is socially possible. In part, the job will be done by default, that is, as a consequence of not overcentralizing the means of indoctrination. Additionally, social institutions based on libertarian assumptions can be expected, for the most part, to positively reinforce the value of privacy.

Moreover, what can be expected to happen is that individuals will not only grow up thinking that they have a *right* to privacy but, also, that they have a *duty* to maintain the privacy of their personal realm. Both employees and employers can be expected to feel that some pretty clear right to privacy needs to be protected. The sensibility of my point here can be illustrated just by observing the kinds of attitudes Americans have about privacy. Not only are they generally insistent on a right to privacy but, for the most part, insistent on the fact that friends who have personal information about them have a duty to keep that information private. Although there are no laws about kissing and telling, people who do so can be expected to be thought less of for doing it. Furthermore, they can often expect to face what Mill called "social sanctions" for their breach of these widely shared, but criminally unenforced, values. We may find gossip titillating but only because it is tinged with the obscene, and those who traffic in it can expect to be avoided and ostracized.

Closely related to concerns about private citizens infringing on each others' privacy rights are those related to private citizens acting in ways that discriminate against others on the basis of race, sex, religion, or irrelevant disability. Does my libertarianism have the consequence that a lunch counter operator can refuse to serve or hire blacks if he or she chooses to do so?

As a matter of history, the depressing fact of the matter is that legislation may not, in practice, be effective against such discrimination. Any persistent bigot can make things so uncomfortable for everyone he is forced to serve or hire that his victims will eventually leave rather than stand on their legal right to stay. Additionally, the kinds of nonlegal considerations about profit and attitudes that I mentioned with respect to privacy rights can be applied here. An owner who refuses to take a black woman's money just because she is black has sacrificed profit (and thereby taxed investors, employees, and customers) for some deranged "moral" purpose.

Moreover, it must be pointed out that to think that government intervention is the cure for racism or other forms of discrimination is, as a matter of history, to confuse the cure with the disease. It was not, after all, the general policy of Woolworth's to refuse service to blacks; that was the policy of local government authorities in the South, as was the policy of making blacks sit in the back of city busses, as was the policy of slavery, and so on. Racism and sexism were largely the handiwork of governments acting to preserve some redneck vision of traditional moral values, not individuals going about their private affairs.

Further still, it has been argued by everyone from Friedman to Jesse Jackson that much of the blame for the continued disadvantages suffered by minorities in the United States is, once again, to be laid on government action. Well-intentioned welfare programs have had the unintentional consequence of virtually destroying the black family. Regulations and licensing policies enforced on behalf of vested interests (e.g., mandatory taxi licenses that go on the open market in some cities for well over $100,000) effectively keep the poor from starting their own businesses.

Finally, there can be little doubt that institutional support of irrelevant prejudice can have serious harmful consequences (up to and including all out civil war) and, thus, institutions arranged under the harm principle should be expected to discourage irrational bigotry. When institutions are arranged so as to encourage hatred of bigotry rather than active endorsement of it (as was done in the public school systems of the South until very recently), bigots will eventually find no rest from argumentative challenge and condescension.

All of these considerations to the side, the severity of the threat of race and class warfare if certain discriminatory practices that *can* be reached by the law *aren't* reached by the law can be turned into a compelling reason for civil rights legislation and even strong affirmative action legislation. For example, it can be argued that the threat of general mayhem posed by the existence of a large class of impoverished, frustrated, and idle youths in the inner cities is immediate enough to warrant some kind of direct governmental action that might remedy the situation. It is, indeed, disturbing that such arguments will pivot on the ability of certain groups to wreak havoc if their complaints are not redressed. Nevertheless, if the practices to be outlawed cannot be argued to avoid harms that outweigh the harms that follow from immanent, racially based civil strife, then my rendition of the harm principle will not stand in the way of legislation necessary to prevent virtual civil war. Also, it must be noted as a grim but undeniable piece of history that no serious redress of black grievances was ever issued out of the kindness of the hearts of white America. In the 1860s and then one century later, even the most minimal (and, largely, merely formal) guarantees of civil rights came only after serious bloodshed.

Fortunately, arguments for programs like affirmative action need not rest entirely on an overt threat of havoc. In fact, considerations that are as firmly rooted in the history of libertarian thought as any others can be marshaled to present a case for strong affirmative action programs (even for explicit quotas) that would be targeted at groups who pose as little threat of bloody insurrection as is the case with middle-class white women. Such considerations, of course, occupy a central place in the writings of Mill. Although previously dismissed as one of Mill's tangential works, his *Subjection of Women* is now getting the attention it should have had all along.

As far as contemporary concerns about the status of women go, this work is remarkable not only because of its originality but also because it, generally, stays within the confines of Mill's (albeit indirect) utilitarianism and his libertarianism. Most of the feminist theory of the last few years has had little to do with utilitarianism, and most of it is decidedly not libertarian. Indeed, at first glance, it is not easy to see how the theoretical tandem of utilitarianism and libertarianism could imply anything other than a strong antipathy to anything as intrusive in the marketplace of private interests as is an affirmative action program. However, the conclusion of the *Subjection of Women* is that if the tendency of any system (including the free market) is the de facto exclusion of half the population from any meaningful role in that system, then something is seriously wrong with that system.

The wrongness of such a state of affairs cannot, for Mill or any other utilitarian, rest, ultimately, on its simple unfairness or injustice. Mill's arguments, for the most part, do not resort directly to any fundamental principles of justice that cannot be founded on deeper utilitarian grounds. This approach is not, on balance, a bad thing, for, as Mill would have been quick to point out, whether or not affirmative action is justifiable under some foundational principle of justice depends upon which principle of justice one chooses. Considerations based on standards of procedural (or formal) justice will tend to weigh in against affirmative action because such programs will, quite often, require the unequal treatment of equals. Considerations based on standards of substantive justice will tend to weigh in for affirmative action because such programs, generally, are designed to level the field on which the procedural rules currently deliver unfair results. Neither of these principles should be given an unqualified precedence over the other. Certainly, *serious* initial inequalities (i.e., serious deviations from the standard of substantive justice) should (but only under certain conditions) be given more weight than *minor* deviations from the principle of procedural justice. Just as certainly, minor deviations from the principle of substantive justice do not warrant serious deviations from the principle of procedural justice. In fact, in some cases, serious deviations from the principle of substantive justice do not warrant any deviations from the principle of procedural justice at all. For example, that murderer A comes from a poorer background than murderer B does not, in itself, entail that A should get a fairer trial or lighter sentence than B. Likewise, an impoverished and mentally handicapped person should not be granted an advantage over a rich and famously talented surgeon for a medical post. Moreover, there are the well-known oddities involved when we confine ourselves to just the substantive level. For example, why should a rich black female be given any sort of hiring preference for any job over an otherwise equally qualified poor white male? How do we sort out who started from the worst-off initial position in such cases? If we commit ourselves to the position that the poor white males in such situations must suffer breeches at the level of procedural justice in order to further the greater collective good to be achieved by the general elevation of the status of women and minorities (even though a particular African American woman may already have started from a social and economic position that was elevated beyond that of a particular European American male over whom she was given an affirmative action advantage), then aren't we engaged in the treatment of individuals (in this case the poor white male) as mere means to an end that so offends most defenders of foundational principles of justice?

As was pointed out in Chapter 3, the utilitarian will argue that the only way to sort out such conflicts is by some sort of appeal to the principle of utility. As such, there would be good reason to suspect that appealing to utilitarianism in the first place might point the way out of the quagmire of competing principles of justice that come into play around the problem of affirmative action. The overall approach should seem even more appealing if it conforms with our present intuitions about who should and should not benefit from affirmative action and if it also conforms to our intuitions about how much procedural justice ought to be sacrificed in order to bring about a better balance of substantive justice. In particular, our current intuitions (as well as our current laws) have it that the appropriate target of affirmative action benefits in any given role would be not just any minority (for this would include left-handers and exclude women) nor just any group that has suffered a history of discrimination (for this would include groups against which discrimination is justifiable, for example, discrimination against very short people who desire to be NBA centers) but, rather, the members of any group that is (1) underrepresented (relative to its current representation in the general population) in some generally desirable socioeconomic role and (2) the victim of a history of general and irrational discrimination against its members. In all of this, Mill's position seems to lead to the intuitive conclusion.

His general line of argument is that the harmful consequences of sexism (and much of what he says about sexism can be extended to cover racism and other forms of irrational discrimination) can be broken down into three main groups. First, and most obviously, are the direct harms to women. When systematically deprived of general social power and any real alternatives to domestic servitude, women are entirely at the disposal of their male masters. As such, the level of straightforward violence against women (and their children) is, for all real intents and purposes, constrained by nothing other than the inhibitions of men against violence. And, certainly, these chivalrous inhibitions are not likely to be strengthened when men know that women have no real alternative to domestic bondage.

Second, the subjection of women poses a range of threats to men. The irrational attitudes men are encouraged to feel toward the whole class of women can be easily generalized to work against certain groups of men. The habit of turning a temporary physical or social advantage into a "natural" moral superiority may well justify procedures designed to keep certain classes of men subordinate to others on the grounds that such subordination is a fact of life grounded in tradition. Another danger to men (though, it is not clear that it is a danger of harm in my narrow sense of the term) is that by barring women from the paths of education and professional success, men guarantee that they will wind up married to narrow-minded, intolerant, and uninteresting shrews. Much more will be said about this line of Mill's argument in Chapter 10.

Third, there are the harms to society at large that follow from the exclusion of half of the possibly available talent in the society. Moreover, as Mill points out in Chapter IV (par. 8) of the *Subjection*, the addition of female influence would result not just in a "greater" effect but a "more beneficial" one than would be brought about by the addition of more men to the pool of talent. Women bring not only their own talent into play, but they also, given the desire of men to impress the women around them, encourage men to use more of their own talent. Also, women bring a different *kind* of influence to the world. Mill argues (as many contemporary feminists do) that, allowing for individual variations, women have a general "softening" influence; they have a higher standard of sympathy and spontaneous generosity to counterbalance the "sterner" male virtues of impartiality and justice (Chapter IV, par. 10). Even though these differences may well be due to the present conditions under which men and women are socialized rather than some innate "nature" of women and men (and Mill believes this to be the case), this diversity of influence is valuable regardless of its origins.

This leads to a much larger theme that runs through all of Mill's social philosophy. Generally, Mill is tied to the Romantic currents of his time, and there emerges from his writings (especially the third chapter of *On Liberty*) a notion of social and individual progress that is quite different from the puritanical views of the "English philanthropists" of his day (many of whom may well have been motivated by a misguided Benthamian paternalism). For Mill, progress was to be achieved through the free reign of human diversity and experimentation. What will turn out to be the best and wisest ways of doing things in the future is not something we can know clearly now. Any culture based on the dogma that it has already found what will be good in the future and, therefore, stunts the natural diversity of human endeavors is, as Mill puts it, doomed "to become another China."[11] The harms attendant to such a "despotism of custom" are among the most serious that any society can face; truly great cultures can fall to the depths of barbarism, boredom, and impoverishment in a short period of time through no cause other than an intolerance of anything new.

Mill, of course, does not take any of this as a warrant to encourage experimentation with alternatives that have a long and obvious history of failure associated with them. So we may, in the atmosphere current in the United States, find no warrant for the claim that discredited forms of superstition and pseudoscience be tolerated by scientists as legitimate science because to do so shows sensitivity and respect for the cultures or subcultures that generated those forms of irrationalism.

Mill seems to think that diversity is something that ought to occur if only a society does not go out of its way to stifle it. In other words, he seems to think that diversity will present itself if only social coercion is properly constrained by something like the harm principle. However, what is becoming clear in this century is that the forces of conformism have become more pervasive than even Mill could have anticipated. As a consequence, it may well be the case that the conditions under which diversity can be expected to emerge must be actively enforced rather than passively allowed to occur. The fears generally associated with coordinated government programs are less bothersome in the case of efforts to bring about greater social and cultural diversity. The Millian fear of pointless homogeneity does not arise when the focus of a government program is to encourage the emergence of a plurality of influences that would have emerged on their own were it not for a history of systematic impediments to diversity.

The elevation of the principles of toleration and diversity to the level of principles that require active governmental support also allows for a stronger position with respect to the sorts of privacy issues discussed previously. This is fortunate, for it would be more than ironic if a general position as committed to the protection of a substantial private sphere as libertarianism is would have the consequence of allowing private entities (like corporations, news organizations, and other assorted snoopers) to trample the privacy of individuals whenever there is a buck in it. The kinds of prudential restraints upon snooping that I appealed to before don't seem strong enough. Indeed, the mechanisms of surveillance extent today seem to require something much stronger; they would seem to require direct governmental protection. Such is justified, once again, on the basis of the tendency of snooping to discourage (and perhaps obliterate) diversity and experimentation. One is less likely to tread along previously unworn paths if one fears that any such deviation from the norm will provoke a disproportionate public attention to one's adventures. A society where whatever titillates or offends is likely to incur full public scrutiny will be one where the engines of conformity will whir the tiresome anthems of personal timidity, public tedium, pointless mediocrity, and, eventually, cultural exhaustion. Indeed, at a certain point of exhaustion, cultures may fully deserve the total collapse they have dumbly engineered because the harms that have befallen their citizens will outweigh any of the harms threatened even by a state of anarchy. But any society that enjoys the combined benefits of plurality, privacy, and peace ought to be able to see that these three things are interdependent. It also ought to be able to forcefully defend its citizens against the real harms entailed by becoming "another China."

Thus, the establishment of laws and institutions that will foster a peaceful diversity of races, classes, genders, and individuals can be given reasonable support on Millian grounds. The defense of strong laws that protect against irrational discrimination and invasions of privacy can be based on an appeal to the harm principle; it need not rely upon an appeal to foundational principles of justice nor to an overarching conception of the good nor to an intolerably vague weave of "moral fabric." Such legislation will, after all, merely guarantee the existence of a level of diversity that should have and, presumably, would have emerged anyhow were it not for a history of socially sanctioned bigotry and intolerance.

Another group of problems for any form of libertarianism concerns the kinds of services and public works that appear to be essential for the creation and maintenance of any substantial standard of living but that would be unprofitable for any investors to provide. The stock examples of such services and works are armies, police forces, courts, roads, and so on. More controversial examples would be water, power, fire protection, telephones, education, and other services that are marginal examples because such services could and, in fact, are commonly supplied without government investment.

To stick to the clear cases, the provision of armies, police forces, and judicial facilities seems to me easily justified under the harm principle. The degree to which public expenditures need to be made for any of these services is, of course, a matter of constant public debate, but only the most extreme libertarian would suggest that any of these services could be effectively handled privately. The case of roads, however, is interesting in that it seems to be the sort of service that marks the boundary between the kinds of goods that simply must be provided by government and those that obviously don't have to be provided by government because, as a matter of fact, they are routinely provided by the private sector.

The case of roads is interesting for another reason: it seems to present a real problem for my theory. Certainly, one could argue that, given our current dependence upon publicly maintained roadways and on the trucks, cars, busses, firetrucks, ambulances, and police cars that travel on them, to not maintain them would be a cause of harm far greater than any benefit that might be derived from diverting highway funds elsewhere (including into the private sector). But how could my theory have justified the construction of all of these roads in the first place? Obviously, great benefits have arisen from public highway projects, but could any argument have been made early in this century that tax funds be diverted in this direction in such a way that the diversion conformed with the harm principle?

I am facing a problem here that most libertarians have not. Adam Smith, for example, simply deemed good high roads "in the highest degree advantageous to a great society"[12] and, on the basis of the obvious benefits that would not come about without government intervention, deemed such intervention justifiable. But what *harm* would have arisen from the *non*construction of any single roadway?

As removed as this issue is from any real practical problem facing us now (since nonmaintenance of roads that are already there would cause harm), an answer to this question is worth pursuing since other issues (especially one concerning nature preserves like national parks, which will come up in Part III) may hinge on how this one is settled. The first line of response is to question the necessity of public road projects from the point of view of the time of their construction. It must be remembered that the rail system in the United States was constructed mostly by the expenditure of private funds. If it was not necessary for the government to build the rails upon which trains travel, then why was it necessary for the government to build the roads upon which cars and trucks travel? Why couldn't the companies that wanted to sell cars and trucks have been the ones who paid to make roads? Of course, the cost of road construction would not have been paid by Henry Ford but by the people who bought Fords. If the Henry Fords and J. D. Rockefellers of the time could not have laid out the necessary cash (which is unlikely), then they certainly could have engaged other investors to make toll roads.

All of this leads to the second line of argument. The fact of the matter is that the automobile and oil industries in the United States have always been subsidized to the tune of whatever road construction has cost over the past century in a way that the rail system never was. As a consequence, the public turned more and more toward cars and away from trains. Cities spread out along freeways and everyone got used to going everywhere (even just down the block) in machines that are responsible for huge taxes, massive depletion of natural resources, fifty thousand deaths annually (in the United States alone) and global environmental concerns. The huge amount of fossil fuels consumed by cars, of course, has the added consequence of making nearly every other commodity more expensive, because car drivers compete with manufacturers for those fuels. In short, it's really not clear that the government's construction of roadways has, on balance, created as much good as is commonly thought. If the government had not been so involved in these projects, then there would now be fewer roads, more railways, fewer cars, more compact but cleaner cities, and who's to say we'd now be worse off because of it?

The larger theoretical point in all of this is that a certain principle that has been taken for granted since the time of Smith may need some reexamination. That principle is the one that government provision of certain services and works is justified when such are "necessary" or "universally beneficial" and when they will not come into existence as a result of the profit motive. This principle, vague as it is, conflicts with the harm principle as I have stated it. If by "necessary" one means "necessary to prevent harm" (as is the case with armies, police, and courts), then there is no problem. With respect to "universal benefit," however, there is a real problem, for, as I have argued before, one has no obligations to provide benefit; coercion (including forced taxation) is justifiable only in order to prevent harm.

But, of course, there are already problems with the notion of "universal benefit." In the first place, if one is going to apply this criterion in a case like road construction, then the benefits are simply not universal since many people never use roads except to walk or ride a bicycle along them. One could argue that everyone except the most isolated hermit really does use the roads since they are necessary for the transportation of food, clothes, building materials, and everything else we consume. Of course, we are so dependent on roads now only because they were coercively financed in the first place in a way that could not have been described as universally beneficial at that time.

This leads to the second problem with the notion of universal benefit, which is that one must be careful not to confuse it with universal *dependence*. We are now certainly dependent upon roadways and their maintenance, but, as I was arguing before, it is less clear that we have really been universally benefitted relative to the alternatives which would have ensued if road construction was not publicly financed.

All of this, in turn, leads to the main line of suspicion that all libertarians share with respect to government intervention, namely, that it tends to be self-perpetuating. Dependencies develop, incentives are affected, and liberties given up in one place tend to result in other liberties being given up in other places. Once the ball starts rolling, not even a restrictive limitation like the harm principle can stop it.

I will finish here with a brief consideration of an issue that has been so thoroughly worked over in the last couple of decades that one can scarcely say anything that is both new and sensible about it anymore, namely, the issue of abortion. I think the way I have formulated the harm principle allows for two *very* small clarifications of the general debate and, especially, of the liberal side of it. As the harm principle is usually rendered, it is inconclusive on the abortion issue because it is not clear that the fetus is or is not something that can be harmed. However, under my formulation, what I have said about burden of proof enters in as a crucial factor. The important burden of proof would seem to fall *squarely* on the shoulders of the antiabortionist. It is up to *them* to prove that the fetus is the sort of thing that can be harmed and, thus, be of direct concern in any calculation of disutility associated with abortion. It is not up to the proabortionist to prove that abortion is harmless. In the absence of a really compelling demonstration that the fetus can be harmed (which, given the continuing divisiveness of the issue, appears to be rather obviously lacking), the issue should be settled in favor of the proabortionist.[13]

Second, my general approach cleanly separates two parts of the abortion issue that ought to be kept far apart. The proabortionist position that follows from my theory is one about *social policy*, not one about *individual choice*. There might be lots of reasons for a woman not to get an abortion, but one of them should *not* be because abortion is *or ought to be* open to any legal or social sanction. This point will receive some clarification in the next chapter.

PART 2

Wisdom

CHAPTER 8

Political Consent, Individual Choice, and Moral Justification

The previous chapters have been concerned primarily with making utilitarianism (in some indirect form) a plausible social ethic. The general strategy was to take two basic Millian principles that have usually been taken as antithetical and make one of them (the harm principle) a mechanism for applying the other (the principle of utility). The intended effect was to limit the range of utilitarianism in such a way as to make it a "political" rather than a "comprehensive" theory of value (to use terms made popular by Rawls in recent years).[1] The basic reason for severing the social and the individual in this way is, at one level, the same as Rawls's. Having originally given the impression in *A Theory of Justice* that individual values could be derived in some reasonably straightforward way from his theory of social justice,[2] he has, apparently, come to see this task as fundamentally opposed to a more basic value associated with liberal pluralism. I too see this opposition, and I too do not think that a theory of the ultimate value of an individual's life ought to be dictated by a social ethic. In fact, as will be clear by the end of this chapter, I see the opposition between the social and the individual level of ethics as being more profound than does Rawls or, more problematically, than do the principal representatives of the utilitarian tradition of which I see myself as a part.

I have already mentioned Bentham's lame attempt to extend his brand of utilitarianism into an individual ethics in his *Deontology*. But I also mentioned that his most famous critic was Mill who was, himself, hardly beyond reproach with respect to confusing social wholes with individual parts. It is, in fact, Mill who is infamous for the inference in the fourth chapter of *Utilitarianism* that "each person's happiness is a good to that person, and the general happiness, therefore, [is] a good to the aggregate of all persons."

But one must be careful in separating composition fallacies from composition *claims*. To make the inference that a hundred different liquors each of which tastes good to one of the hundred people who threw two ounces of it into a vat would produce two hundred ounces of a liquid that would be palatable to any of them (let alone *all* of them) is to commit a fallacy unless all one hundred people threw in the same liquor or, at least, ones that complimented each other. Given the variability of pleasures and their causes, Mill's claim must be taken as fallacious. However, given the similarity of harm and its causes, things are not so clear. One hundred people who each throw two ounces of battery acid into a vat ought to produce two hundred ounces of battery acid, which is distasteful to each and all. Moreover, there are threshold effects to consider. Two ounces of New York City water thrown into 198 ounces of pure and fine scotch might not be noticeable by any taster, but a fifty-fifty mix of the two would be noticed as different from the pure stuff by almost anyone.

I have argued so far that pleasure or happiness is something too vague to play any more than a restrictive role in the determination of social policy. It, in all of its facets, can only serve to weigh *against* social restriction. It cannot, even if there is temporary unanimity about the fact that a certain alternative will bring about universal pleasure, be used to restrict individual action unless there is the requisite demonstration of serious harm. Pain, death, and suffering, on the other hand, I have argued to be things universally distasteful enough to serve as the ground for social consensus. But even here there are threshold effects to take into account. The suffering of one, one hundred, or even one thousand humans may count for little in the cosmic scheme of things. Thus, utilitarian calculations (concerning estimates of either pain or pleasure) must be aimed not at single actions but at something of more consequence, like legislation.

There is one further aspect of harm (defined narrowly as pain, suffering, and death) that separates it from pleasure and makes it fit as the foundation of a social ethic. Not only is the dislike of it universal at any given time, but this dislike can be counted on to continue through time from generation to generation. Thus, the elimination of the common causes of unjustifiable pain, death, and suffering is a project that can form the basis of what Rawls calls "an overlapping consensus."[3] There will be a little more to this consensus over time in my scheme of things, namely, a continued commitment to the values of toleration and diversity engendered by the institutionalization of my rendition of the harm principle. But there will be nothing like a continued commitment to anything as comprehensive as Rawls's principles of justice or the even more comprehensive value systems of strong communitarians.

In response to Rawls's criticism[4] that this neo-Hobbesian foundation is not enough to either support social unity as a matter of principle or describe the social unity that, as a matter of fact, has held Western democracies together over the past three centuries, I would argue that, as a matter of history, there really is nothing other than a progressive extension of sympathy and understanding regarding the suffering of others coupled with an increasing respect for individual differences and toleration that has held any western state together. Certainly, nothing like agreement on Rawls's principles of justice can be seen as having played a central role in social cohesion; after all, they can't find anything like unanimity even among professional liberal philosophers.

The issue of an overlapping consensus is connected to another large problem that, once again, is rooted in the utilitarian tradition. In the same chapter of *Utilitarianism* where Mill falls into a problem with composition, he gets tangled up in what Moore would tag "the naturalistic fallacy." The "sole evidence," Mill argued, "that anything is desirable, is that people do actually desire it." As the argument of that chapter unfolds, Mill's argument becomes a little more complicated and the issue of naturalism looms larger. His full claim is not just that happiness is desired but that it is the *only* thing that is desired. Moreover, it is the only thing that, as a matter of "psychological constitution," we are *capable* of desiring as an end in itself.

In order to make this claim plausible, however, Mill was driven to continually broaden the notion of pleasure so that all human pursuits could be rendered as instrumental means associated with that one end. Eventually the notion becomes so broad as to be meaningless, and the associationist explanations start to look like so much question begging. In the end, the notion of happiness that emerges from Mill's works is so mixed up with other values (and especially with the value of individuality) that his overall view can still be called hedonism only with substantial difficulty.

Nevertheless, if Mill's argument is altered so as to focus on the intrinsic undesirability of harm rather than on the intrinsic desirability of pleasure, it runs more plausibly and produces more interesting consequences. The most interesting consequences for my present purposes concern questions of ultimate justification and explanation of values. Questions of justification cannot be confused with ones of explanation, but Mill's naturalism, when connected with Rawls's concerns about overlapping consensus, raise an important point of connection between the two.

For convenience, I will divide theories of justification into two groups: constructivism and nonconstructivism. Among the nonconstructivists I include naturalists, neonaturalists, moral realists, intuitionists, and divine command theorists. Although there are many varieties of constructivism, what I take as common to all of them is the thesis that moral values are to be justified on the basis of some kind of agreement or consensus. Most constructivists would make the claim stronger by insisting that it is *unanimous* agreement among rational or reasonable agents that really serves as the only adequate justification of fundamental moral claims. Unanimity, in turn, can be argued to be securable under either actual or hypothetical conditions. Rawls's move involving consent behind a veil of ignorance puts him in the hypothetical constructivist camp. The neo-Hobbesian moves I have made put me in the actualist constructivist camp.

The actualist is going to have a problem the hypothetical constructivist does not, namely, that of *explaining* why we should believe that there are any really universal values when the lack of agreement about anything moral is so apparent in the actual world. Moreover, when political values are brought into the picture, the hope of an overlapping consensus about any such values seems extremely dim given the variability of beliefs over generations. The hypothetical constructivist can largely ignore actual disagreements and proceed to argue that all individuals *would* consent to certain values or principles *if* they were all fully rational or reasonable. The problem with such an approach, of course, is that it runs the danger of circularity. Individuals will be deemed rational or reasonable if and only if they act in accordance with the principles or values that are to be justified on the grounds that all rational or reasonable individuals would choose them.

Mill's move is to put forward a theory of psychological rather than rational necessity, but, as I argued earlier, his particular theory seems to face its own problem of circularity. By shifting attention away from the psychological necessity of the intrinsic desirability of pleasure to the psychological and physiological necessity of the intrinsic undesirability of harm (narrowly defined as pain, suffering, and death), I think the circularity can be avoided. For one thing, it must be understood that the range of action I claim to be explainable in terms of harm avoidance is much smaller than that alleged by Mill to be explainable in terms of the pursuit of pleasure. He winds up explaining *all* behavior, whereas, I would assert, very little of our behavior can be explained in terms of harm avoidance. I need only claim that harm, when it is not instrumental to some perceived greater good, will, as a matter of fact, be avoided by any *tolerably* (not *ideally*) rational and well-informed individual.

However, this naturalistic maneuver commits neither Mill nor me to anything beyond constructivism as a theory of justification. What *justifies* moral standards is universal agreement and consent.[5] It is this, not correspondence with any Platonic or natural fact, and certainly not any intuition or divine command, that makes moral claims reasonable and justifiable. From the constructivist's point of view, the entire purpose of doing ethics in the first place is to secure agreement so that people may be led by reasonable persuasion rather than brute force. So, even if moral judgments are ultimately *based on* certain natural desires and aversions, they are not *about* those mental states; they are about persuasion and the attainment of rational and moral agreement. Moreover, even if some natural referent or a Platonic Form of the Good could be found, its only value (practical or otherwise) would have to be anchored in its usefulness in securing agreement. What, in turn, *explains* the actual fact of present and future agreement is a claim about the natural and physical properties that humans (and many other animals for that matter) have and will have in the future.

Two important objections arise at this point, and the response to them will bring me to the central thesis of this chapter and a main point of this whole book. The first is a Rawlsian concern about autonomy. Rawls, following in the Kantian tradition, rejects the idea that a valid moral consensus could arise from choices that are not really free choices. If consensus is in any substantial way determined either by coercion or by natural compulsion, then the choices that make up that consensus are heteronomous, not autonomous. The second objection is that a theory that links questions of justification to a natural inclination to avoid harm will leave too many moral issues beyond the pale of justification. All kinds of claims about the good life will be unresolved and, in fact, unresolvable as a matter of principle.

The answer to the first of these problems is embedded in the very statement of the second one. The fact is that under my theory, indeed, little of our behavior as individuals will be dictated by the legitimate demands of social morality. But the whole point of a restrictive libertarianism about social ethics is precisely to leave a large realm of activity that is genuinely free of real social control. My concern all along has been the real political guarantee of real day-to-day autonomy. In this large realm of activity, individuals will not be able to appeal to compulsion as an excuse for their action; they are genuinely free and responsible only to their own autonomously chosen standards. That there is a small range of activity where real compulsion is justified because of a universal aversion to a natural evil does not imply any real threat to autonomy. In fact, I'm not sure it poses any real threat to autonomy even at the elevated theoretical level of concern of the Kantian. That I, by nature, choose to avoid painful contingencies does not make those choices any less real than my choice to obey the law of gravity when I am rock climbing. That my freedom here is forced does not make it any less real.

As regards the second objection, it is indeed true that little in the way of claims about the good life can be justified on my theory. But this is an inherent characteristic of any genuine theory of liberalism. There is a limited range of activity that the state or the community can make a legitimate claim to be able to control on the basis of its wrongness. Of the rest of life, not only does the community have no right to control the lives of individuals, it has no right to even proclaim them as wrong. As Mill was especially aware, the mere social proclamation of wrongness will carry what he called a "social sanction" against the "wrong" activity even if there is to be no warrant for an official government condemnation of the activity and none could be sensibly defended in public.

The private sphere is not just that area where the government can't officially move; it is, in fact, the area where the morality of others has no business. It is the area precisely where the individual need have no justification or even explanation for what he or she does. It is the area where the consensus of others is completely irrelevant and where there is just no fact of the matter concerning the rightness or wrongness of a person's actions. The only explaining or justifying one need do concerning private affairs is to oneself.

To take anything other than this radical position about the status of individual ethics is to have something less than a fully liberal political philosophy; it is to pay mere lip service to the whole idea of a private sphere. The private sphere is not something that exists only because of the logistical difficulties of regulating certain individual actions. It is something founded on a serious claim about the epistemology of ethics and on a serious assertion that certain kinds of moralizing are not only annoying but also intellectually groundless.

This view fits well with what is generally perceived by ethics professors as a kind of sappy and intellectually irresponsible relativism that we find in our undergraduate students. Generally, unless they are under the sway of some stern religious code, they seem to come to us with a view of relativism about most moral issues (like abortion, homosexuality, pornography, certain kinds of lying, obligations to give to charity, obligations to vote, and so on) that stops cold at a certain point (racism, robbery, fraud, brutality, intolerance, and so on). Under my theory, such an ethic is not at all sappy or intellectually lazy. It is exactly what we ought to expect of young people raised in a liberal society. And, from my experience, when students are at ease around professors who no longer have any influence over their grades, they will articulate their liberalism fairly well with claims like: "As long as I'm not breaking the law and I'm not hurting anyone, what I do is none of your damn business."[6]

None of what I have said implies that individuals will not, on many occasions, find it *prudent* to justify or explain themselves to others. They may do this for a couple of perfectly good reasons. In the first place, we are constantly making commitments to other private citizens that we seek to maintain for very good prudential reasons. In situations where we may appear to be on the verge of violating an important commitment, we may find it necessary to apologize, explain, and justify our actions. In the second place, one may seek to justify and explain in order to convince others (and perhaps oneself) that one has not violated one's own personal standards. But if one chooses to drink or lie away a job, a friendship, or a marriage, then no *moral* criticism is in order unless it is to be leveled by oneself or one has violated a socially distinct and assignable obligation. Lord Acton's claim that "freedom is not the power of doing what we like but rather the right to do what we ought" must be rejected by any liberal, just as much as Burke's claim that democracy need not imply the enfranchisement of anymore than an enlightened minority who can vote in the best interests of the masses must be rejected by any real democrat.

All of this leads to the main topic of the remainder of this part of the book. Just because the range of social morality, where there is a genuine fact of the matter about right and wrong,[7] stops at the private sphere, that doesn't mean that normative consideration stops altogether at that point. We are still capable, as individuals, of freely adopting comprehensive philosophies of life that we feel binding, prudent, or productive of fullness, richness, or integrity. On these matters, however, in a liberal society we form no more than a consensus of one, and, no matter how deeply we may feel right about our private choices, we may not insist that those who live differently are *really* wrong or immoral. We may only try to persuade that our way is better because it is wiser.

The rest of this part of the book is about wisdom in this sense. It is about how one ought to live one's own life, regardless of how others live or ought to live theirs.

CHAPTER 9

Egoism, Altruism, and Virtue

Leaving aside the claims about justification in the previous chapter, it is important to point out that the realization that questions about social ethics and individual values are not straightforwardly reducible to each other is hardly original to me or, for that matter, to Enlightenment value theory generally. In fact, the separation of these two levels of concern is evident as early on as Plato's *Republic*. Although there is, for Plato, some overarching Form of the Good in which all good things somehow "participate," when it comes to the specific definitions of justice offered in the *Republic*, Plato gives not one but three different definitions.

First there is his definition of justice for the individual, which has it that justice is a result of and constituted in the rule of reason over the other elements of the soul (spirit and appetite). He comes to this conclusion as a result of having examined justice "writ large," that is, as a consequence of looking for what it is that makes a just state just. This is, he tells us, the state of affairs brought about by the rule of the reasonable element of the state (the Guardian class) over the other elements of the state (the Auxiliaries, who represent spirit, and the merchants and artisans, who represent appetite). So, in both cases, justice is a matter of a specific kind of balance and harmonious integration of elements.[1]

But these two definitions imply that the vast majority of people are incapable of being just. If justice for the individual is a matter of maintaining the rule of reason in the soul, then the vast majority of people will never be just because they are, by nature, ruled by other elements of the soul. Moreover, Plato gives every indication that he feels this incapacity for full justice to be a matter of heredity. Guardians are, for the most part, born to be reasonable just as Auxiliaries are born to be spirited and the rest are destined to be ruled by appetite. However, there is Plato's third definition of justice under which everyone can be just. This third view is that justice is a matter of everyone doing their jobs and not meddling in the jobs of others.[2]

This third definition, in essence, *requires* people who are unjust under his first definition of individual justice to stay that way. For either the Auxiliaries or the moneymakers to pretend that they are people of reason and then act as though they ought to have a meaningful role in government is for them to act unjustly by meddling in affairs that are properly left to the Guardians. The third definition, then, is sort of a bridge between the other two definitions. Only a small part of the population can be fully just as individuals if justice is to be maintained in the state. The rest, however, can be just in the sense that they are serving their proper function in the just state.

There is one more twist in all of this. I think it is fair to say that Plato was, primarily, concerned about questions of justice because of the bearing of these questions on ones about wisdom. This was, in fact, an ordering of issues common to all the ancients. Certainly, questions about how states ought to be set up and how the actions of individuals ought to be orchestrated in order to maintain social order were never thought to be trivial, but still, the important thing for any Greek was *eudaimonia*, personal well-being and the means by which it can be achieved. Plato's answer for the common Greek was: know and keep your place in a well-ordered state. But for the philosopher-king, who hates practical politics, his or her place will not bring maximal fulfillment. The person of reason would rather be left to contemplate than be forced to rule. But politics is the social duty of the philosopher-king because his or her rule is required in order for everyone else to wind up doing those things that their talents and inclinations best suit them to do. Moreover, although others might be inclined to rule, only the philosopher has the talent to rule.

So, when the first definition of justice for the individual is applied to the philosopher, it prescribes (as a requirement of justice and as a means to *eudaimonia*) abstinence from public life, whereas the second definition prescribes political leadership. For everyone else, the first definition either requires them to become philosophers or it tells them that they can't possibly be just (or achieve *eudaimonia*), whereas the second definition tells them that justice (and *eudaimonia*) will result from their being the best at what they are fit by nature to be.

The tangle of individual and social ethics is apparent even before Socrates attempts to define justice in the *Republic*. It emerges at the end of the first book of the *Republic*, and it is at this point in the dialogue where Plato begins his argument (which will take the remainder of the *Republic* to conclude) against the most obvious theory of wisdom about how to achieve *eudaimonia*. That theory is first put forward by Thrasymachus, who winds up arguing that justice has little to do with personal well-being or happiness.[3] Happiness may well involve fooling others by *appearing* to be just, but only a fool would think that the way to happiness is to be truly just. Happiness, says Thrasymachus, is a consequence of being able to outwit, control, and take advantage of others.

Socrates' reply to Thrasymachus at the end of Book I is hopelessly confused. He argues that a society full of unjust people who are always trying to outwit and take advantage of everyone else would produce more strife and misery and less happiness than would a society full of just people. But, as Glaucon points out in the beginning of Book II, Thrasymachus's position never had it that the result of *everyone's* being unjust would be more happiness than would arise if *everyone* was just. Rather, Thrasymachus was claiming that, *regardless of how others behave*, it is wisest for *me* to be unjust. The reasoning here is exactly like that going on in the prisoner's dilemma discussed in Chapter 2 and, as a result, Glaucon is rightly seen as the first advocate of a social contract theory that is, in many important details, just like that of Hobbes.

If everyone else is unjust, then *I* am better off by being unjust as well. If everyone else is just, then so much the better, because then they are easier to take advantage of and *I* am still better served by being as opportunistic as their stupidity will allow *me* to be. In between are all of the partial compliance scenarios under each of which, again, it seems wisest to be of unjust intent.

Glaucon goes on to assert, as Thrasymachus had before, that justice is simply a device used by the weak to protect themselves from the strong and, in the end, a device used by the strong to lull the weak into a false sense of security. It is a necessary evil invoked to prevent the open warfare of all against all, but the one that the wise person will circumvent whenever she or he can do so with impunity. It is, at most, according to Glaucon, a compromise that "stands between the best and the worst, the best being to do wrong without penalty and the worst to be wronged without the power of revenge."⁴ Thusly, Glaucon opens a wide rift between the right and the wise that, from Plato on, moral philosophers have tried to span.

The elaborate argument of the next eight books of the *Republic* has turned out to be the most widely accepted response to the "Why be moral?" question posed by Thrasymachus and Glaucon. In the tenth book he gives the old "Because the gods will get you if you're immoral" answer, but this can be written off as a disappointing anticlimax to the real answer that begins in the fourth book and culminates in the ninth. Yet the bottom line of both arguments is the same, namely, that the surest way to *not* get happiness is to pursue it with an egoistic vengeance. This basic theme runs through the writings of all of the ancients, especially the stoics and Epicureans. It is also found in the East among the Buddhists and in modern Westerners as diverse as Mill and Nietzsche.

But Plato is not content to point out a common platitude about how not to get happiness. His argument is intended to show that the unjust person is doomed to profound unhappiness because of a certain kind of *ignorance* about the nature of the soul that egoists act upon. This brings us to the moral psychology developed in the fourth book. As mentioned before, Plato pictures the soul as the composite of three parts: reason, spirit, and appetite. Everyone's soul contains all three components but in different states of balance. According to Plato, in the vast majority of people, the psychological balance of power rests in the appetites. It is not as though appetitive people are without a capacity to reason, for, indeed, one cannot get much money, power, sex, security, or other appetitive satisfaction without some modicum of control and intelligence. Likewise, appetitive people cannot be lacking in the sort of ambition that characterizes the high-spirited Auxiliary.

But the appetitive person will take a serious interest in abstract truths only if there is some appetitive payoff in doing so. He will learn calculus, but only in order to earn a high salary as an engineer or architect. Learning mathematics or anything else just for the sake of gaining knowledge will be seen by him as oddness. The same goes for ambition. The idea of doing something simply because one is a "man of action" will seem weird. The kind of "irritability" Plato attributes to the military psyche of the Auxiliary will seem like some sort of psychosis. The appetitive person will do things only because such things help him get something linked to the satisfaction of an appetite (and, indeed, the desire for leisurely inactivity may well be one of these appetites).

In the ninth book, Plato's analysis turns to the grim side of the appetitive life. Most appetitive people go through life constrained by law (if nothing else) to what we can call the "normal" appetites such as those for food, shelter, wealth, power, sex, and so on. There is, however, a dark side to the appetites that Plato refers to simply as "lust." The desires for enough food, shelter, and wealth turn into gluttony and outlandish extravagance. The desire for power turns into brutality. The desire for sex turns into the desire for debauchery, incest, and rape. As Plato describes the situation, lust is always lurking just beneath the social veneer of the appetitive person. Occasionally it emerges in dreams, but in the wakeful company of others the very possibility that one might come to act on such slimy impulses is confidently denied.

However, this confidence is based on ignorance. The capacity for mindless destruction is in every soul, and the appetitive person is far closer to vice than he or she thinks. In the first place, the appetitive life is characterized by a lack of reasonable control from the outset. Reason may intrude to balance one appetite against another, for example, a strong desire for wealth may cause restraint of desires for liquor, luxury, sex, or anything else that costs money or impairs capital accumulation. (Plato ascribes this kind of balancing to the "oligarchic man.") But at some level the appetites go unchecked by reason. The basic appetites will vary from one person to the next, but, whether it is money, sex, power, leisure, or something else, the appetitive person will never feel compelled to offer reasons for his or her selection of one appetite as basic rather than another. In fact, in what Plato refers to as "the democratic man" (who is controlled by this appetite and then that one but is not yet controlled by lust), any suggestion that reasonable justification is required as a base of one's selection of one appetite over others will be met with hostility and resentment. But the problem is not so much that the appetitive person should not be called upon to offer justification for the selection of basic appetites; rather, that none is possible.

In the second place, and in addition to the fact that the appetitive person is not in the habit of thinking deeply about motivation and justification, the line that separates "normal" desires from the "abnormal" ones rooted in lust is not at all clear as a matter of conceptual distinction. More importantly, it is far easier to cross than the "normal" appetitive person will admit or know. Contemporary social psychology supplies dreadful confirmation of this claim. The obedience experiments of Stanley Milgram provide a case in point.[5] The upshot of Milgram's experiments was that most people (65 percent of them) will willfully deliver painful electrical shocks to an innocent stranger who has screamed out the fact that he doesn't want to be shocked and who may well be dying as a result of the shocks. And they will do it for no better reason than that they are told to by someone in a position of questionable authority. One must wonder what the obedience rates would be if the penalty for not delivering the shocks was loss of one's job or of one's life. I suspect that almost everyone would harm strangers if required to do so at the point of a gun.

Once over the line, familiar mechanisms of rationalization will take over. Eventually, one will rest content with the realization that one's barbarity is not only justifiable, but fun too. Indeed, violence and brutality seem to have a sort of excitement about them that is simply not to be found in the desire for and satisfaction of "normal" pleasures. The thrill of marital sex pales in comparison with the excitement of an affair. Downhill skiing is boring when compared with the adrenalin rush of a convenience store hold-up. Normal life is just not capable of providing the excitement of life on the edge of danger, debauchery, drunkenness, and death.

Of course, the "normal" appetitive person denies that any of this is so, as though she knows all about the addictive capacity of vice. She knows her own strength of will and reason better than a million drunks, rapists, and murderers who all thought themselves incapable of addiction and who all suffered for their stupidity and unfounded confidence that it is they who control the appetites, not the appetites that control them.

The issue of control brings us to an important piece of analysis of the concept of freedom that unfolds in the eighth and ninth books of the *Republic*. Plato delineates five forms of government and five corresponding types of person: the aristocrat (who is ruled by reason), the timocrat (who is ruled by spirit), the oligarch (who is ruled by the appetite for wealth), the democrat (who is ruled by a congeries of "normal" appetites), and the tyrant (who is ruled by lust). The aristocrat considers real freedom to be a matter of self-control or autonomy. As we go down the scale we find a different notion of freedom emerging. By the time we get to the democrat, the notion of freedom has become a matter of what we now call "negative freedom," which is constituted in a simple lack of control or absence of restraint. The tyrant is characterized by an utter lack of restraint.

This idea of freedom as lack of restraint is one of the main targets of Plato's moralizing about the appetitive life. The appetitive person feels that she is free to the extent that she is uncontrolled by others or by her own reasoning (which will be seen as a source of prudish inhibition). But this kind of freedom is, for Plato, sheer illusion. To leave the appetites unchecked and, thusly, to be dictated to by them is to be free only in the way that a drunk is. In a sense, a drunk is the freest of all people, because she is unrestrained. But in another sense, she is the least free of people because she has lost all self-control. Eventually, if the drunkenness continues, self-respect will vanish as well, which will make her even more free in the negative sense but, again, less free if freedom means self-control; she no longer really has much of a self to be concerned about or inhibited by.

So, the appetitive person, that is, the person who goes through life judging it to be a success to the degree that various personal appetites are satisfied, winds up leading a life that is without fulfillment, happiness, real freedom, or dignity. Moreover, the appetitive person is always on the verge of complete calamity and, for the most part, held barely at the brink by law and the threat of criminal punishment.

There is more. If one evaluates one's life in terms of desire satisfaction, then it seems that the best way to guarantee maximal satisfaction and minimal frustration is to simply have as few desires as one can manage. This, in fact, is the practical wisdom offered up by Epicurus. Unlike Plato, the Epicureans held that we are *all*, by nature, appetitive. Nevertheless, we can try to stifle the appetites and, especially, the imagination that inflates our hopes of satisfaction and our fears of frustration. This might sound like a path to even more frustration inasmuch as one would now be led by a desire to not have any desires. But this problem is based on a misunderstanding of the moral psychology held by Plato and, in large part, by Epicurus as well. Desire is a product of the appetitive part of the soul, which is at war with the reasonable part of the soul. None of the Greeks were suggesting that one develop an appetite to not have any appetites. Rather, the suggestion is that reason be cultivated in such a way as to keep the appetites in line. To the degree that the reasonable part of the soul is strengthened, the appetitive part loses its power.

There is some metaphorical sense in which one can have intellectual desires and even a love of reason, but these desires and loves are different in kind from those associated with the appetites. The major point of difference is to be found in the fact that intellectual desires can be satisfied, whereas, appetitive desires are inherently frustrating. As Plato points out in the ninth book of the *Republic*, ordinary desires for food, drink, sex, and so on bring greater satisfaction to the degree that the period before the having of food, drink, or sex was characterized by the absence of food, drink or sex. For example, a meal is most enjoyable after a period of relative hunger. So satisfaction is dependent upon and directly proportional to prior frustration. When the moments of frustration are subtracted from the moments of satisfaction, the result is a wash. This is not the case with intellectual pursuits; one does not have to go without reading for a week in order to get the most out of Plato. In fact, the more one reads Plato, the more one will get out of him. But the more food, drink, sex, or money one gets, the more one's expectations go up and the more difficult satisfaction becomes.

I have spent a lot of time on Plato's arguments against Thrasymachian egoism because this position poses a serious threat to all other theories of wisdom. Indeed, given that a theory of wisdom is simply a theory about how one can secure personal well-being, it is hard to see how any theory could be any better than the one that asserts that the individual ought to simply pursue the satisfaction of his or her own desires. However, the plausibility of the theory hinges on the nature of the desires that direct the pursuit. Broadly speaking, personal well-being must only be a matter of desire satisfaction; but if the desires to be satisfied are simply those that emerge from what Plato called the appetites, then their satisfaction will not lead to a life that is either very happy or very interesting. Indeed, what the appetitive person longs for, namely, a life of unrestrained appetitive satisfaction, is the most miserable of all lives.

A thesis that really stretches beyond all of Plato's psychological premises has been called the hedonistic paradox.[6] The claim here is that the surest way not to be happy is to try to be. Happiness comes to us when we least expect it and when we are absorbed in the pursuit of something other than our own happiness. Plato's thesis is narrower than this inasmuch as his claim is merely that the attempt to get *a certain kind* of happiness (appetitive satisfaction) is futile. Certainly he thought that other routes to happiness (for example, that toward the life of reason) could be consciously pursued with reward.

Irrespective of whether the hedonistic paradox can find support in the moralistic arguments of Plato, it does bring us to the doorstep of a realization that is found not only in Plato but also in modern writers like Mill and Nietzsche. Regardless of the fact that *some* kinds of well-being can be reached by conscious pursuit, the kind of well-being *most* people attempt to achieve (i.e., appetitive satisfaction) cannot, generally, be gotten by trying to get it. As Mill put it in his *Autobiography*, "the best theory for all those who have but a moderate degree of sensibility and of capacity for enjoyment, that is, the great majority of mankind," is what he describes as Carlyle's "anti-self-consciousness theory."[7]

> Those are only happy (I thought) who have their minds fixed on some object other than their own happiness; on the happiness of others, on the improvement of mankind, even on some art or pursuit, followed not as a means, but as itself an ideal end. Aiming thus at something else, they find happiness by the way. The enjoyments of life (such was now my theory) [in 1827, that is, at the time Mill was coming out of his depression] are sufficient to make it a pleasant thing, when they are taken *en passant*, without being made a principal object. Once make them so, and they are immediately felt to be insufficient. They will not bear a scrutinizing examination. Ask yourself whether you are happy, and you cease to be so. The only chance is to treat, not happiness, but some end external to it, as the purpose of life. Let your self-consciousness, your scrutiny, your self-interrogation, exhaust themselves on that; and if otherwise fortunately circumstanced, you will inhale happiness in the air you breathe, without dwelling on it or thinking about it, without either forestalling it in imagination, or putting it to flight by fatal questioning.[8]

This "best theory for . . . the great majority" shares some affinities with ancient virtue theories. The idea is, as Aristotle had suggested, that one should strive to stifle the appetites *as a matter of unreflective habit.*[9] These habits, in turn, would bring one into harmony with oneself and others. For example, as one goes through life struggling to find the mean between the vices of rashness and cowardice, of profligacy and meanness, and of a long list of other pairings of vices, one ingrains in one's behavior the virtues of courage, generosity, and others in such a way that one finds the limits of one's talents and develops one's "excellence" in a way fortuitous for oneself and for others whom one benefits by the prudent deployment of effort.

In the modern tradition, and especially in British philosophy, the harmony of individual virtue, prudence, and social benefit was given a new twist by introducing utility as the factor that linked all three levels. Aristotle certainly felt that there would be a natural harmony between the virtuous individual and the just state, but (unless one misdefines "*eudaimonia*" as "happiness" in the modern sense) one cannot find any explicit utilitarianism in Aristotle. But in Mill, and before him Bentham and Hume, the utilitarian link is explicit. Hume claims in the *Treatise*, that moral distinctions depend entirely on certain peculiar sentiments of pain and pleasure, and that whatever mental quality in ourselves or others gives us satisfaction, by the survey of reflexion, is of course virtuous; as every thing of this nature, that gives uneasiness, is vicious. Now since every quality in ourselves or others, which gives pleasure, always causes pride or love; as every one, that excites uneasiness, excites humility or hatred: It follows, that these two particulars are to be consider'd as equivalent, with regard to our mental qualities, *virtue* and the power of producing love or pride, *vice* and the power of producing humility or hatred.[10]

In the second *Enquiry* the utilitarian underpinnings of virtue are detailed at length as Hume describes how several virtues ranging from intelligence to honesty to cleanliness are virtues because and only because of the tendency of such character traits to maximize aggregate happiness as well as the happiness of the virtuous individual.

Now, given the theory of utilitarianism outlined in Part I of this book, I am compelled to find fault with part of the reasoning here. There is good reason to think that, as a matter of practical wisdom, the development of virtue will be beneficial for the virtuous individual. The development of habits that tend to increase the happiness of those around a person can be expected, in most cases, to meet with the approval and reciprocal benevolence of those other people. Although there is clearly more than this sort of extended prudence at work in the Golden Rule or in Kant's theory, just as clearly there is considerable prudential wisdom in treating others as one would like others to treat oneself, in treating others as ends in themselves rather than as mere means to one's own ends, and in acting according to rules that one would be willing to have made universal. Not only can one expect that what goes around will eventually come around, but if one acts with routine malevolence, one will find it hard to go through life without assuming that others are equally opportunistic even in cases where they really aren't. This, in turn, can lead to the sort of paranoia that Plato attributes to the soul tyrannized by lust in the ninth book of the *Republic*.

In the cases of virtues that are more abstract than simple benevolence, like those of honesty, industry, modesty, intelligence, and even cleanliness, one can still expect that, in general, these virtues will meet with the approval of others who benefit from one's exercise of them. Moreover, given that, even under the harm principle, institutions that encourage the development of and respect for simple benevolence and other virtues, like honesty and industry, can be justified, one has even more right to expect approval of others. Of equal importance, one will feel at ease with the values inculcated by one's moral upbringing and will be spared the psychological tumult that usually accompanies value rejection and reformulation.

Nevertheless, even though there may be good reason to set up institutions that inculcate various virtues, from the point of view *of the individual*, the reason to be virtuous is ultimately a matter of *personal* well-being, not *aggregate* utility. It is through the development of various virtues that one will be made happy (even though, as Mill points out, they must be pursued, scrutinized, and made the object of self-examination for their own sake and in their own right). To think that one's own virtue or lack of it will have a discernable effect from the point of view of the aggregate sufferings and strivings of all sentient beings present and future is, as I argued in Part I, to engage in a kind of self-aggrandizement that, in general, cannot withstand analysis. That cosmic utility would be affected by *everyone's* having a certain virtue might be an argument for establishing institutions and practices for the inculcation of various virtues, but not for *me* to be virtuous.

Moreover, in order for the virtuous life to pay, one must not only not think about virtue in terms of its expected personal utility but one must, as Mill also pointed out, be "fortunately circumstanced." He might have in mind the simple Aristotelian point that in order to fully exercise the virtues, one must be blessed with a certain amount of luck with respect to one's place in the world and one's natural talents. A certain amount of wealth, wit, agility, and attractiveness is required in order to develop many virtues. One cannot reach an impressive level of generosity if one is hopelessly poor. One cannot excel at finding the mean between rashness and cowardice if one is either chronically stupid or too physically feeble or squeamish to face real danger. One will not be able to find much virtue in sexual temperance if one is too ugly to attract anyone else.

It must be pointed out that this Greek idea of virtue is quite at variance with Christian notions that would follow. From the point of view of Christianity, one neither had to be nor strive to be an aristocrat to be virtuous. As Nietzsche would point out at bellicose length, the major moral breakthrough of Christianity was to make a virtue of poverty, chastity, boredom, and fully deserved humility, and then count as "evil" many of the virtues that the Greeks and Romans associated with nobility. Nietzsche's sarcastic intent aside, Christianity, indeed, did make it possible for the vast majority of people to pursue virtue in a way that was really impossible under the Greek and Roman virtue theories.

There is a possibility of stretching another interpretation out of Mill's point so as to get a more interesting insight into the relationship between virtue and fortune. The value of virtue rests in its harmonious relationship with self-interest, which, by a curious twist of psychology, cannot be gotten if directly pursued. But what if one's life is visited by the misfortune of circumstances where the relationship is not at all harmonious. Regardless of how easy the Christian theory of virtue makes things, one might still be plagued by a common problem that was touched upon in Chapter 6, namely the partial compliance problem. What should one do in situations where acting in accord with simple virtues brings extreme suffering to the individual because the social arrangements one lives under are not at all in accord with the practice of virtue?

The advantage of acting from virtue is that a certain separation of virtue and direct egoism takes place. One does not, on each occasion, act on the basis of what's in it for oneself. One does not even spend much, if any, analysis on whether the life of virtue will be rewarded. But how great can the separation of virtue and personal well-being be before any reasonable person should be expected to succumb to the pressure to give up virtue?

The best wisdom here is probably that people often overestimate how bad things are and break down too easily. For example, many Europeans were too quick to infer that the triumph of Nazism was permanent. Ultimately, they were thought much less of than those who clung to virtue under severe, but endurable, pressure. On the other hand, many people were simply unceremoniously shot for resistance. Many prisoners of war who undergo torture without revealing information sought by the torturers die or are driven insane as a result of refusing to divulge an inconsequential piece of trivia. Many corporate whistleblowers simply ruin their personal and professional lives without effecting even a slight correction of the corruption they sought to expose.

What does one do in such cases? I have stated before that such cases really fall within the domain of a theory of wisdom, not a theory of right and wrong. What follows from the virtue theory of wisdom is really only a slight clarification of the perplexity that arises in such cases, namely, that such cases always put virtue at odds with the prudential basis of virtue in such a way that we are faced with a continuum of cases ranging from those where only slight personal sacrifice is required in order to maintain one's virtue to those where virtue requires pointless and painful death. How far one should be willing to travel along this continuum in partial compliance cases is something no theory should pretend to settle a priori for all individuals and all cases. The best that can be expected is that the confusion created by such cases is located in the right place.

.

CHAPTER 10

Individualism

The idea that some things (like happiness) can be gotten only by not pursuing them is given an interesting exemplification by Elster.[1] He likens the pursuit of happiness to the pursuit of sleep. When struck by insomnia, the course of action least likely to succeed in inducing sleep is to concentrate on going to sleep. The first retreat from this direct approach might be to try something like counting sheep, reading, or something else, that is not being pursued for its own sake but, rather, in the hope that while we are distracting ourselves sleep will creep up and grab us as it so often does when we really want to get something counted or read.

Although this might work most of the time for most people, there will be times for some people when it won't because, no matter how hard we try to concentrate on the reading, we know that we are only doing it to trick ourselves into sleep and, so, the hope of going to sleep is still recognized as the real motive behind the reading. Finally, one might resign oneself to the probability of never sleeping again, start reading for the sake of reading, and then probably fall asleep almost immediately.

In terms of the discussion of the previous chapter, this final recourse to counting sheep for the sake of counting sheep is something like pursuing virtue for its own sake and ultimately being happy. And, whether pursuing sleep or happiness, this strategy is, as Mill says, "the best theory for . . . the great majority." But one must wonder about the minority for whom this strategy will not work. One must assume that Mill did not consider himself one of "the great majority." What about those who have more than just "a moderate degree of sensibility and of capacity for enjoyment," those who are too sensitive and introspective to trick themselves into believing in the intrinsic value of counting sheep?

The question is, of course, much more troublesome when directed toward the pursuit of virtue than when directed at the pursuit of sheep counting. Sheep counting is obviously of no inherent value, whereas virtue, under the theories of Hume, Bentham, and Mill, is of value inasmuch as it is linked with the happiness of others. But still, as Mill is at great pains to point out in the third chapter of *On Liberty*, the happiness of most people is something informed largely by their unreflective, habitual commitment to convention. Thus the reflective individual will, at some point, have to come to the belief that virtue is of no more inherent value than the desires of others that it is directed at satisfying. This realization would appear to be the immediate cause of Mill's depression in 1826. If reflection continues, and the realization comes that the ultimate value of virtue is the self-interest of the virtuous, then the trick of achieving happiness by not pursuing it will no longer work. This realization would appear to be behind Mill's claim that the pursuit of virtue is the best strategy only for "the great majority," that is, for those with just "a moderate degree of sensibility and of capacity for enjoyment." For those who think too much, the strategy will not work.

In addition to the problem caused by the fact that virtue (as construed in the previous chapter) ultimately rests on convention and conformism, which, more often than not, is acted upon without reflection, Mill is keenly aware of the self-destructive social disutility of mindless conformism. The principal disutility of such conservatism, as we saw in Chapter 7, is that it will stifle the experimental journeys of those who are discontent with the norm. To repress these individuals, in turn, will rob society of the opportunity of progress, which, in Mill's mind, is to be accomplished not by goose-stepping toward some preestablished social ideal but by observing the successes and failures of social mutants. Any society which suppresses every mode of life it deems "abnormal" or "eccentric" is doomed, as Mill put it, "to become another China."

However, the philosophically surprising line of argument in the third chapter (par. 2) of *On Liberty* does not concern the social utility of individualism but, rather, Mill's claim that individuality is not only socially and instrumentally valuable but *intrinsically* valuable. The great "evil," Mill asserts, is "that individual spontaneity is hardly recognized by the common modes of thinking as having any intrinsic worth, or deserving any regard on its own account. The majority, [are] satisfied with the ways of mankind as they now are . . ." What is surprising about this claim is that it seems to fly in the face of his claim at the beginning of the second chapter (par. 2) of *Utilitarianism* "that pleasure, and freedom from pain, are the only things desirable as ends . . ."

The surprise is compounded not only by Mill's individualistic rhetoric in *On Liberty* but also by the infamous line of argument that immediately follows his endorsement of simple hedonism in *Utilitarianism*. In opposition to Bentham's claim that "quantity of pleasure being the same, pushpin is as good as poetry," Mill asserts that it is "better to be Socrates dissatisfied than a fool satisfied." This is offered in support of Mill's claim that some *kinds* of pleasures are not just *quantitatively* better than others but *qualitatively* better.

But the Socrates platitude makes it clear that Mill doesn't just believe that some pleasures are better than others, for Socrates' life may be devoid of any pleasures at all and still be of more worth than a fool's life in paradise. Mill is, in fact, asserting that some kinds of *lives* are better than others. Living in a certain way, namely, in the mere pursuit of "higher" pleasures, is better than living in such a way as to actually obtain satisfaction of various "lower" pleasures.

In order to flesh this claim out, it must be noted that Mill's reference to Socrates is hardly incidental, for it was Socrates who argued that "the unexamined life is not worth living," and it is precisely the Socratic life of reflection, introspection, and examination that Mill is endorsing in *Utilitarianism* and, especially, in *On Liberty*. This is connected to Mill's individualism inasmuch as individual identity is formed precisely in the autonomous choice of values. Who one is as a person is a matter of how one chooses to order one's beliefs, desires, and tastes about religion, politics, ethics, art, literature, music, and a host of other things that are not predetermined by physiology. That one has a taste for food, sex, or the absence of pain does not make one an individual; it does not even separate one from a pig. Likewise, one who simply adopts conventional wisdom about religion, ethics or music without ever thinking about *why* one ought to do so has character "no more than a steam engine has character."

Aside from the link between Mill's position and that of Socrates, there is also a link worth noting between Mill and Kant. Kant's fundamental reason for rejecting the utilitarianism of Bentham was that happiness, as Hume and Bentham discussed it, could not be good for its own sake. In the first place it might not be deserved. In the second place, happiness was not an end toward which we are directed autonomously. We are, Kant thought, directed toward the pursuit of our own happiness by nature and, thus, acting on this natural impulse is no more deserving of moral credit than a knee jerk. That we would direct ourselves to the pursuit of the happiness *of others* is, generally, no more than the facilitation of mindless, and heteronomous, knee jerking for others.

Where Kant and Mill differ radically is not on the issue of the fundamental value of autonomy but on whether reflection and autonomous choice should be expected to produce any substantial uniformity at the level of legitimate individual choice. Under the usual reading, Kant's position is that all rational individuals would choose identical duties and, moreover, would arrive at univocal applications of these duties on matters like suicide, lying, conditional benevolence, and the cultivation of talent. Mill certainly didn't hold this position with any consistency. To the contrary, he went out of his way to argue in his major works that "energy of character" was always recognized in terms of personal "originality."

Another feature of Mill's thought would seem to distance him from both Kant and Socrates (perhaps more clearly from Plato). In both Plato and Kant there is an extreme suspicion about the effect of passion and impulse on the cultivation of moral character. Mill's thought, on the other hand, was thoroughly marked with the Romanticism of his day. Although impulsiveness surely has to be controlled by a strong will, it is, nonetheless, "the raw material of human nature." Strong passion makes us "capable, perhaps of more evil, but certainly of more good."

The influence of Romanticism aside, this feature of Mill's thought brings his view, in an important way, close to that of Aristotle, who held that rationality and introspection are inherent prerequisites of the development of virtue but they are not sufficient for it; emotion is also necessary to bolster a strong commitment to virtue and a revulsion about vice.[2] In a much more important way, Mill is even closer to the Aristotelian tradition in that the meaning of life (at least for some) is not straightforwardly reducible to the simple pleasures of others or any feelings of happiness or peace one might feel oneself as a consequence of pursuing the welfare of others. Rather, the fully meaningful life is one characterized by the pursuit of individual excellence, which, according to Aristotle as well as Mill, can be achieved only by rational examination of ends and by living through actual situations where those ends are acted upon and one's true talents, commitments, and limits are tested. No individual is in a position to prescribe for all that they ought to do things as he does, for some do not have his talents and some are not constrained by his limitations. Just as surely, no individual ought to be judged in terms of the talents and limitations of the lowest common denominator.

All of this leads to a final question, namely: Given that worthwhile individual ends are prescribed by neither physiological nature nor by mere custom or unreflective common wisdom, how are such ends to be found and what kinds of ends are likely candidates? The answer to the first part of this question supplies the answer to the second. Individual ends are to be found by searching for them through philosophical reflection and by trial-and-error testing of oneself in the real world. To the degree one takes this experimental attitude to life seriously, one comes to realize that living this way *is* the end of the good life. The reflective questioning and experimentation never ends for the true individual. The desire to have it end in some neat set of prescriptive platitudes that can be mechanically followed is the desire to become a steam engine. What fails for "the great majority," namely, thinking about happiness and how it can be gotten, is the only way some people can find any real value in their lives at all.

Indeed, the individual who lives this way may experience little of the calm and relaxation so easily attainable in the middle classes of modern society. But just as surely, such an individual is not likely to be as bored or as boring as are the devotees of televised bowling tournaments. Indeed, the true individual, by her words and deeds, will pose threats—perceived and real—to the ethical upholstery so cherished by conservatives and collectivists. But, as Mill pointed out, "society has now fairly got the better of individuality; and the danger which threatens human nature is not the excess, but the deficiency, of personal impulses and preferences." When the ultimate imperative for everyone becomes, "What would the average person do in my position?" or, at best, "What would Rambo (or some other mannequin for middle-class social fabrics) do?" then the tyranny of the majority will have triumphed.

None of what I have said here does anything to absolve the fundamental blunder involved in Mill's claim that some pleasures are qualitatively better than others. Richard Taylor was right in arguing that to claim that some *kinds* of pleasures are better than others is to abandon pleasure as the measure of all things; it is, indeed, to abandon hedonism. Although, as I argued in Part I, a significant part of hedonism can still be a part of a viable social ethic, Mill, for all important purposes, abandoned it as a theory of individual ethics. Mill's theory of wisdom (to impose my term) is clearly centered on the value of individual discovery and growth.

CHAPTER 11

Sublimation

Nehamas describes Nietzsche as "the first modernist at the same time that he was the last romantic."[1] As I understand it, one of the principal points of demarkation between these two movements is supposed to be that romantics (like Mill) were obsessed with the discovery and development of human nature whereas modernists (like the existentialists who would so revere Nietzsche) denied that any individual had any "nature" to discover or develop. The self, according to the typical modernist, is, first of all, created rather than discovered and, secondly, inherently fragmented and in a state of anomie; there is no intact "noble savage" beneath the veneer of civility. The theme of self-creation figures prominently in most existentialist philosophy (especially in Sartre), and the theme of personal fragmentation runs through a lot of existentialist literature, often in tandem with themes from Eastern thought (Hesse is a good example).

However, in spite of Nietzsche's frequent references to the "soul as subjective multiplicity,"[2] I am inclined to think that much of the difference between Mill and Nietzsche on this issue is rhetorical rather than substantive. Indeed, Mill often refers to that object of existentialist dread: "human nature." But there is nothing in what he says about human nature that is at all deterministic or at all intended to free individuals of any responsibility for their choices, characters, or actions. In fact, Mill's standard of ethical responsibility (the harm principle) can, as I have argued, be made quite coherent and reasonably precise, whereas existentialists are notorious for insisting on personal accountability without being at all clear as to whom or what one is accountable.[3] This may well be because they are even more confused than other modern philosophers about the distinction between social ethics and wisdom. What they have to say about values is, I believe, almost always more interesting if it is taken as a series of suggestions about wisdom rather than as any serious proposal about social moral standards.

This is certainly the case with Nietzsche, as most of the major commentators on his work argue.[4] To take any of Nietzsche's hyperbole as containing even the seeds of a social ethic is to render his work incoherent and, moreover, positively dangerous. (Perhaps this is precisely the motivation of those who would reduce his thought to the claim that we all ought to act more like Attila the Hun.) What is now routinely taken as the main reason for rejecting the idea that Nietzsche could have seriously held any definite social or political philosophy is his "perspectivism."

This view amounts to a thoroughgoing relativism about everything, not just social values but also science, mathematics, geometry, semantics, and even logic.[5] There is no truth independent of an overarching point of view and, it would seem, no way to even talk about values, science or anything else without assuming a particular perspective for the purpose of saying something. This position may account for the complete lack of objectivity in Nietzsche's style of exposition. For Nietzsche, an objective style cannot exist. So, if one is going to say something about values, one must say it from a certain point of view. In the case of ethics, Nietzsche thinks the points of view are historically limited to two: master morality and slave morality. Thus, in order to write about morality one must, if one is Nietzsche, adopt the point of view and the literary style of either a master or a slave. Nietzsche's choice is pretty obvious, and that, I think, is why works like the *Genealogy of Morals* and *Beyond Good and Evil* come off like descriptive ethics written by a barbarian. But the adoption of such a persona does not necessarily imply a moral endorsement of the perspective it is drawn from any more than Kafka would have been endorsing the perspective of a huge cockroach had he written "The Metamorphosis" in first person.

If I am right about this, then a slighting remark made by Hilary Putnam has a rejoinder. According to Putnam, "Many thinkers have fallen into Nietzsche's error of telling us that they had a 'better' morality than the entire tradition; in each case they only produced a monstrosity, for all they *could* do was *arbitrarily* wrench certain values out of their context while ignoring others."[6] Under my interpretation, Nietzsche's central works were not pretended by him to be deliverances from an omniscient, ahistorical, and objective observer but, rather, broadsides from the grave of Attila the Hun. By conjuring up, as best as he could (and he did it shockingly well), the condescending perspective and literary persona of an enlightened barbarian, he was not attempting to step outside of the entire tradition. Rather, he was turning an ancient part of the Western tradition (Aristocratic master morality) against another part of that tradition (i.e., the slave mentalities produced by Christianity and modern science). Even the fact that he planned a four-part "Revaluation of All Values" does not show that he had in mind anything other than the revaluation of all *prevailing* values (i.e., all modern slave values) from the point of view of master morality. In fact, the pretense of objectivity and the denial of subjectivity would have to be a mark of slavishness on Nietzschean grounds.

Whether or not there is anything to my suggestion about Nietzsche's style is a matter I will leave to the scholars (and there are a great many

Nietzsche scholars these days). There is, however, one interesting line of thought in Nietzsche about a phenomenon common to both master and slave moralities that bears directly on my concerns in this part of the book. What is of interest, I think, is his view about myth (which is closely linked to the whole idea of perspectivism) and, more particularly, a few passages where he talks about sublimation.

In this century, the notion of sublimation has been almost entirely shaped by the thought of Freud and his followers. It has come to signify the channeling of immoral or socially disapproved impulses (e.g., sexual desire) into other impulses (e.g., desires to write books). For something to be subliminal, then, is for it to be concerned with the subconscious rather the conscious mind. Although this notion of sublimation can find some application in Nietzsche's thought (especially in connection with his basic idea of the will to power), it does not fully capture what Nietzsche had in mind by introducing the notion into modern psychology. Moreover, it imputes a sort of involuntary and neurotic mechanism about the process that Nietzsche didn't intend—at least I'd prefer to think that he didn't intend it.

It seems reasonable to suppose that Nietzsche's ideas about sublimation would have much more to do with the idea of the sublime as it was developed in the aesthetics of Burke, Kant, and Schopenhauer than it would with twentieth-century clinical technique. This is, at any rate, the angle I will be pursuing. As was the case with my discussions of Mill, I am much more interested in developing a line of thought that is independently plausible than I am in constructing an interpretation that is faithful to the actual Nietzschean texts. (Being "faithful to Nietzsche" may well constitute an utter oxymoron anyhow.)

In the aesthetics of the eighteenth and nineteenth centuries, the sublime was explained in terms of its difference from the beautiful. In Burke, Kant, and Schopenhauer, the beautiful was reckoned to be the cause of some sort of "disinterested satisfaction" (to use Kant's term). The beautiful was something that freed the mind of all concerns about the practical, empirical, or sensual. In Schopenhauer's colorful terms, the beautiful leaves us in

> the painless state which Epicurus prized as the highest good and the state of the gods; for we are for a moment set free from the miserable striving of the will; we keep the Sabbath of the penal servitude of willing; the wheel of Ixion stands still.[7]

To look at a painting and only wonder about its market value, to listen to a piece of music and only fantasize about performing it oneself, or to watch a movie only in order to be sexually turned on is to not experience the artwork as beautiful. To experience the beautiful is to lose oneself and to be free of all mundane egoistic concerns about money, power, fame, or sex.

The sublime has the same effect, but it comes only with a "struggle," as Schopenhauer sees it. The beautiful seduces us by drawing our attention away from the ordinary; the sublime assaults us and forces us to come to terms with the insignificance of our ordinary concerns. A painting lures us; a volcanic eruption confronts us, as does a fierce storm, a first glimpse of Yosemite Valley, or a full realization of the vastness of the heavens. The feeling of the sublime is grounded in a feeling of awe that impresses upon us our smallness, impotence, and unimportance, a feeling that the world was not created *for us*. As is the case with the appreciation of beauty, the feeling of the sublime requires a certain detachment. One is not likely to feel much sublime awe when in the path of a lava flow, when in a rowboat during a storm, or when falling off of El Capitan. In these cases, one feels only fear and an intense concern for one's own survival and the mere continuance of ordinary life.

A crucial insight into the nature of the sublime belongs to Kant. Following from the epistemology of the first *Critique*, Kant argues in the third *Critique* that, upon reflection, our feeling of the sublime cannot be a result of any simple encounter with some brutally vast thing in itself. The world is inherently a partial creation of the perceiver; it involves the work of a priori forms of intuition, the imagination, and the understanding much more than it involves mere sensibility. This is especially true in the case where infinity is attributed to some thing "out there." Infinity is not, on Kantian grounds, a property that inheres in space itself. Instead, it is a property the mind attributes to space. Space is neither finite nor infinite but rather infinitely extendable.

What this has to do with the sublime is that when we are awed by the infinitely vast or the infinitely powerful we are really in awe of our own reason, we are awed by the feeling that the world *was* created for us. I think Kant's claim is made particularly compelling by the example of the contemplation of the heavens. The sublimity a child feels when she or he first realizes that space can go on forever (at least in a child's Euclidean universe) is not so much a result of realizing how great the distance between earth and some star really is but rather a result of grappling with the very notion of infinity. Children are first inclined to think that outer space must end somewhere only to realize that there must be something on the other side of wherever that somewhere is. In other words, sublime awe is a product of something *we* do, not something *it* does.

The effect of making something sublime, of *sublimating* it, is to make it more than it "really" is. What something "really" is is what it is under the simplest explanatory story. For example, Yosemite Valley is an arrangement of dirt, rocks, and plants. A more detailed explanation would involve a discussion of carbon, chlorophyll, and, eventually, electrons and strings. What Yosemite "really" is is as boring as a park ranger's geological serenade. Yet hardly anyone sees it for the first time without being stunned (even when it is barely visible through the smog). What is stunning is obviously more than the spectacle of a few more rocks and electrons. Moreover, realizing *that* Yosemite is stunning is, in some way, a lot more important than being able to explain *why* it is so.

Nietzsche seems to think that sublimation is involved even in the mere construction of "reality" to begin with (as indicated by what he has to say about the nature of scientific "truth"), but he certainly thinks that it is involved in the valuation of anything that may be posited as real. Nothing can simply be as it is, no thing, no human action, certainly no human's pain and suffering. According to Nietzsche, the Greeks found in their gods not only the reasons for the existence of elements and phenomena, nor only the reasons for the tragic sufferings of great men and women. More important than a reason was an *interpretation* of these things that made them more important, more noble, than a simpler explanation of them would have made them. Life, for the Greeks, was not merely dramatic, nor was it mere "real life drama." It was drama itself; it was art in its purest and finest form. The noble Greek, "was on a stage and knew himself to be; virtue without a witness was something unthinkable for this nation of actors."[8] The aristocrat's life was every bit as sublime as that of any fictional character in a Hollywood film because his life *was* fiction; it was truly *larger* than life.

Likewise, Christianity facilitated the sublimation of life. But, as Nietzsche is so fond of pointing out, the underlying fiction of life was not one devised by or intended for nobles. Christianity was the fiction of the slaves, by the slaves, and for the slaves. And it reflected the psychological illnesses of the slaves. The Greek aristocrats needed an audience for their virtues and their tragedies. In the bargain, they got psychological absolution for their stupidity and arrogance (for their *hubris*). They acted stupidly because of the devious machinations of the gods, and they paid mercilessly in *this* life because of this divine manipulation. There was then, according to Nietzsche, no need for them to feel much guilt; the gods took that in return for the punishment they inflicted even upon the best men and women. The Greeks didn't have to psychologically torture themselves; their gods would take it out on them in real blood spilled upon real ground.

In Christianity, the order is reversed with devastating psychological consequence. God takes upon himself the most heinous of all punishments: the torturous death of an only son. In return, *we* take the guilt, much like a child whose parents refuse to allow her to pay for damage done to the family car and then insist that they not take a long-planned and much dreamt of vacation in order to pay for the repairs.

This homey example hardly does justice to the cosmic proportions of true Christian guilt, though. As it turns out, we are responsible not only for our own irremovable *evil* (which, as Nietzsche points out, has a self-inflicted moral horror about it that the simple *stupidity* of the Greeks did not), but also for the death of God's only son and, eventually, every evil that can possibly befall other humans. *All* evil ultimately can find its origin not in God, but only in us. In particular, it finds its root in our freedom of will. Thus, that in Christianity which appears to have absolutely no remotely *logical* explanation (a virgin birth, a deity that can be in Jerusalem and not in Bethlehem but everywhere in the universe all at the same time, a good and omnipotent and omniscient God who allows evil to exist) has a perfect *psychological* explanation.

The basic engine of all life for Nietzsche is what he calls "the will to power," which is an animalistic "instinct for freedom" that, in turn, is a desire to dominate, manipulate, and opportunistically overcome obstacles. Slaves live under conditions that prohibit any real exercise of this will in the real world. They resent those who do have the opportunity to exercise such control, and they call them "evil" for actually dominating and manipulating the world and its slaves. Any impulse the slaves then find in their own souls to dominate and manipulate (e.g., impulses toward aggression, sex, or anything artistic), they also must deem evil. Since the will to power necessarily exists in every living thing, according to Nietzsche, the slaves are faced with the necessity of evil in their own souls and so they must resent, hate, and dominate themselves. They do this through the mechanism of guilt, which is elevated to the level of sheer madness by the Christian fiction of a God who is as neurotically self-punishing as they are. He must punish himself because no amount of punishing mere mortals can atone for the punishment God has inflicted upon himself for our sake:

> suddenly we stand before the paradoxical and horrifying expedient that afforded temporary relief for tormented humanity, that stroke of genius on the part of Christianity: God himself sacrifices himself for the guilt of mankind. . . . You will have guessed *what* has really happened here, *beneath* all this: that will to self-tormenting, that repressed cruelty of the animal-man made inward and scared back into himself . . . this man of the bad conscience has seized upon the presupposition of religion so as to drive his self-torture to its most gruesome pitch of severity and rigor. . . . All of this is interesting, to excess, but also of a gloomy, black, unnerving sadness, so that one must forcibly forbid oneself to gaze too long into these abysses. . . . Too long, the earth has been a madhouse!⁹

Perhaps it is fair to suggest that the second essay of the *Genealogy of Morals* makes for better literature than it does serious psychology, but, of course, Nietzsche's principal thesis is that our most deeply held perspectives concerning ourselves and the significance of our actions are thoroughly informed by the fictions, the myths, of our times. The Greeks had their myths, which gave a certain sort of significance to their lives and actions, and the Christians had theirs. And, as Nietzsche makes clear in the third essay of the *Genealogy of Morals*, one must not underestimate the degree of richness the Christian myth added to the life of the medieval priests and peasants who lived under its influence. As psychologically debilitating as it was, Christianity made deep sense of feudal life. The questions, Why am I here? What will happen to me? What is the meaning of life? Why are my actions significant, and why should I do right? Why do we all suffer so much? all had straightforward answers: God put me here. I will die and go to heaven to be with God. My life is given meaning by serving God. My actions are being watched by God, and he will send me to hell for doing wrong. We suffer because we are evil, but our suffering is only a small part of what it ought to be.

In modern times, these questions baffle even the most thorough philosophers, and some of the best answers from the best thinkers have run something like this: There is no reason why you are here; you are just a member of a species of temporarily adaptive mutants. You will die and become food for worms. The question about the meaning of life is meaningless. Your actions are not really important, but if you ask "Why *should* I do what I *ought* to do?" then you are just confused about the nature of moral discourse. We suffer because we are alternately stupid and unlucky, and there is generally no redeeming value that arises out of suffering; there is no purpose or reason for it.

This bafflement is, according to Nietzsche, a consequence of what he describes, with his usual sense of melodrama, as "the death of God." What, I take it, he meant when he proclaimed the death of God was not some necro-metaphysical claim but, rather, a statement of the social fact that the Christian myth has become obsolete. As the institutions of Christianity have had to adapt to Roman culture, then northern European culture, then modern science, then capitalist and industrial revolutions, and then sexual and feminist revolutions, the weight of the guilt enforced on Christians became unbearable and had to be abandoned. That Christians now hold positions of political power, believe in the big bang theory, lend and borrow money, hustle for economic influence, work on Sunday, kill in self-defense and in defense of economic interests, have sex without reproductive intent, and believe that women are not chattel means that they have abandoned almost all of the central psychological tenets of Christian slave morality. Power, passion, creativity, and aggressiveness are, if not virtues, at least no longer evils for most twentieth-century "Christians." When compared with Americans of even the nineteenth century, Americans today feel little guilt about anything and are told by their gurus and psychoanalysts that they ought to feel even less.

Nietzsche would probably think that this constitutes no small step toward the prospect of psychological health for us all. However, the demise of the Christian myth has come at the cost of bafflement and a profound meaninglessness that has been commented upon ad nauseam by a long parade of existentialists, social scientists, and nostalgic fundamentalists in this century. Nietzsche was a little more perceptive than many of his intellectual heirs have been, however. Most modernist thought seems to have been erected on the assumption that the cause of our twentieth-century angst is that we no longer have any myths to inform our experience. The old fables have all fallen to scientific realism, and one now appeals to the nonfactual only at the peril of being considered uneducated and, probably, uneducable.

Nietzsche's worthwhile insight in the third essay of the *Genealogy* is that the modern scientific world view *is* a myth. Although it may show signs of improvement over the "madness" of Christianity, the basic "sickness" that formed the psychological basis of Christianity is also at work in the new myth. This "sickness" Nietzsche calls "asceticism." Asceticism, "the worship of chastity," is, at a deeper level, the basic self-denial that is at work in the Christian fiction. In many ways, the self-denial, the denial of the role of the will to power in life, is even stronger in the modern scientific fiction than it was in Christianity. At least in the Christian universe we and our lives were center stage in the grand cosmic drama. Even though our role was that of the most unworthy sort of moral slime, the history of the entire universe and, in fact, the universe itself, revolved around the drama of our sliminess and its ultimate forgiveness at the horrible and bloody ending of time. What a show!

On the stage of the scientific drama, we are of as much importance as dust in the curtains. We are temporary holders of an ecological niche that opened up long after the play started and will vanish long before it is over. We are scrambling around on a tiny and insignificant speck of dusk that orbits a nowhere star in a remote corner of a bush league galaxy, which is in the middle of nothing important. Our loves are nothing but the product of errant hormonal secretions, our children no more than bearers of some of our mutant genes, our highest aspirations no more than chemical and electric reactions in the slow and soggy computers between our ears, our cultures no more than glorified ant farms, and our part in this theater of the absurd could end at any time with one good hit from a medium-sized chunk of flying ice that happens to pass our way for no good reason.

When asked why we have painted ourselves into such a lowly corner, the defender of science will engage in the same piece of bad faith reasoning that the Christians did. Just as the Christian would say, "It's not my fault that we are all so sinful that God's only son had to be tortured to death because of it; that's just the miserable *truth*," the adherent of the scientific myth will say, "It's not my fault that we are of no real significance; that's just the miserable *truth*." In either case, according to Nietzsche, the truth is only as good as the initial assumptions that go into its derivation. Whether the system of derivations gives us the Christian world view or the scientific one, it will be based on various axioms, observational protocol, and psychologically and socially conditioned motivations. The results will then be, in large part, dependent upon what is initially *willed* by us before any "facts" are derived. Modern science, no doubt, is largely conditioned by a desire to manipulate the physical world for various economic, military, and political reasons, and it is, to that degree, "healthy" on Nietzschean grounds. But underneath it all, the same "sickness," the same "self-belittlement of man," and the same "will to nothingness" festers. So after the money has been made, the artillery tested, and the world made safe for the ideology of the day, we are left to wallow in the consequences of the scientific myth that have nothing to do with practical affairs. Ironically, after growing out of a healthy exercise of the will to power, science turns on us to derive, in science after science, the conclusion that we are powerless in the face of natural forces and, ultimately, as is the case with much of twentieth-century psychology, that we have no will. Thus, science "makes common cause" with "herd instincts."[10]

In these matters (namely, those concerning the ultimate significance and willfulness of human life), science really should have nothing to say. Instead it falls into a verbal confusion that Carnap accused Heidegger of and proclaims "nothingness" as a "fact of life." Many in this century have attempted to back away from the conclusion that "nothing" is sacred by restricting the implications of science to technology and then resurrecting the old myths. Science may smash as many molecules and build as many bridges as it can, they think, but when it comes to questions of spirituality, morality, and the meaning of life, only God and Jesus can give answers.

The only problem is that just about everything God and Jesus said that is at all clear is not just underivable from the modern gospel of "nothingness," it is incompatible with the cosmogony, the cosmology, the methodology, and, more importantly, the psychological and social motivations of modern science. As modern philosophers from Hume and Kant onward have insisted, one cannot look to science to confirm propositions about the supernatural, but, what is far worse, in giving scientific explanations one must *assume* that the miraculous just doesn't happen. Any scientist who claims that some theory works only on the assumption of occasional divine intervention will be laughed out of the laboratory. As far as motivation goes, one cannot believe that the love of money is the root of all evil and that, when struck, one should turn the other cheek and then say that science is good because it allows us to become wealthy and blow up anyone who tries to take away our stuff. No matter how much modern Christians try to reinterpret the Bible, the success of any such reinterpretation will be judged in terms of how well it renders scripture compatible with science and the motivations behind science and technology. Ultimately, the core of any gospel will have to be interpreted literally to death.

Many other myths have been suggested over the last couple of centuries. In Nietzsche's day, the Romantic movement manufactured all sorts of fables about "noble savages," "free spirits," and various idols of nationalism and racism that would play a hideous role in some of the darkest moments of the twentieth century. For all of it, Nietzsche reserved some of his harshest language, deriding Romanticism's "nostalgia for the old days"[11] and its "lack of philosophy and science."[12]

All of this brings us to Nietzsche's doctrine of the eternal return, "the most *scientific* of all possible hypotheses."[13] I will take it here that this doctrine cannot be understood literally as a hypothesis about cosmology, in spite of some of Nietzsche's feeble arguments that it should be taken as a serious empirical hypothesis.[14] I am inclined to agree with Nehamas's interpretation, which has it that the eternal return is "scientific" only to the extent that believing in it does not require the denial of any really empirical claims of modern science.[15] At one level, it is at least compatible with the antiteleological presuppositions of Galileo and his heirs; it postulates no purpose or final cause for either the existence of the universe or of us, only that this pointless story will infinitely repeat. Nietzsche probably also thought that it was compatible with an almost fatalistic determinism that runs through some nineteenth-century scientific thought.

But at a more serious level, the doctrine is compatible with the most anti-Christian corollaries of modern science. We can no longer believe that the universe was created just for humans to play out some drama under the eyes of a watchful God. More frightful still,

> In our hearts we all know quite well that, being unique, we will be in the world only once and that no imaginable chance will for a second time gather together into a unity so strangely variegated an assortment as we are.[16]

This passage not only indicates that Nietzsche did not believe that we have any good reason for thinking that we will actually experience any eternal return to this world but also that we can no longer really believe that we will actually be "gathered together" for some afterlife in any other world. And even if some immaterial part of us could go to heaven, what kind of rewards could be offered that would be at all interesting for us moderns? Maybe St. Thomas can be happy as a pure soul, but how could anyone who cherishes the material values that motivate science and technology be happy without eyes to see rich colors, ears to hear beautiful music, or various other organs whose stimulation we so value? Not only can we not believe in a Christian afterlife we, like Huck Finn, reckon we might have more fun in hell.

The function of the doctrine of the eternal return is like that of any myth. Myths need not be demonstrably true. Indeed it is part of the meaning of myth that it is known to be false and is believed not for its truth but for the exhilaration of believing it. But it must exhilarate without requiring a serious sacrifice of the goods we hold dear. This is why the Christian myth can no longer work for us. It might bring exhilaration to believe that one is being watched over by the God of Abraham or Paul, but not enough to outweigh the boredom of the lifestyle which that God demands. The eternal return, however, does not require any such abstinence. In fact, the remarkable effect of believing it is that it would seem to encourage not being bored or boring. Boredom in this life will not be rewarded in another; it will just be repeated again and again and again. Experiences that present no challenge or novelty will recur again and again and again. Decisions not to change one's life will be made eternally.

The curious thing about this myth is that believing it shouldn't have any effect on our lives given the motivating values of our culture. If we really believe that, as an old beer commercial claimed, we will only go around once and should grab for all the gusto we can, then it shouldn't make any difference whether or not we believe in the eternal return. What subjective difference can there be between going around once and going around an infinite number of times, each time being totally unaware that we are eternally returning? It shouldn't make a difference, but for many it does. If the medieval monk was really only interested in the cultivation of piety and spiritual closeness to God, then it shouldn't have mattered that God was watching his every move, but it did. If the ancient Greek was really interested in the cultivation of virtue, then it shouldn't have mattered that the gods were active in the life of Greece, but it did. In all of these cases, the function of myth is to heighten one's appreciation of the values of one's culture and to purge any irrational inhibitions that stifle the pursuit of them.

Thus, Nietzsche's

> formula for greatness for a human being is *amor fati*: that one wants nothing to be different, not forward, not backward, not in all eternity. Not merely bear what is necessary, still less conceal it—all idealism is mendaciousness in the face of what is necessary—but *love* it.[17]

In our times, wishing for things to be different, wishing that a god was watching, wishing for a better life after death, wishing we weren't so evil, wishing life was easier is to wish away what we deeply believe to be the hard "truth." The function of the myth of the eternal return is to sensitize us to the possible presence of some psychological remnants of the eleventh century and make us face up to the realities of the modern world and love it. It requires us to be happy with the way we are or fix ourselves so that we could honestly desire only to do it all again.

In this way, then, the myth of the eternal return serves as a mechanism of sublimation in the era of science. Our actions become much more significant than they "really" are, although there is no real *reason* why the myth ought to have that effect, any more than there is any real *reason* why one ought to be awed by a first view of Yosemite Valley; one either feels sublime or one doesn't, and that's all there is to it. There's no point in trying to convince someone that they ought to be awed if they aren't. But there is another, and deeper, level at which the myth operates, namely, that of the kind of concern raised at the beginning of this chapter about the nature of the self.

The demise of the Christian myth creates a gap not only with respect to the significance of our actions but also with respect to the thing that is supposed to tie our actions and, indeed, our simple sensations together. The Christian doctrine of the soul provided not only a simple and compelling explanation of this unity of consciousness but also an entity that could undergo a rich, fateful, and eternal drama. The fiction of the soul was so simple and compelling that, of all the remnants of Christianity, it has survived the best. Despite the onslaught of Hobbesian materialism, Hume's theory that the self was a mere "heap" of sensations, Freud's fragmentation of the self, the influx of Eastern fragmentation theories, modernism, and strong artificial intelligence theses, the soul has held on. It lived on as the Cartesian "thinking thing," the Kantian "transcendental unity of apperception," individual human nature, and the subconscious. Even Hume had second thoughts about being able to fully dispense with some nonsensible thing that ties our sensations together.

Indeed, it is hard for us to even imagine, let alone articulate, a coherent picture of the mental that does not involve a unified mind behind it all. "But there is no such substratum; there is no 'being' beyond doing, effecting, becoming; 'the doer' is merely a *fiction* added to the deed—the deed is everything."[18] Indeed, common sense and even science for "all its coolness, its freedom from emotion . . . still lies under *the misleading influence of language* and has not disposed of that little changeling, the 'subject.'"[19] The connection between the self, language, and logic is taken up at length in *The Will to Power*, where Nietzsche claims that "beings," generally, are apparently necessarily "part of our perspective . . . The *fictitious* world of subject, substance, 'reason,' etc., is needed . . . to order, simplify, falsify, *artificially* distinguish."[20] If, "belief in the 'ego' stands or falls with belief in logic" and if "the ego proves to be something in a state of becoming: then—"[21]

But, neither common sense nor science give us any reason to believe that we are anything but some sort of heap. At most, what seems to be required is nothing any stronger than what Derek Parfit has called "reductionism,"[22] which is, in part, the view that "we are not separately existing entities . . . our existence just involves the existence of our brains and bodies, and the doing of our deeds. . . ."[23] What holds our mental states together is nothing any stronger than "psychological continuity." Given this view, although logic and language will get in *my* way every time *I* deny personal substantiality, Nietzsche tells us that the only real individuals are those who are "new, unique, incomparable, who give themselves laws, who create themselves."[24]

But what rational point can there be in taking any interest in one's own creation if one can have no guarantee of one's persistence into the future? Why should I care about who I am if, in five years, the person stages I will be connected to by nothing but psychological continuity can't be reasonably said to be *mine* anymore? It is this line of questioning (which Parfit reels out with all of his "repugnant" answers) that Nietzsche's doctrine of the eternal return might be seen as answering.

Even though we have no reason to believe that *we* will "really" be around very long into the future, we would be linked, by strict identity, to an infinite number of previous and future recurrences of ourselves as we are now. Of course, this isn't much of a *rational* answer to Parfit's questions inasmuch as we have no independent and empirical reason to believe in the eternal return. Moreover, it doesn't directly address Hume's problems with personal identity *at any given time* (as opposed to the problem of identity *over time*).[25] But then, it's just a myth. And, as a myth, the important criterion of its worth is not posed by the question, "What empirical reason is there to believe that it is true?" but, rather, "Why should I act *as though* it is true? What *value* is there in believing it?"

The answer to this question is, in Nietzsche, pretty clear: you should believe it because the alternative (as Parfit argues) is to believe that you are "really" nothing, to take one's stand with Schopenhauer who "*said No to* life and to himself."[26]

> It was precisely here that I saw the *great* danger to mankind, its *sublimest* enticement and seduction—but to what? to nothingness?—it was precisely here that I saw the beginning of the end, the dead stop, a retrospective weariness, the will turning *against* life, the tender and sor-

rowful signs of the ultimate illness: I understood the ever spreading morality of pity that had seized even upon philosophers and made them ill, as the most sinister symptom of a European culture that had itself become sinister, perhaps as its by-pass to a new Buddhism? to a Buddhism for Europeans? to—nihilism?[27]

It is not at all surprising that the last section of Parfit's *Reasons and Persons* should be entitled "Buddha's View." A "Buddhism for Europeans" has, indeed, arrived, and the "ascetic ideal," the morosely ironic "will to nothingness," is as alive and well as it was in the twelfth century. Parfit argues that, "in various ways, our reasons for acting should become *more impersonal* . . . it would often be better for everyone."[28] The radical altruism Parfit argues for is precisely what Nietzsche derides as the core of "slave morality," which grows out of "herd instincts."

It is interesting to note that Parfit's project is seen by him as a continuation of Sidgwick's. In Parfit's words, the argument of the *Methods of Ethics* ultimately compelled Sidgwick to the conclusion that

> when morality conflicts with self-interest, there is no answer to the question of what we have most reason to do. When he compared moral and self-interested reasons, neither seemed to Sidgwick to outweigh the other.
>
> Sidgwick held this view because he believed the separateness of persons to be a deep truth. He believed that an appeal to this truth gives a Self-interest Theorist a sufficient defence against the claims of morality. And he suggested that, if we took a different view about personal identity, we could refute the Self-interest Theory. I have claimed that this is true.[29]

Parfit winds up refuting the self-interest theory by annihilating the self. I, to the contrary, am not interested in reconciling self-interest with social morality.

I have been arguing from the outset of this book that, in essence, Sidgwick was right about this irreconcilability. But I have, in this chapter, been suggesting that he was wrong about the "deep truth" alleged to underlie personal identity. In other words, I have been suggesting that Parfit is right about this issue. And it is, precisely, for this reason that I have done my best to elaborate on Nietzsche's view. On that view, "in truth," there is no real identity of the person over time, but that is all the more reason to struggle for some admitted myth that, if believed, could make sense of the desire to define and create oneself. Given what we know of psychology, biology, and neurophysiology, one cannot continue to cling to the hope that there is "really" some ghost in the machine. Nor can we hang much weight on Mill's clearly metaphorical notions about growth. The idea that the self is like some noble oak that will flourish if only it is allowed to explore its natural limits is charming, but sheerly poetic. The self will not just "naturally" emerge and blossom if passively allowed to; it must be constructed and reconstructed at every moment, not because that will ultimately make us "happy," but because, if we don't, *we* won't even exist.

Ultimately, the self is doomed to be parted out into functional states, neurophysiological correlates, and binary operations. Even if these reductionist projects will never be completely satisfactory, the scientific world view will certainly proceed on the assumption that they can be, just as physics will proceed on the assumption of the possibility of a complete theory of physical reality in spite of the fact that our species and all of its science may well perish before that happens. Such is the nature of the will to power, Nietzsche would say. In our desire to break things apart, manipulate them, and make them do what we *will* them to do is the seed of that medieval masochism that is driven to the denial of the very will that makes science possible and, moreover, *valuable*. One can talk only so long about the "utility" of scientific theories before one must admit that questions of value ultimately underlie all questions of truth. Simple "truths" are cheap; *important* truths are what science and philosophy are about, and importance can be gauged only in terms of *our* interests.

If we are to face the dissection that the cognitive sciences are about to perform on us with humble resignation, then, perhaps, Parfit is right. We ought to start viewing the welfare of our future time-slices ("our" being used loosely here) as no more important than the present and future time-slices that are psychologically continuous with other "people." We ought to "commit ourselves" (whatever that could now mean) to something like the virtue theory I outlined two chapters back, not just because it will distract us long enough to have happiness unintentionally descend upon us but, rather, because that is the only "rational" thing to do. It's not that, from the cosmic point of view, the individual could really have any morally significant effect; it's just that, from all points of view (all perspectives), the individual will have been obliterated.

If we are to live with the myth of science—and, as we seen over the last few centuries, the modern world will force us to do that, at the point of a gun if necessary—and still survive free of the "illness" of "Buddhism for Europeans," still ask with Nietzsche, "What is the *value* of morality?"[30] then there must be some fiction that can be willed which does not presuppose what science will destroy. Afterlives and romantic growths will not work, and, perhaps, neither will something as simple as the eternal return. It is more believable than other myths, however, because, as I argued above, it's acceptance *shouldn't* make any difference. No law of physics need be rewritten on its account. Although (contrary to the embarrassing arguments in *The Will to Power*), science neither implies nor is implied by the myth, it *could* be true. More importantly, it is *worth* believing. For the individual who cannot take altruistic diversions seriously and cannot believe that the self will just spontaneously generate, it beats Buddhism.

CHAPTER 12

Friendship, Love, Marriage, and Gender

Over the past three chapters I have outlined four theories (straightforward egoism, altruism, individualism, and Nietzsche's sublimation theory) about personal well-being that I have been calling theories of wisdom. What I want to do here is draw some central parallels between these theories of well-being and things that most people believe to be, if not an absolutely essential element of well-being, at the very least, a principal cause of its intensification.

At the simplest level, friendship, love, and even marriage may be based on simple mutual self-interest. Probably most relationships that people refer to as "friendships" and "loves" are of this sort. Really all that is going on in such cases is mutual *use*. There need be nothing exploitative about such relationships inasmuch as both friends or lovers may be well aware of the fact that they are being used by the other but consent to being used under the reckoning that they are gaining an advantage worth whatever sacrifices are being called for. The services rendered in such relationships are as varied as the provision of company, entertainment, money, security, sex, or whatever people generally are inclined to want from one another.

When such relationships are coupled with a mutual understanding of exclusivity (as they usually are in the cases of romantic love and marriage), they are, of course, only as strong as the benefit of the relationship to either party when measured against the opportunity costs of staying in the relationship. When either friend, lover, or spouse sees greener pastures elsewhere, the entire basis of the relationship is in doubt. Moreover, the relationship may be even weaker than is indicated by the real bargaining equilibrium to the extent that one or both of the people in it are veterans of a few broken relationships. A partner who is at all "worldly" may then be on a hair trigger and develop the strategy of bailing not just at the point where the relationship has actually stopped yielding optimal returns but at some prior point where it is perceived that a nonoptimal point is immanent and, thus, there is no point in waiting for the inevitable collapse of the relationship, which is right around the corner.

Illustrations of this dynamic are, I assume, familiar to all of us—familiar to the point of sexual (and sexist) stereotype. Most of us have known men who routinely exit romantic relationships as soon as things cross the sexual threshold. At this stage they figure that the point of diminishing erotic returns is just a few weeks away. Accordingly, they infer that there is no point in actually going through those weeks plagued by the dreadful knowledge that everything will end soon. Likewise, most of us have known women who have developed the strategy of exiting relationships before they become sexual for the pretty good reason that they can expect most men to exit upon the commencement of sex. Recursion has done its worst to many people, and a great many of them have dutifully drawn all of the miserable conclusions and, as a consequence, just don't expect to be involved in any serious relationships with members of the opposite sex anymore.

Women often protest that it is simply "impossible" for them to have any male friends. Inevitably, they report, any friendship with a man will go along fine for a while, but then the fated sexual proposition will be made, at which point the only rational thing to do is terminate the friendship. What is actually going on is that by "friendship," what was meant was "a good mutual user relationship." He would have the company of a woman at the movies or at a bar, and she would have the company of a man that would spare her from the incessant advances of lecherous drunks or, better yet, from having to hang around drunks at all. But at a point he figures: "as long as we're just using each other . . ." and makes his sexual proposal. She figures, rightly enough, that she would be screwed in more ways than one if she accepted. She has just been offered a very bad deal compared to what she has become accustomed to from him. Given that the reproductive consequences of sex are to be borne by her and that a sexist double standard about promiscuity and venereal disease is still alive and well, she figures that he is so insensitive to the plight of women generally, and to hers in particular, that any future dealings with him would be suspect. And so, with the extreme suspicion that he will be Machiavellian in his future pursuit of sex, she terminates the "friendship" and goes on to greener pastures where yet another man will wonder how much he has to spend on her before he is warranted in propositioning her. And so it goes.

Fortunately, most couples get beyond the realm of hard bargains, for a while anyhow. Unfortunately, many relationships, even those that eventuate in marriage, often become hopelessly mired in the assumption that if the relationship is not mutually advantageous then it is not worth preserving. Of course, there is a certain level of misery that no one should be expected to endure just for the sake of preserving a relationship (even a marriage where children are involved). But this position might be based on a different principle than the one that any marriage ought to end when its returns, for either partner, are likely to become suboptimal. Often, the business of marriage is analyzed in the popular media with all the warmth, tenderness, compassion, and humanity of a trade war. And, like most American business partnerships, most American marriages now end in dissolution.

Of course, mutual user relationships can just as often provide intense bonds that last for many years. Most of us have lifelong friends who demand little from us and from whom we demand little other than occasional "moral support," professional guidance, or the simple sharing of old memories. The exchanging of such pleasantries is easily maintained around a suitable equilibrium. Still, if all one knows in life are such relationships, then one is not likely to experience much of the joy and satisfaction that love and friendship have, over the ages, been claimed to provide. It is, indeed, hard to view one's friends and lovers as being, at all times, greener than the greenest available pasture and even harder to be, at all times, greener than all competing pastures.

Fortunately, most of us have known more. Specifically, most of us have experienced a friendship or love affair serious enough for us to have weighted the happiness of the friend or lover above our own. The bliss that accompanies this sort of devotion is not surprising given the line of argument I ran in Chapter 9. Given that happiness is not likely to come to those obsessed with its pursuit and that "the great majority" are better served by the pursuit of the happiness of others, it is easy to see that many of the most intensely blissful moments of our lives would come as a result of the kind of intense pursuit of the happiness of another that we engage in when in love.[1]

Generally, what happens is that we do much more than show an elevated level of concern for the happiness of the lover. At first, at any rate, we tend to do little second-guessing about what would "really" lead to our lovers' happiness, and we take their simple preferences as our guide; their wishes become our commands. Things often start to fall apart when we start second-guessing. When we start to engage in the paternalistic correction of our lovers' desires and start to weight highly only those preferences that we think are "really" productive of their happiness, we are often met with resentment. The resentment is, of course, fully understandable since our lovers now perceive that we are no longer really interested in *their* happiness but, rather, in what *we* think *should* make them happy. That is, we are no longer interested in what our lovers want but, ultimately, what we want, namely, that they be the way we want them to be. Even if we may not want them to be that way for straightforwardly selfish reasons, there is still a second-order selfishness about our paternalism: *we* have placed a certain value on *their* being a certain way and, so, in being that way they are serving *our* interests since we *prefer* that they be the way they *ought* to be (which we now perceive to be different than the way they *are* and the way *they* think they *ought* to be). This is a rather common reason for the collapse of love and friendship in relationships where paternalism is a built-in threat, namely, relationships between parents and children.

Although paternalism may often be behind the collapse of adult friendships and romances, the reasons for failure at this level are usually more straightforward. For whatever reasons, we just quit assigning more weight to our lovers' preferences than we do to our own. We even quit assigning more weight to what we think ought to make them happy than we do to what really does make them happy. We just quit caring about them as ends in themselves altogether and lapse into straightforward self-interest. If lovers can even remain friends after this has happened, it is only because there is some basis for a commodious mutual user relation.

The account I have given so far is somewhat parallel to that given by Aristotle in the eighth and ninth books of the *Nicomachean Ethics*. There are two important differences. First, Aristotle didn't think that mutual user relationships should even be counted as true friendships, let alone anything that could answer to the name "love." Second, unless we mistranslate "*eudaimonia*" as "preference satisfaction," he did not believe that holding an intense interest in another's desire satisfaction counted as love or friendship either. He believed that true friendship was a matter of taking an intense and sincere interest in the development of the friend's virtue, by which he meant, the friend's "excellence."

I will not endeavor here to give any satisfactory account of what, exactly, this sense of virtue amounts to. Rather, for better or worse, I will spend most of the rest of this chapter in an attempt at an account of friendship and love that is, I think, in many important ways close to what Aristotle had to say. Specifically, I will do so in terms of the individualistic theory of Mill. Much of this discussion may well apply to the theory of Nietzsche inasmuch as many of the differences between Mill and Nietzsche are, as I pointed out at the beginning of the last chapter, more rhetorical than real. But, for reasons I will make clear as we go along, I will not be going out of my way to develop any Nietzschean theory of love and friendship. However, I will eventually get around to some Nietzschean considerations that, when taken in contradistinction to the ideas of Mill, have much to do with contemporary debates about gender and gender difference.

In spite of Mill's romantic metaphors about individual nature, most of what makes the individual truly an individual is, as I claimed two chapters ago, a matter of choice and willful *creation* for Mill. What Mill may have been (rightfully) sensitive to in a way that Nietzsche and most of his existentialist heirs are not is the fairly apparent truth that choice will be, to some considerable degree, made possible or restrained by heredity and behavioral history; no congenital idiot will win the Nobel prize for physics and no uncoordinated five-foot, two-inch physics professor will play in the NBA. Nevertheless, Mill's view seems to be that these possibilities and limitations will tend to be, respectively, underestimated and overestimated and, largely, a product of a powerful and destructive social prejudice against anything unconventional. On the other hand, what Nietzsche may have been sensitive to in a way that Mill and, perhaps, the British generally are not is the manner in which the rational rests upon the irrational—the manner in which reflective wisdom rests upon myths that will not bear much reflection. But still, there is little in Mill to suggest that some preestablished set of specific personality traits will *inevitably* emerge as one goes through life. As much as Nietzsche, Mill seems committed to the view that what we wind up as is, almost entirely, a matter of what we make ourselves—not just once but again and again and again as we go through an unscripted life.

That I will cast my discussion on the assumption of a fair amount of indeterminism about the self is the major reason for my not wanting to attribute much of what I have to say to the Greek tradition. In both Plato and Aristotle there is much more than a hint that they both feel that nobility of character is something innate. Aristotle was so bold as to assert that half of the human race (i.e., women) could never really achieve it.[2] Plato allowed for the possibility of a fully excellent woman but only at the expense of a prior assumption that aristocratic excellence is something hereditarily restricted to a very small portion of the general population.

With respect to Nietzsche, I think that someone who is sympathetic to his theory of the self may also find reason to be sympathetic to the theory of love, friendship, and marriage that comes out of Mill. But, I am reticent to even insinuate that much of Mill's theory can be sensibly ascribed to Nietzsche. In the first place, Nietzsche thought Mill was a "flathead." In the second place, as we shall see, so much of what Nietzsche has to say about love, friendship, and marriage is so different from Mill that there is just no sense in belaboring strained points of agreement between the two.

As for Mill, his *Autobiography* speaks eloquently and decisively to the role played by Harriet Taylor in Mill's life. And in order to understand why, exactly, she had the effect on Mill that she did, we must turn to a work that, certainly, she must have influenced: *The Subjection of Women*. In the last chapter of that work, Mill lays out a truly ingenious and, he was sure, politically effective line of argument. Figuring that men will, by and large, be insensitive to the sorts of suffering that oppression causes to women, he cuts to the chase involving the most likely vehicle of moral and rhetorical success: the self-interests of men.

The reason why men ought to allow for the full development of female potential is not just because it would be unfair not to or because such would allow women to bring more money into individual male-dominated households but, rather, because if such is not allowed, then almost all men will wind up married to morons who will, in turn, make their husbands imbeciles. According to Mill, the lowly intellectual status that women in the bourgeoisie of nineteenth-century Britain were allowed to attain, combined with the increasing domestication of men had

> thrown the man very much more upon the home and its inmates, for his personal and social pleasures. . . . His desire of mental communion is thus in general satisfied by a communion from which he learns nothing. An unimproving and unstimulating companionship is substituted for (what he might otherwise have been obliged to seek) the society of his equals in powers and his fellows in the higher pursuits. We see, accordingly, that young men of the greatest promise generally cease to improve as soon as they marry, and, not improving, inevitably degenerate.[3]

Worse than learning nothing and becoming more stupid as their middle-class days go by, men can also expect that their wives, having been allowed to have no identities of their own, will insist that their husbands conform to the most scrupulous pursuit of conformist respectability. Any meandering of moral conscience that detracts from the husband's accomplishment of bourgeois acclaim will lead to the nondescript wife's fancy that "nothing prevents her and her husband from moving in the highest society . . . except that her husband is unfortunately a Dissenter, or has the reputation of mingling in low radical politics."[4] Thus,

> A man who is married to a woman his inferior in intelligence, finds her a perpetual dead weight, a drag, upon every aspiration of his to be better than public opinion requires him to be. It is hardly possible for one who is in these bonds, to attain exalted virtue. If he differs in his opinion from the mass—if he sees truths which have not yet dawned upon them, or if, feeling in his heart truths which they nominally recognize, he would like to act upon those truths more conscientiously than the generality of mankind—to all such thoughts and desires, marriage is the heaviest of drawbacks, unless he be so fortunate as to have a wife as much above the common level as he himself is.[5]

If he is not to have such a wife then, perhaps the best he can hope for is to have not a woman with whom he shares "that *idem velle, idem nolle*" ("wanting the same and not wanting the same") essential to any good relationship between equals but rather "a woman who is so complete a nullity that she has no *velle* or *nolle* at all."[6] Although, "dulness and want of spirit are not always a guarantee of the submission which is so confidently expected from them."[7]

What, then, constitutes the ideal marriage and also the ideal of love and friendship? The following passages supply the core of Mill's theory:

> when each of the two persons, instead of being a nothing, is a something; when they are attached to one another, and are not too much unlike to begin with; the constant partaking in the same things, assisted by their sympathy, draws out the latent capacities of each for being interested in the things which were at first interesting only to the other; and works a gradual assimilation of the tastes and characters to one another, partly by the insensible modification of each, but more by a real enriching of the two natures, each acquiring the tastes and capacities of the other in addition to its own. This often happens between two friends of the same sex, who are much associated in their daily life: and it would be a common, if not the commonest, case in marriage, did not the totally different bringing-up of the two sexes make it next to an impossibility to form a really well-assorted union. Were this remedied, whatever differences there might still be in individual tastes, there would at least be, as a general rule, complete unity and unanimity as to the great objects of life. When the two persons both care for great objects, and are a help and encouragement to each other in whatever regards these, the minor matters on which their tastes may differ are not all-important to them; and there is a foundation for solid friendship, of an enduring character, more likely than anything else to make it, through the whole of life, a greater pleasure to each to give pleasure to the other, than to receive it. . . .[8]
>
> What marriage may be in the case of two persons of cultivated faculties, identical in opinions and purposes, between whom there exists that best kind of equality, similarity of powers and capacities with reciprocal superiority in them—so that each can enjoy the luxury of looking up to the other, and can have alternately the pleasure of leading and of being led in the path of development—I will not attempt to describe. To those who can conceive it, there is no need; to those who cannot, it would appear the dream of an enthusiast. But I maintain, with the profoundest conviction, that this, and this only, is the ideal of marriage; and that all opinion, customs, and institutions which favour any other notion of it, or turn the conceptions and aspirations connected with it into any other direction, by whatever pretenses they may be coloured, are relics of primitive barbarism.[9]

A number of threads connect these passages with previous points made about the four theories of wisdom I have discussed. First of all, Mill is claiming that an essential sign of love is the weighting of the lover's well-being above one's own. And so his theory is, in an important way, incorporating the idea that love is an intense variation of the idea that it is wise to pursue one's own well-being indirectly through the well-being of others. Secondly, given the kinds of examples Mill provides of the sorts of actions that the standard marriage will stifle (consorting with

"Dissenters" and "mingling in low radical politics"), one of the important consequences of a good and supportive marriage between equals would appear to be that it, in turn, supports the pursuit of the well-being of others generally. So, if one is operating under that theory which Mill thinks best for "the great majority" (i.e., the virtue theory described in Chapter 9), then a good marriage or friendship will keep one on the right track to one's own well-being by bringing the friends or lovers to new heights of sensitivity and benevolence.

Mill talks about this as a likely consequence specifically of male-female relationships. Benevolence requires not just a stern sense of impartiality and justice but also the capacity of partiality, empathy, and immediate generosity. In these latter traits of character, the standard of women is, generally, "higher than that of men; in the quality of justice, somewhat lower . . . though the statement must be taken with all the modifications dependent on individual character."[10] The effective pursuit of virtue requires both of these tendencies: the tendency to be hurt by the sight of a beggar and the tendency to figure that the simple dispensing of alms in a specific case may not, in the long run, really be in the best interests of the beggar or, even, most effectively prevent harm to him or her. Mill takes the fact that women, generally, have a greater capacity to feel the immediate hurt of such situations (along with the fact that they are shut out of other pursuits) to account for the fact that women are more inclined to be involved in charity work than men. Men, on those occasions when they are outraged at the state of the disprivileged, are more inclined to think that the appropriate resolution of the problem is to be found not in immediate aid but, rather, in the adjustment of social policy. Indeed, until very recently, any woman who would cross the line that separates charity work from political activity would find herself the target of male suspicion for arrogating to herself what men thought to be their social turf.

A lot of what Mill is saying here would be picked up by feminist writers in the 1970s and 1980s. Many feminists, Carol Gilligan and Annette Baier for example, based their views on the observation that the fundamental moral attitudes of men and women tend to be opposed; women tend to base their moral assessments on the kinds of sentiments that are fundamentally important in personal relationships (empathy, trust, affectionate support, etc.), while men (as demonstrated by the kinds of ethical theories they have historically developed) tend to base their moral judgments on the kinds of considerations required in the development of coercively enforced social policy (fairness, impartiality, duty, honor, obligation, obedience, etc.).[11] Hence, if a woman is told by her husband that he is staying in the marriage out of a sense of duty and obligation, she will be inclined to think that things have gone terribly wrong, whereas the man might think that nothing stronger than duty and obligation can act as a bond and, at any rate, there can be nothing *wrong* about fulfilling one's duties and obligations when there is a strong inclination to move to greener pastures.

I think that the point underlying Mill's claims and those of the feminists I have mentioned is an important consequence of the main thesis of this book. Although, as everyone with any sense realizes, things don't split entirely along gender lines, there are a number of important distinctions to be drawn relative to questions of *social justice* as opposed to ones about character and *personal relationships*. I have been discussing many of these distinctions in terms of the (usually underappreciated) dichotomy between theories of social *ethics* as opposed to theories of individual *wisdom*, and one may well speculate that the reason these distinctions have been almost totally blurred in the history of moral philosophy has something to do with the domination of the field by men who tend to view the antithesis of the personal and partial with the impersonal and impartial as a problem that must somehow be resolved in favor of the latter.[12]

At any rate, there is clearly more going on in the previous passages from *The Subjection of Women* than the claim that love will refine and bolster the pursuit of virtue (as understood under the altruistic theory of wisdom). When Mill talks about how love "draws out . . . latent capacities" on the basis of "reciprocal superiority . . . so that each can enjoy the luxury of looking up to the other, and can have alternately the pleasure of leading and of being led in the path of development," he seems to have more in mind than the path of development fit for "the great majority." It is hard not to think that the sort of relationship he had in mind was the one he himself had with Harriet Taylor. Although she may have had a considerable influence in the expansion of his benevolent sentiments (especially those involving the plight of women), that was not her primary effect on him. Benevolence of a fairly radical kind had been drilled into him since birth by his father, Bentham, and the Benthamites.

By Mill's own autobiographical testimony, Taylor became a major part of his life and of his very being after the virtue theory had failed him, after he had become depressed as a result of the realization that a world full of hysterically happy idiots would not have made him happy—even if they all received their happiness by delivering happiness to other idiots—after he had come to the conclusion that it was better to be an unhappy Socrates than a happy pig. What exactly is it, then, that a Taylor adds to a Mill?

The answer, I think, is twofold. In the first place, in the pursuit of self-definition, one will be in need of a partner who can accurately assess and question the present state of one's self-identification free of the blinders imposed in mutual user relationships or relationships based on the assumption that the desires of others have some built-in value to them. People interested in the merely congenial using of others are prone to employ artificial flattery or meanness in order to get what they want out of the used. Thus, the picture one gets of what one has made of oneself will tend to be alternately overly charitable and then overly uncharitable, depending on what one's mutual user figures to be the most efficient means of manipulation. If one is primarily interested in the happiness of others, then one will tend to evaluate all personal traits on the basis of the actual preferences of the other, even though one may have come to reject the idea that the preferences of the dull should form the basis of any life. True lovers, however, will take a more impartial interest in one another's personal discoveries and development. First, because they will want to emulate any good characteristics and adopt any important insights that have been discovered by the other and, second, because valuable discoveries are a cause to look up to the loved.

Mutual users can only experience the joy of using and being used in an optimal manner. Lovers locked into the virtue theory must confine themselves to the joys of a limited and, ultimately, unquestioning kind of loving without the expectation of being equally loved in return. True lovers, however, enjoy all of the fullness of being both lovers and loved. Their concerns are for the autonomous self-definition of the other without which their own self-definition would be retarded and uninteresting.

This brings up a related benefit that true lovers give to each other, namely, an example. We have all met people whose individuality, originality, and energy come across with such force that we are given to a long moment of reflective envy. We may at first be put off or threatened by such people, and we may ultimately dismiss them as pompous bores. But, every once in a while, we are driven to an examination of how sheepish and conventional we have become. Even if we don't endeavor to be just like them (which would be a sheepish and conventional thing to do), they do force us to think about who we are and about how much latitude we really do have in becoming something different. In those moments Mill speaks of where the loved becomes the respectful lover, this sort of thing happens. Moreover, and this is Mill's most important point, anyone who takes self-definition seriously is in need of a constant source of such ennobling humility and respect.

In short, what private life is all about for Mill is personal identification. This involves a life devoted to the examination of our actual motives and the autonomous choice of motives we think best. It involves the examination and choice of what things we will find pleasant, important, and worth pursuing; these choices will determine who we are. What love is all about is the mutual search for the things that make life meaningful, free, and worth living.

I mentioned before that points of agreement between Mill and Nietzsche on the topic of love are likely to be few and strained. The following passage from *Ecce Homo* ought to make this clear enough:

> May I here venture the surmise that I *know* women? That is part of my Dionysian dowry. Who knows? Perhaps I am the first psychologist of the eternally feminine. They all love me—an old story—not counting *abortive* females, the "emancipated" who lack the stuff for children.— Fortunately, I am not willing to be torn to pieces: the perfect woman tears to pieces what she loves.—I know these charming maenads.—Ah, what a dangerous, creeping, subterranean little beast of prey she is! And yet so agreeable!—A little woman who pursues her revenge would run over fate itself.—Woman is indescribably more evil than man; also cleverer: good nature is in a woman a form of degeneration.—In all so-called "beautiful souls" something is physiologically askew at bottom; I do not say everything, else I should become medi-cynical. The fight for equal rights is actually a symptom of a disease: every physician knows that.—Woman, the more she is a woman, resists rights in general hand and foot: after all, the state of nature, the eternal war between the sexes, gives her by far the first rank.
>
> Has my definition of love been heard? It is the only one worthy of a philosopher. Love—in its means, war; at bottom, the deadly hatred of the sexes.
>
> Has my answer been heard to the question of how one *cures* a woman—"redeems" her? One gives her a child. Woman needs children, a man is for her always only a means: thus spoke *Zarathustra*.
>
> "Emancipation of women"—that is the instinctive hatred of the abortive woman, who is incapable of giving birth, against the woman who is turned out well—the fight against the "man" is always a mere means, pretext, tactic. By raising themselves higher, as "woman in herself," as the "higher woman," as a female "idealist," they want to lower the level of the general rank of women; and there is no surer means for that than higher education, slacks, and political voting-cattle rights. At bottom, the emancipated are anarchists in the world of the "eternally feminine," the underprivileged whose most fundamental instinct is revenge.[13]

But Nietzsche's "definition" of love as war has more going for it than this facile, and hopelessly bourgeois, inference that, since all that any woman really wants is children, the really "clever" and "evil" (and, thus, "perfect") woman is the one who manipulates and "cuts to pieces" whatever men may serve as a suitable means to the end of childbearing. The idea that love is, at base, some kind of war is Nietzsche's peculiar, and *literary*, way of exalting love and, moreover, of making it something exalting. Love as war is something he opposes, predictably, to "a slavish love that submits and gives itself; that idealizes, and deceives itself—there is a divine love that despises and loves, and reshapes and elevates the beloved."[14] In fact, in the passage of *Ecce Homo* that appears just before the one already quoted at length, Nietzsche derides,

> that gruesome nonsense that love is supposed to be something "unegoistic."—One has to sit firmly upon *oneself*, one must stand bravely on one's own two legs, otherwise one is simply *incapable* of loving. Ultimately, women know that only too well: they don't give a damn about selfless, merely objective men.[15]

Elsewhere, Nietzsche writes, "Only the most complete persons can love; the depersonalized, the 'objective,' are the worst lovers (—one has only to ask the girls!) . . . one must be firmly rooted in oneself."[16]

One has to search hard for a ray of romance anywhere in Nietzsche, and it is probably a mistake to make too much out of these passages. That women don't give a damn about selfless men doesn't imply that they do give a damn about other men. The set of men worth giving a damn about may well be empty. After all, selfishness (of some sort) is only suggested here as a necessary condition of being worthy of female love, not a sufficient one.

Moreover, when taken as a whole, Nietzsche's analyses of love leave little room for any romanticism about a really "divine" love that really "elevates the beloved." A passage from the *Will to Power* entitled "On the Machiavellianism of Power" makes it clear that

> sexual love, too, belongs here: it desires to overpower, to take possession, and it *appears* as self-surrender. Fundamentally it is only love of one's "instrument," of one's "steed"—the conviction that this or that belongs to one because one is in a position to use it.[17]

One might protest that this passage is confined to *sexual* love and not anything answering to "true" or "divine" love. But, then, one must contend with all of the passages (like the long one from *Ecce Homo* quoted previously) where Nietzsche claims that almost everything that passes for love has a hidden sexual or reproductive motive. Elsewhere, Nietzsche talks about love as "a fever that has good reason to transfigure itself, an intoxication that does well to lie about itself."[18] This is an idea that runs all through German thought from Schopenhauer to Freud. Love is really nothing but a set of grimy sexual and reproductive impulses that are subconsciously dressed up in fictions about something else.

In spite of all of this, however, there is a sensible ambivalence about this analysis in Nietzsche. Whatever there may be in his writings that renders love down to something primitive, biological, and animalistic, there is also a fundamental doubt: "For two lovers in the complete and strong sense of the word sexual gratification is not essential and is really no more than a symbol . . ."[19] Love, Nietzsche goes on to argue[20] is something that gets in the way of socially sound reproductive policy. The institution of the family "can be founded on the sex drive, on the property drive . . . on the drive to dominate . . . never, absolutely never . . . on an idiosyncracy . . . on 'love.'"[21] So, any straightforward link between sex and love "in the complete and strong sense of the word" is being denied. Sexual and reproductive drives may be all or most of what there is to a "respectable" marriage, but it is tangential to love.

What, then, are we to make of Nietzsche's "theory" of love? Not much, I would suggest. What about his "theory" of sex in the context of real love? Here, I would suggest, something of interest can be *strained* from Nietzsche. The sad fact is that when Nietzsche claims that, between real lovers, sex is no more than a "symbol," he has elevated sex to a plateau far higher than the one it currently rests on. Contemporary Euro-American culture has, quite unsuspiciously, bought into the German way of thinking about sex. Sex is simply so much quasi-reproductive gyration that, for some undoubtedly irrational and medieval reasons, we still take more seriously than we ought to. We know in our hearts that the old Christian fable that had it that God, the eternal voyeur, was insuring that every single sex act (including instances of masturbation) either had reproductive intent or would result in a sentence in hell is simply unbelievable.

Yet, once again, the loss of the old myth brings a profound emptiness. Sex had a truly cosmic significance in the Christian myth. Now, as Allan Bloom has lamented,[22] we see it as a sign of health and progress when we proclaim that "sex is no big deal." Indeed, to make it as big a deal as it was in the Christian myth is to court psychological disease of unmanageable proportions.

> Beautiful feelings, sublime agitations, are, physiologically speaking, among the narcotics: their misuse has precisely the same consequences as the misuse of any other opiate—neurasthenia—[23]

But still, is the *wisest* course to make it *nothing*, not even a meaningful "symbol" of something really worthwhile? Isn't making sex into nothing a little like seeing Yosemite for the first time and saying, "No big deal; rocks, trees, dirt; I've seen it before"? "Physiology" aside, we are, indeed, in need of something to save us from our own cynicism about sex, at least, the sex that occurs between lovers. (The rest of it may deserve cynicism.) Perhaps the difference between the sex that merits cynicism and that which doesn't would be made clear by wondering after each occurrence of either kind: "Would I be willing to have that and all of its *unavoidable* consequences (*unlike* childbearing—for that is avoidable—but, *like* having future conversations with one's partner—for someone almost always says *something* reasonably important to *someone* after sex) recur again and again and again?" If the answer is "no" then that sex was, perhaps, no big deal. If the answer is "yes," then *maybe* that sex was not just good sex but, more importantly, at least a symbol of something important. Whatever that "something" is, I would be inclined to think that is something other than "nothing."

I will close here by offering up a general distinction that is admittedly and grossly general but nevertheless, I think, generally accurate, useful, and, moreover, central to some of the issues that will come up in Part III of this book. Furthermore, as overly general as this distinction may be, it is playing a central role these days in discussions about gender difference and the proper meaning of the tag "feminism."

What Mill has to say about relationships between men and women represents pretty well a certain kind of feminist theory. Usually (and quite properly) called "liberal feminism," I will dub this position "modernist feminism." Under this position, men and women are, ideally, equal partners in the struggle to live lives worth living. Whatever general differences we may, at present, observe between men and women that are in any way relevant to the different positions open to various individuals in our society, these differences may well be nothing but the product of differential socialization. Certainly there is no reason to believe that each and every woman is innately incapable of holding any particular high-status social position. There is no clear scent of any gender warfare about this theory; the oppression of women is an outgrowth of stupidity and immorality that generally serves the interests of men no better than it does women. Moreover, modernist feminism views the subjection of women as an evil precisely because such oppression constitutes an outright violation of the basic tenets of modernism and Enlightenment liberalism.

Nietzsche's views are obviously different. So are those of the theorists I will lump together as "postmodernist feminists." Regardless of the obvious fact that Nietzsche's bombast doesn't answer to anything that could be called "feminist," Nietzsche's deconstructive perspectivism looms large behind everything postmodern—including postmodern feminism. The basic idea that every perspective, especially the *scientific* perspective, is just another myth—just another mode of narrative usually driven on by deep psychological disease—is the real axiom of postmodern thought.[24] If we add the premise that the scientific myth constitutes a distinctly *masculine* form of narrative, then we have the theoretical core of what I intend to denote by the term "postmodern feminism." Add in the historical correlates of the scientific revolution (like industrialism, urbanization, capitalism, colonialism, and individualism), and we have a reasonably complete picture of the diverse target of postmodern feminist scorn.

So as not to oversimplify this variant of feminism beyond recognition, it must be pointed out that most feminists who drift in this direction are not simply parroting some monolithic party line. In fact (and as to be expected given the pluralism inherent in anything postmodern), postmodern feminists often link up with Marxists and other defenders of the thesis that all knowledge (including scientific knowledge) is "socially constructed," as well as with what Allison Jaggar has called "radical feminists," to create an extremely eclectic range of positions.[25] Even when there appears a discernable common core among postmodern (or at least nonliberal) feminists, there is always some tension. Donna Haraway, for example, gently distances herself from the organic holism common among nonliberal feminists:

> Both nineteenth- and twentieth-century western feminist theorists have argued that the self-contained, autonomous, western masculinist self, and the knowledge of the world he produces, is somehow truly opposed by women's putatively less rigid selves, issuing messages in another voice. The knowledge of the world imagined to come from this point of view, called women's, is variously described as more holist, less hostile to the body and to nature, promising a healing touch for alienation in industrial societies. . . . In complex sympathy with these claims, the feminist philosopher of science Sandra Harding (1986) noted that contemporary criticism of "western" science by Afro-American theorist Vernon Dixon aligns him neatly with organicist ideologies of contemporary white women. . . . In these arguments, there is little or no analysis of the historical and textual forms of power and violence built into "holist," "non-western" frameworks. . . . [There is a] sordid history of organicism and rejection of "dualism" in explicitly racist, fascist twentieth-century movements . . .[26]

Still, there is a discernable core to what I am calling postmodern feminism, and this core will emerge rather clearly as we move on to discussions of postmodern environmental ethics and ecofeminism in the next part of this book.

In all of these discussions it will be useful to keep in mind what I have been attempting to show up to this point. Part I was largely an attempt to show that the domain of the morally wrong should be construed to cover far less normative territory than is usually admitted. What is morally wrong, it was argued, is wholly a matter of what ideal social policy ought to arrange to publicly condemn. Lacking a serious demonstration that real institutions should target, in some concrete way, a certain type of behavior is perfectly good reason to believe that there is nothing *morally* wrong with that behavior. Part II, on the other hand, has centered on the idea that the realm of prudential wisdom can be extended to cover much more normative turf than is often thought.

But, beneath these two points is a third one, which is at the center of an ongoing concern of the whole book, namely, that the confusion of issues connected with moral wrongness with those connected with individual wisdom is behind a lot of mischief in moral philosophy. As serious as are questions about how one ought to live one's private life, charges of imprudence carry a different sort of normative force than do charges of immorality. This is due largely to the fact that one has to do less to justify a charge of imprudence than a charge of immorality. To charge another of lacking wisdom, one only has to *assert* one's *opinion* that he or she thinks that the other would be better off by doing things differently. To accuse someone of immorality, on the other hand, is to pretend to have a good *argument* based on real social *facts* about why we all ought to compel the wrongdoer to do things differently.

Nowhere in philosophical ethics has the line between wrongness and wisdom been so blurred as it has in discussions of the environment. This blurring of environmental vision has been made all the worse lately because of the entanglement of environmentalism with two other blurry doctrines just touched upon above: feminism and postmodernism. It is to this intellectual tangle that we now turn with an eye to sort out serious claims about the wrong from serious claims about the wise. Whatever is left over is, I will argue, just not serious at all.

PART 3

Wilderness

CHAPTER 13

Anthropocentrism and Ecocentrism

In order to get a handle on how, exactly, feminism and postmodernism have come to be woven into debates about the environment, it is necessary to retrace some of the formative steps in the development of environmental ethics over the last thirty years. By the early eighties, theories of environmental ethics had come to be arrayed along a continuum between two positions known as "deep ecology" and "shallow ecology." At the "shallow" end of the scale are theories, such as those of John Passmore,[1] that are "anthropocentric," that is, they approach the issues of pollution, overpopulation, and other forms of ecological degradation in terms of human interests. Degradation, then, for these theorists is to be defined as affecting the environment in ways which are bad *for us*. At the "deep" end of the scale are theories, such as those of J. Baird Callicott,[2] Arne Naess,[3] John Rodman,[4] Holmes Rolston III,[5] Christopher Stone,[6] and (as he is usually interpreted) Aldo Leopold,[7] that are "ecocentric," that is, they attempt to define ecological degradation in terms of what is good for the ecosystem, not just in terms of what is good for the human members of the "biotic community" (to use Leopold's term). In between these extremes are various forms of what Callicott calls "extensionism."[8]

Leaning in from the anthropocentric end of the extensionist spectrum are positions, like those of Bentham,[9] Feinberg,[10] Tom Regan,[11] and Peter Singer,[12] that extend the base of normative considerability beyond that formed by the interests of humans to that formed by the interests of sentient animals. Callicott has dubbed the basic position here as "first-stage extensionism." I will, following Singer, hereafter refer to this position as "animal liberationism."

Leaning toward the ecocentric end of the spectrum are positions, like those of Albert Schweitzer[13] and Paul Taylor,[14] that extend the base of moral considerability beyond animals and to anything living, but they stop short of extending direct considerability beyond *individual* animals and plants to the *whole* of the biosphere as ecocentrists do. Callicott calls the basic position here "second-stage extensionism," but it is generally known as "biocentrism." This is the term I will use to denote this position.

The principal motivation for moving from anthropocentrism to animal liberationism is that the basic criterion for inclusion in the moral community found in theories like utilitarianism (and, Regan argues, Kantian rights theory) naturally includes animals. In particular, if a utilitarian is going to assert that pleasure is intrinsically good and pain intrinsically evil, then, on the reasonably obvious observation that animals feel pain and pleasure, it follows that their pain and pleasure is as intrinsically important as ours. To derive a different conclusion can only be seen as irrationally discriminatory. In fact, Singer likens the denial of moral considerability to animals to the racist's irrational denial of moral standing to nonwhites and calls human chauvinists "speciesists."

The motivation for moving to biocentrism is that pain and pleasure cannot be viewed as valuable in themselves. The capacity of animals to feel pleasure and pursue it as well as to feel pain and avoid it is, after all, just a survival mechanism bequeathed to the animal kingdom by the process of evolution. In the end, the good of pleasure and the evil of pain are not intrinsic but instrumental to the more fundamental value of survival.[15] Since plants and nonsentient animals participate in the struggle to survive as much as sentients do, the failure to extend direct moral consideration to them would seem to be as irrational as speciesism. (I understand that Feinberg has been accused of being a "kingdomist.")

The motivation for moving to ecocentrism is that any form of extensionism overlooks the importance of a *holistic* perspective on environmental issues and misplaces concern on the *individuals* that make up various ecosystems and the biosphere as a whole. The first level of failure will be that the extensionist cannot establish the appropriate amount of concern about species preservation. The extensionist will not be able to explain why we should be more concerned about the survival of the few remaining members of a rare species of condors than we should be about the life of a common Swift's Butterball. For that matter, the ecocentrist will argue, there are many species of plants that we ought to be more concerned about than we are about dogs and cats. Moreover, aside from not accurately reflecting the importance of rare and ecologically important species (which may, according to Norman Myers,[16] be disappearing at a rate of one hundred per day by the end of the century), an indiscriminate concern for the welfare of individual animals or plants could be ecologically disastrous. The proliferation of certain kinds of plants and animals in environmentally sensitive areas might well ruin those areas. In other words, from the point of view of the environment, it might be best to control (by killing them off) certain human-introduced plants and animals as well as certain native plants and animals that are unnaturally flourishing because of human activity.

To consider things in the other direction, the motivation for not going to ecocentrism is twofold. First, there is the concern expressed by Regan that ecocentrism leads to a kind of "environmental fascism."[17]

Judging things from the point of view of the "integrity, beauty and stability of the biotic community" (to use Leopold's phrase) would require wholesale slaughter of many sentients and, especially, of humans. Indeed, from the biotic standpoint, maybe there should be something on the order of a 90 percent "dieback" of humans and their domestic animals.[18] This realization put the environmental ethics movement at odds with the animal rights movement as evidenced in the titles of two important articles in the early eighties: Callicott's "Animal Liberation: A Triangular Affair"[19] and Mark Sagoff's "Animal Liberation and Environmental Ethics: Bad Marriage, Quick Divorce."[20]

The second motivation for rejecting ecocentrism cuts against the first and, moreover, also counts as a reason to reject biocentrism. The concern is that it is implausible to attribute direct moral considerability to any entity that cannot reasonably be said to have any interests of its own. The reasoning that establishes this implausibility is straightforward enough; unless an entity can be ascribed reasonably complex mental states (especially important is the mental capacity to have beliefs and desires), then that entity cannot be said to have interests of its own. The lack of such mental states in insects, plants, and ecosystems is obvious enough and, thus, so is the lack of interests these entities could have. This cuts against Regan's concern about fascism inasmuch as no action at all (let alone brutal "diebacks") could be said to be in the interests of the biotic community if the biotic community is simply not the kind of thing that can have any interests in the first place. This cuts against the move toward biocentrism for the same reason; plants and insects just cannot be argued to have any interests.

The simple power of this line of argument cannot be denied. Unless some plausibility can be attached to the idea that things other than humans (and a few other mammals) can be attributed interests of their own, then environmental ethics ceases to be at all *philosophically* interesting. The only sensible position would be anthropocentrism or, at best, animal liberationism. Any talk about the health or welfare of plants or ecosystems would have to be viewed as merely metaphorical ways of talking about enlightened anthropocentric (or mammalian) interests.

In the next chapter I will attempt to reconstruct some of the arguments that have led several important philosophers to believe that we can get beyond mere metaphor. Moreover, I will be attempting to cast these arguments in a way that does not presuppose in any way any sort of prior deconstruction of modernist or, for that matter, liberal perspectives. The moves I will be making are, in fact, utterly dependent upon an assumption of the soundness of several distinctly modernist premises.

CHAPTER 14

Modernist Biocentrism and Ecocentrism

As the debates of the 1980s unfolded, the associated quandaries about what did or did not have interests, direct moral considerability, inherent worth, or intrinsic value were analyzed nearly to death. Yet, beneath it all, rested the question of why any of this debate was really central to any really serious concerns about our attitudes or policies toward the environment. To take the debates about what did or did not have intrinsic value as an example, does it really matter whether the earth as a whole, individual plants, individual insects, individual mammals, or just individual humans have *intrinsic* value? After all, questions of intrinsic value are not tied in any easy way to questions of *ultimate* value. A straightforward hedonist, for example, would grant that pain is intrinsically bad and that money is "only" instrumentally good but, nonetheless, think that the ultimate good of a large sum of money clearly outweighed and was thus preferable to the ultimate bad of a minor pain. Likewise, is there any need to argue that the sun is intrinsically important when we can all agree that it is *damned important* to us that it keep burning?

In short, the distinction between things that are intrinsically valuable and those that are "only" instrumentally valuable does not seem to imply, in any interesting way, a rank ordering between things that are, respectively and qualitatively, *more* valuable and those that are *less* valuable. In fact, given the general perspective detailed in the first part of this book, I am not even committed to the view that humans, per se, are intrinsically valuable (even though certain of their mental states, like pain, may be intrinsically disvaluable). The entire point in my laboring over the distinction between intrinsic and instrumental value in Part I was to produce a basic ethic that would meet with unanimity among social contractors. The claim that only pain, suffering, and death are bad *simpliciter* would have no chance of receiving unanimous agreement. However, the claim that only pain, suffering, and death are *intrinsically* bad has something going for it.

Generally, the ethicists for whom the question of intrinsic value is vital do not come from the hedonistic tradition I do. Many of them do, however, come from a generally *modernist* and also a generally *liberal* tradition, namely, that of Kant. To take things in the theoretical order established in the last chapter, it is central to Regan's animal rights theory[1] that animals have inherent worth because nothing without inherent worth can bear the rights of a genuine individual. In Taylor's biocentrism it is important that all living things have intrinsic value because no thing that lacks intrinsic value—or a good of its own—can be the object of *respect*.

An important movement of Taylor away from the animal rights position of Regan is constituted in his refusal to make biocentric ethics turn on the concept of rights. In this, he is making a theoretical turn that, as we shall see, becomes more obvious, and more important, as we progress toward ecocentrism. In this progression we shall see a gradual decrease in concern about rights, duties, and principles along with a corresponding increase in concern about attitudes, feelings, and general "sensibilities" (to use a term of Rodman's).

Although Taylor remains concerned with the formation and defense of moral principles (along with our duties to act according to them), it is clear that his more basic concern is for the *attitude* of "respect for nature" that directly underwrites all of the principles he lays out. Duties such as noninterference (generally violated when we intrude into nature and redesign it for our own ends) and fidelity (specifically, and interestingly, violated when we deceive animals in the process of hunting or fishing them for sport) are specifically disrespectful to nature for exactly the same reason these activities would be disrespectful if directed at people; they betray a disregard of the legitimacy of the autonomous ends had by the entity who is the target of the interference or deception, as well as a willingness to treat that entity as a mere means to our own ends.

The obvious retort to Taylor at this point is that, aside from people and perhaps a few other animals, the whole issue of the legitimacy of the autonomous ends of natural objects is stupid; questions of legitimacy and autonomy just don't arise with trees, for example. Autonomy, it will be argued, is impossible for entities that don't make any choices or have any desires. For the biocentrist to respond with the fabrication of some quasi-mental state possessed by trees would be to engage in the most embarrassing sort of anthropomorphism.

But Taylor, and biocentrists generally, have something more compelling than anthropomorphism to offer in their defense: they have a rather central tenet of modern science, specifically, of evolutionary biology. This tenet is the one that has it that no organism possesses any adaptations for the sake of any other organism; populations of living creatures pick up the evolved characteristics they do because those characteristics enhance the inclusive fitness of the creatures that have them.

Certainly, organisms can pick up characteristics that are also of use to other organisms as well as characteristics that are useless even for the organism that has them. But characteristics that also benefit other organisms (e.g., the structure of the horse makes it useful for humans) do so only incidentally. For example, there is no sense in which horses have the properties they do *because* those properties are useful for humans; they were not *designed* (presumably by God) to fulfill any human desires. This, of course, is central to the anti-Aristotelian spirit of Darwinism as well as to the accurately perceived anti-Christian spirit of the theory of natural selection. The main point to derive with respect to the defense of biocentrism, however, is this: it is a clear consequence of Darwinism that all living things have some *good of their own* that explains why they have the evolved characteristics they do.

The next line of argument against the biocentrist is likely to be that the words "autonomous" and "good" are being abused; "autonomous" should mean something like "freely chosen." Likewise, "good" should have some connection with free choice. The activities of most living things are obviously neither autonomous nor, in and of themselves, good in any morally important sense. But here the biocentrist can appeal to a line of argument mentioned in the last chapter. It is, again, a clear consequence of Darwinism that human mental activities like believing, desiring, and choosing occur in a larger biologically context. Cognition generally must be seen as something fairly tightly connected with our inclusive fitness as living things. From a biological point of view, the mechanisms involved in believing, desiring, thinking, judging, and deciding are, in principle, on a par with porcupine quills, poison oak toxin, and the mechanisms behind rapid asexual reproduction in bacteria; these are, each and all, the mechanisms of survival. The sense in which the natural proclivities of people, porcupines, and plankton equally well constitute autonomous goods is the only sense in which words like "autonomy" and "good" will be accepted by the biocentrist.

To define "autonomy" strictly in terms of certain mental activities that are biologically fortuitous for humans or to define "good" in terms of exclusively human activities is to openly beg the main question at stake for the biocentrist. There are, after all, other ways of defining the phrase "autonomous good" so that all organisms can be (and must be, if Darwinism is right) said to have goods of their own. To go on insisting that the only respectable way of speaking about autonomy and goodness is to do so within the confines of anthropocentric assumptions is just to be proudly guileless about one's chauvinism.

Ultimately, however, chauvinism is rarely dislodged by an argument. What is usually required to shake sheer prejudice is a change in what John Rodman calls "sensibility."

The term "sensibility" is chosen to suggest a complex pattern of perceptions, attitudes, and judgments which, if fully developed, would constitute a disposition to appropriate conduct that would make talk of rights and duties unnecessary under normal conditions . . . When perception is sufficiently changed, respectful types of conduct seem "natural," and one does not have to belabor them in the language of rights and duties. Here, finally, we reach the point of "paradigm change."[2]

To invoke the notion of paradigm change is, of course, to invoke Kuhn. What is central to the notion of a paradigm change (and to the associated notion of a gestalt switch) is that the change (or switch) is not a consequence of *rational* reexamination. In the standard examples of the gestalt switch (a drawing of a cube that appears first to point up and to the right and then down and to the left; a drawing that looks like two faces and then like one goblet; a drawing that looks like an old person and then like a young one, etc.), one is not compelled by *reason* to see things one way and then another. Moreover, the raw sensory data (the lines in the various drawings) have not themselves changed at all. Nevertheless, the gestalt, the pattern of perception and judgment, does change. Kuhn became famous for arguing that great leaps in the "progress" of science are much more a matter of these sorts of nonrational switches than they are a matter of a slow accretion of theoretical confirmations and refutations. A Copernicus or an Einstein does not just (if at all) add to the sum total of available observations but, rather, changes the prevailing gestalt that orders the available observations and thereby revolutionizes the very mode of perception; the same data just mean something different than they did before. The kind of gestalt switch that is important in ethics would seem to be a *sympathetic*, rather than a visual or conceptual one. One can look at a tree, a cow, or another person and see nothing but a resource with a few imaginable uses. Or one can put oneself in the position of the other and, thusly, move in the direction of being respectful of that other and the ends it has onto itself. It can be argued rather easily that the real impetus for real change in civil rights laws in the 1960s was far less a matter of the public's understanding that racial discrimination was logically incompatible with the spirit or letter of the Constitution than it was a result of a kind of mass empathetic gestalt switch. For whatever reason (probably the televised spectacle of police brutality during civil rights actions in Birmingham and Selma had a lot to do with it along with other things, like the identification of whites with blacks that occurred as a consequence of large numbers of whites listening to distinctively black music) European Americans stopped viewing African Americans as "animals" and started to view them as people who were like whites in all morally important ways.

A few years down the road, many people took the next empathetic step and stopped viewing a lot of animals as "just animals." One more step gets us the biocentrism of Schweitzer and Taylor. Rodman intends for us to take yet another step.

> It seems to me an observable fact that thistles, oak trees, and wombats, as well as rainforests and chaparral communities, have their own characteristic structures and potentialities to unfold, and that it is as easy to see this in them as it is in humans, if we will but look ... a forest may be in some ways more nearly paradigmatic than an individual human for illustrating what it means to have a *telos*. A tropical rainforest may take 500 years to develop to maturity and may then maintain a dynamic, steady-state indefinitely (for millions of years, judging from fossils) if not seriously interfered with. It exhibits a power of self-regulation that may have been shared to some extent by millennia of hunter-gatherer societies but is not an outstanding characteristic of modern humans, taken either as individuals or as societies.[3]

But this switch—the ecocentrist switch—really constitutes a double—and doubly demanding—switch. First, we must move beyond the biocentrist and admit that even nonliving entities can be objects of empathy; we must struggle to take seriously the image of John Muir, spread-eagle on a chunk of granite in Yosemite, "thinking like a rock." Secondly, we must take the *holistic* leap. This is the move that most radically reorganizes evaluation. To admit that a tree or a rock or a cloud must count for *something* is one thing, but to admit that some dirt and a few weeds may count *more* than a human because that particular weedpatch is more environmentally important than a given human is quite another—and this is exactly what the holistic switch will require.

In one of the most important, and surprising, articles of the 1980s, Callicott poses the conflict between ecocentrism and all previous forms of ethical extension as follows:

> Some indication of the genuinely biocentric value orientation of ethical environmentalism is indicated in what otherwise might appear to be gratuitous misanthropy. The biospheric perspective does not exempt *Homo sapiens* from moral evaluation in relation to the well-being of the community of nature taken as a whole. The preciousness of individual deer, as of any other specimen, is inversely proportional to the population of the species. Environmentalists, however reluctantly and painfully, do not omit to apply the same logic to their own kind. As omnivores, the population of human beings should, perhaps, be roughly twice that of bears, allowing for differences of size. A global population of more than four billion persons and showing no signs of an orderly decline presents an alarming prospect to humanists, but it is at present a global disaster (the more per capita prosperity, indeed, the more disastrous it

appears) for the biotic community. . . . The extent of misanthropy in modern environmentalism thus may be taken as a measure of the degree to which it is biocentric. Edward Abbey in his enormously popular *Desert Solitaire* bluntly states that he would sooner shoot a man than a snake.[4]

It is interesting that critics of holism draw the same sorts of consequences from the theory but intend these derivations to count as a reductio ad absurdum of the theory. Regan, for example, attacks Aldo Leopold's holistic dictum that "a thing is right when it tends to preserve the integrity, stability, and beauty of the biotic community," by pointing out that if

> . . . the situation we faced was either to kill a rare wildflower or a (plentiful) human being, and if the wildflower, as a "team member," would contribute more to "the integrity, stability, and beauty of the biotic community" than the human, then presumably we would not be doing wrong if we killed the human and saved the wildflower.[5]

Regan uses this inference to support his contention (mentioned in the last chapter) that ecocentrism constitutes a sort of "environmental fascism."

Callicott has an answer to this objection. In order to see how it works, it is useful to reconstruct the metaethical foundation of his system. Callicott sees himself coming out of distinctly modern tradition, specifically, that of Adam Smith, David Hume, and Darwin. First of all, he adopts the generally emotivist sentiment theory of Smith and Hume. Under this view, when it comes to moral argumentation and persuasion, reason is, to use Hume's famous phrase, "the slave of the passions." Passion, in turn, is rooted in certain primitive sentiments, which, for Smith and Hume, break down into two general types: egoistic and altruistic. Moreover, as Hume was at great pains to point out, altruistic sentiments are not appropriately understood as simple extensions of egoistic ones. There are really two psychologically *independent* springs of action.

Hume's principal reason for rejecting psychological egoism was that the theory failed to deliver the sort of empirical simplicity that was supposed to be the theory's main virtue. The explanatory contortions the psychological egoist must go through in order to reinterpret every action, no matter how apparently altruistic it might be, as an egoistic action make the whole account far less simple and intuitive than the easy theory that egoistic actions are generally motivated by egoistic sentiments and altruistic actions by altruistic sentiments. Other objections against psychological egoism have become standard (e.g., Butler's objection, the objection that the theory is question begging, and the one that it is irrefutable, though, presumably, empirical).

But, aside from any reason Hume (or anybody else) might have for *rejecting* the idea that all motivations spring from a single self-regarding source, there is a more important reason Hume and, after him, Darwin had for *accepting* a nonegoistic account of the sentiments. What Hume would speak of in terms of "the constitution of human nature," Darwin could couch in the vocabulary of natural selection:

> In however complex a manner this *feeling* [i.e., the altruistic or "social" sentiment] may have originated, as it is one of high importance to all those animals which aid and defend one another, it will have been increased through natural selection; for those *communities*, which included the greatest number of sympathetic members, would flourish best, and rear the greatest number of offspring.[6]

To elaborate a bit on a pretty simple idea, we can imagine three different groups of humans who have evolved in isolation from one another. Suppose Group 1 had evolved (contrary to Darwin's claim that such would not be at all likely to happen) so that all of them were propelled by solely egoistic sentiments. Group 2 (again, contrary to Darwinian hypothesis) had evolved so that all of them were propelled by solely altruistic sentiments. Group 3 (as Darwin, and Hume, suppose to correspond to the realities of evolved human nature) had evolved so as to be propelled by a combination, refined over time by natural selection, of egoistic *and* altruistic sentiments. Without much imagination, we can see the logic of the suggestion that if all three groups had to live under equally demanding conditions, Group 3 would do better than either of the first two groups. Furthermore, if all three groups somehow happened upon each others' turf and commenced upon a course of competition and, eventually, warfare with each other, then even less imagination is needed to construct the scenario under which Group 3 would quickly come to dominate (and outreproduce) the others. At the risk of begging a few questions on behalf of Hume and Darwin, we have every reason to believe that this scenario does, indeed, represent the reality of humans evolution because we have, indeed, turned out to be propelled by the twin fountains of egoism and altruism.

There is an important qualification to enter at this point that will be important to keep in mind as we proceed to considerations of the relevance of the Hume-Darwin view to environmental ethics. Although, at the level of *motivation*, altruism cannot be reduced to egoism, at the level of *explanation*, specifically, at the level of explaining why it is that we have the motivations we do, altruism really does have a plain reduction to egoism. The reason why we, *as individuals* (and we must keep in mind that a central tenet of evolutionary theory is that no *individual* organism is set up to pass on its genetic legacy for the sake of any other *individual* organism), have evolved a motivational structure containing both egoism and altruism is that our ancestors were, *themselves*, well-served by that motivational makeup and, thus, survived well enough to pass on to us whatever genes underlay that motivational makeup. In other words, human populations have evolved altruistic sentiments because to do so was good for those altruists, not because it was good for others. In yet other words, altruistic sentiments did not evolve for altruistic reasons. However, this does not in any way suggest that the immediate motivation of any altruistic action is really egoistic. Altruistic acts will generally be performed without any conscious connection to one's own self-interest; generally we will act out of a genuine love of others just because that is how we are psychologically and physiologically set up to act—every once in a while.

We are now in a position to understand the state Callicott winds up calling "bioempathy." Given an evolutionary explanation of how opposing springs of motivation (egoistic and altruistic) can come to reside in the same organism, it is not hard to imagine evolutionary explanations of other distinct, psychologically nonreducible types of motivation. Bioempathy might amount, at base, to something as simple as a primitive sort of love of the nest, *amor loci*, a spontaneous affection for the surroundings in which one flourishes. Again, the *explanation* for the existence of such a primitive affection might well turn on a series of egoistic (or at least anthropocentric) premises. Again, this will have nothing to do with the phenomenology, the feeling, of the bioempathetic *motivation* that prompts the actions of an organism bent on protecting its place.

If Callicott is at all right about this foundation of the land ethic (regardless of whether or not Leopold really had anything like it in mind, as Callicott insists he did), then the prominence that environmental concerns have come to have in public policy disputes over the last few decades signals the most fundamental moral upheaval since the dawn of serious moral analysis. Moral theory, and simple moralizing for that matter, really only arises as a consequence of the necessity of sorting out egoistic and altruistic motivations and, more importantly, of sorting out egoistic and altruistic *justifications*. The whole point of trying to tell someone that they *ought* to do x rather than y (and threatening some kind of social sanction if they refuse to do x rather than y) is brought on by the clash of self-interest with the interests of other reasonable agents. The main project of the first part of this book was entirely wrapped up in an attempt to sort out this sort of conflict—so were the main projects of Plato's *Republic* and Aristotle's *Nicomachean Ethics*. Without the existence of a series of conflicts of interests between rational individuals, there would simply be no point in doing ethics. For the Humean, such conflicts are rooted in the underlying tug not only between competing egoists but also between the egoistic and altruistic sentiments deeply buried in the nature of each of us.

If we admit the existence of yet a third type of irreducible and basic sentiment, then the fundamental modalities of what will count as a legitimate moral dispute will have changed; the very "patterns of perception" will be different, as different as they had become for the first humans who started to belabor the clash between the interests of the individual and those of the community. Moreover, we can expect that those who now claim to speak for the earth will appear every bit as preposterous to Americans obsessed with various social problems as the missionaries of social order must have seemed to a nineteenth-century Coloradan whose nearest neighbor lived thirty miles across the Rockies. It's not that this Coloradan wouldn't have had any altruistic sentiments. Rather, he just wouldn't have ever noticed any collision between his own interests and those of others (because he hardly ever saw anyone else). Similarly, members of small, tightly knit communities may never notice any serious conflict between their own interests and those of the community because individual and communal interests are so tightly bound together by a strenuous process of communal indoctrination. It cannot be a mere coincidence that it is only when humans start living in relatively large and diverse communities (like the Greek *polis*), that serious speculation about ethics, as we have come to know it, begins.

Likewise, it cannot be a mere coincidence that it is in times of increasing human exploitation of natural resources that the voices of environmental concern emerge. It cannot, for example, be just chance that produces the lake poets at a time when the Thames had been turned into a sewer, Muir at a time when the Sequoias were being hacked down for firewood and amusement park displays, Leopold at a time when all of the top soil of the central United States seemed to be either floating or blowing away, or the Rio Conference at a time when alarm about atmospheric change, resource depletion, and species extinction has become general and global. It is at times like these that the latent land sentiment emerges in public policy debate. It has always been there, "woven into our breasts" as Hume would say, but it is only under pressure that we are seeing with any clarity the full dimensions of the conflict between egoistic motives and justifications, altruistic ones, and ones connected with the preservation of the land.

What is especially significant for Callicott is the *holistic* nature of the land sentiment. Although bioempathy may, on occasion, look like an individualistic (or biocentric) concern for this tree or that mountain, it is fundamentally a love of *place* that is involved. Concern about the individual fixtures of a place are incidental to the welfare of the place itself. (Note that this is a reversal of Taylor's biocentric position that has it that eco*systems* warrant concern only because the individuals in those systems are deleteriously affected by what might be perceived as systemic deterioration.) Moreover, as common knowledge of the interconnectedness of individual living things grows, concern about the nest becomes concern about the locality, which becomes concern about the bioregion, which becomes, finally, concern about the whole biotic community—the planet.

We are now in a position to reconsider Regan's view that ecocentrism constitutes an ecofascism. Any time there is a pronounced public demand that self-interest be sacrificed in some new way we can expect cries of "fascism," "One-Worldism," "Bolshevism," "leveling," or whatever else taps into the jingoism of the day. A century ago, for example, only outright socialists and communists were calling for things like progressive income taxes, old age pensions, and some sort of welfare for the poor. Today, in the United States anyway, income taxes are loathed but not because they are "fascist" or anything of the sort. There is an enforced *balance* now between egoism and altruism that almost everyone recognizes as necessary and justifiable and that entails some new altruistic duties (e.g., taxes), some new egoistic freedoms (e.g., sexual liberty), but nothing approaching the *elimination* of self-interest in the name of the community.

Similarly, what we can expect now, if Callicott is right, is not a fascistic demand that self-interest or humanistic altruism be *eliminated* in favor of bioempathetic motivations but, rather, that these newly strengthened sentiments will at least come onto the table during policy disputes and be given some serious weight as we *balance* the interests of ourselves, others, and our places. The kind of balancing we can expect has already emerged as a template in discussions of environmental problems local and global. Locally, it is now common for residents in some relatively pristine environs to attempt to keep others out (by enforcing strict limits on residential and commercial growth), not just because this would benefit current residents (although it would certainly do that) but also because this would be "good for the environment." Although these sorts of arguments may often be disingenuous smokescreens for keeping property values high, there is no reason to suspect that this is always the case; at least some of these self-proclaimed defenders of the environment are probably in earnest. Here we see how egoistic sentiment may unite with bioempathy against altruism.

At the global level, the same sort of three-way conflict arises when environmentalists in industrialized countries try to persuade developing countries ("developing" here meaning only that these countries are, in their official national policies, seeking to industrialize) to slow their developmental acceleration because their rapid industrialization will be bad for the planet (it may deteriorate the ozone layer and aggravate the problem of global warming, for instance). Many of these developing nations (China is notable) are, to say the least, suspicious of this newly found love of nature in the West and have openly proclaimed that the real motivation for wanting a moratorium on Chinese coal burning, for example, has less to do with some theory about global warming than it does with the knowledge that the West will not be able to compete in many international markets with an industrialized China. And, of course, the West really *does* have to worry about a nation the size of China producing everything from cookware to cars at a fraction of the cost these items now carry around the world.

Another line of analysis that leads us away from the conclusion that policymaking is simply a matter of balancing egoism and altruism is that made famous by Garrett Hardin.[7] Although Hardin himself casts his concerns in fully anthropocentric terms, it is easy to see how his arguments expose the threefold competition of egoism, altruism, and bioempathy. The easiest place to start is with Hardin's arguments concerning what he calls "the ratchet effect." Basically his argument is that it is a mistake (for egoistic and altruistic reasons) to be propelled by the pangs of immediate altruistic sympathy into sending aid to famine stricken parts of the world. Food aid will only alleviate suffering long enough for fertility rates to increase, which will, in turn, just ratchet the level of misery up to a new plateau. If the response to this new level of suffering is even more aid, then things will just ratchet up to an even more homicidal level. In the end, the givers of aid have sacrificed needlessly and, tragically enough, the intended benefactors of that aid have suffered in greater numbers than would have been the case had they not been given the aid. Eventually, the Malthusian graveyard is filled anyway; it's just a matter time, space, and the tenacity of misguided altruistic delusion.

It is easy to see the bioempathetic dimension in this sort of tragedy. Each time the population ratchets up, there is greater environmental damage, and this damage will occur not just in the place of the famine. Resources will be used and pollution created in the process of producing the aid elsewhere and in shipping it to the source of the need. It is important to keep in mind that I am not really interested in defending Hardin's basic assessment of the hopelessness of aiding the victims of famine nor any of the details of his ratchet-effect argument. I am most interested in pointing out that what he views as a three-pronged conflict between egoism (on the part of aid givers), long-term rational altruism, and short-sighted knee-jerk altruism can be seen as all of that along with bioempathetic sentiments weighing in against short-sighted sentimentality.

An even more complicated ethical landscape is provided by a rethinking of Hardin's famous analysis of the tragedy of the commons. The tragedy of the commons is a close cousin of another tragedy, namely, the prisoner's dilemma. The prisoner's dilemma was discussed in some detail in Chapter 2. Then, the dilemma was useful for an understanding of social contract theory. But there are other uses for the dilemma. (The fact that there are so many uses for it explains why so much ink has been spilled analyzing it.) Specifically relevant to Hardin's concerns is the usefulness of the dilemma in understanding certain features of the market mechanism.

We are all familiar with Adam Smith's claim that market transactions are driven by an "invisible hand."

> he [the capitalist] intends only his own gain, and he is in this, as in many other cases, led by an invisible hand to promote an end which was no part of his intention. Nor is it always the worse for society that it was no part of it. By pursuing his own interest he frequently promotes that of society more effectually than when he really intends to promote it. I have never known much good done by those who affected to trade for the public good. It is an affection, indeed, not very common among merchants, and very few words need be employed in dissuading them from it.[8]

And we are all familiar with the fact that the invisible hand often fails to work its magic in the real world. The main reason for this is that participants in the market—both producers and consumers—do not act in fully rational ways; they do not pursue well enough their own self-interest. Producers often do "affect to trade for the public good." Consumers, for their part, often act on the basis of preferences that are ill-informed, short-sighted, or coerced. Other things can go wrong, but the usual line from the economists is that these problems are all open to *technical* solutions. Specifically, all of these problems can be solved by simply letting the market play out to its logical conclusions. Do-gooder capitalists will (unless the government moves in to prop up their philanthropy) either do-good themselves into the poor house or sink in a sea of unintended consequences. Ignorant or short-sighted consumers can be benefited by the development of new markets where information is bought and sold.

What intrigues Hardin is the class of market problems that have no such technical solutions. These problems have no technical solutions precisely because they are caused by the very mechanisms that, otherwise, make markets self-correcting. Even more troublesome is the fact that the more efficiently markets can be made to work, the worse the problems become. In order to get a handle on the sort of mechanisms involved in these kinds of problems, consider the following, admittedly simplistic, scenario: A certain market for pins is controlled by two pin manufacturers (A and B). Demand for pins is high enough for both A and B to sell as many pins as they can make and remain profitable (but just barely so). A and B have both pondered the possibility of taking firmer control of their market by colluding to fix prices. If they each cut pin production in half, then their overhead would go down and scarcity of pins would drive up the price. As a consequence, their profits would actually go up. However, if either A or B went to half production while the other stayed at full production, the one at half production would lose many customers and, quite likely, go out of business. The situation, then, is as follows:

		B	
		HP	FP
A	HP	2, 2	0, 3
	FP	3, 0	1, 1

where FP stands for full production and HP stands for half production.

This is where the workings of the invisible hand come into play. Although both A and B would be better off if they both pursued half production, neither party could have any trust in any subcontractual agreement to fix prices. Moreover, the only way to effect a contract would be to appeal to some party powerful enough to enforce that contract. As long as the government stays out of the marketplace and, further, prohibits the existence of nongovernmental enforcers (which could be done by the enforcement of ordinary laws against extortion, murder, etc.), no further measures are necessary in order to maintain producers at the equilibrium outcome.

In other words, unless A and B can get the government to help them fix prices, they will both be driven to full production, which is suboptimal in the context that includes only A and B but very good news when the context includes pin consumers who now will have lots of cheap pins. When the interests of pin consumers are taken into account, the outcome is Pareto optimal and should remain so. Thusly, A and B are led by the invisible hand to promote an end (the welfare of consumers) that is no part of their intention (which is simply to maximize their own profits).

But, suppose that instead of talking about pins, or any other reasonably plentiful commodity, we imagine that A and B are involved in the production of some good made from raw materials that are obviously finite and, furthermore, diminishing rapidly. Suppose, for example, that A and B are competing oil or timber companies. (We will have to assume as well, for there is continuing empirical controversy about the issue, that oil and timber are in increasingly short, almost critically short, supply.)

What the invisible hand will do is predictable enough. The invisible hand will drive A and B to maximal depletion of oil or timber stocks. It might very well be understood that not just A and B but even consumers would be better served by having A and B restrain production. It would be better for A and B because it would increase their profits and lengthen the period of time they could stay in their respective businesses. It would be good for consumers because their long-term interests are not best served by the quick elimination of oil or timber from the world either.

Even if the government moves in to impose production quotas (i.e., it moves in to help A and B fix prices), there is trouble. Although A and B (as well as the general public) are best served by a government-imposed contract, A and B will both be rationally disposed to lobby intensely for exceptions to the contract that would put their competitors at a disadvantage. If they are successful, then the contract will be nickel-and-dimed to death. The tragedy unfolds as follows:

1. A and B both recognize that the invisible hand is forcing an outcome that is suboptimal not just for them but for the general public as well.

2. A and B persuade the government that everyone, not just A and B, will be best served if the government imposes production limits on A and B. (They might even start running TV commercials that talk about how precarious our supplies of timber or oil are and plead that A and B want to do not only what's good for A and B but what's "good for nature" as well.)

3. The government imposes production limits, that is, it forces A and B to fix prices.

4. A starts approaching politicians with arguments that it is unwise (for whatever reasons A can lay its hands on) to hold A to the production limits, although the limits are, generally, a good idea and "good for nature" too and, thus, ought to still be imposed on B. (A might start running TV commercials assuring the nation that there enough trees— or oil deposits—to allow A to increase its production.)

5. B starts doing the same thing as A.

6. Piece by piece, the regulations that limited production are dismantled. Everyone's back where he or she started; precious resources are cheapened and squandered to the advantage of no one.

As Hardin (quoting Whitehead) once pointed out, the essence of a true tragedy is not unhappiness or ordinary stupidity; what is truly tragic is the perverse rationality of life, "the solemnity of the remorseless working of things."

Hopefully, it is now getting clear that environmental issues pose a special sort of economic problem. The kinds of quandaries we are dealing with are ones that, even in the rarified air of pure theory, set the marketplace against its own goals. Mechanisms that, ideally and perhaps even usually, are part of the self-correcting apparatus of the market turn out to *be* the problem. The mechanism just discussed (that drives producers to equilibrium outcomes) can, ideally and perhaps even usually, be expected to break up cartels, which is important in the maintenance of freedom and efficiency in the market. To the degree things work as they're supposed to, however, they fail; efficiency and freedom turn to waste and enslavement to depletion. And yet, we have only seen the first act of the tragedy.

As it turns out, the mechanism described above is only a part of the self-correcting apparatus of the marketplace. Something else is needed in order to insure that cartels are broken up. To see why this is the case, consider the following, again admittedly oversimplified, example: Imagine there to be two ranchers who use a commons to graze their cattle. This commons will support a maximum of one thousand head of cattle. However, as the number of cattle on the commons increases, profit per head will go down because of increased supply and because each animal will have less to eat and, thus, weigh less. Although things will never be this neat and linear in the real world, let's summarize the characteristics of this situation as follows:

Number of Animals on the Commons	Profit per Animal	Total Profit
100	$100	$10K
200	90	18K
300	80	24K
400	70	28K
500	60	30K
600	50	30K*
700	40	28K
800	30	24K
900	20	18K
1000	10	10K
1100	0	0**

At six hundred head (indicated by *), the point of diminishing returns has been reached and at eleven hundred head (indicated by **) the commons simply collapses.

A prisoner's dilemma arises here around the point of diminishing returns.

		B	
		200	*400*
	200	14K, 14K	10K, 20K
A			
	400	20K, 10K	12K, 12K

The equilibrium outcome is the one where A and B are each grazing four hundred head, even though A and B would both be better off by cutting their herds to two hundred. At this point the invisible hand is doing it's job (providing maximal benefit for consumers while also providing equilibrium—but not optimal—outcomes for producers). A conspiracy to fix prices (without the aid of an outside third party) should fail. This is too simple, though, and the following table shows why:

		B	
		300	600
A	300	15K, 15K	6K, 12K
	600	12K, 6K	0, 0

This is *not* a prisoner's dilemma. The equilibrium outcome is a result of A and B each putting three hundred cattle on the commons; this is also an optimal outcome and it is, furthermore, a sustainable outcome. As long as one of the ranchers (say, A) holds at three hundred head, B doesn't have much to gain by putting more cattle out on the commons. If B goes to four hundred, then his profits will increase to sixteen thousand dollars, but at five hundred they will go back to fifteen thousand dollars. In short, there is no good reason for either A or B to move away from the equilibrium, optimal, and sustainable outcome.

So, there is some good news. The market will not necessarily drive competitor's toward the ruin of the commons. But, of course, this is bad, for it means that the market is not really being fully efficient from the standpoint of the consumer. The consumer is best served by A and B pushing the commons to its limit, that is, by A and B together producing not six hundred but, rather, a thousand head.

As the remorseless engine of fate would have it, consumers need not worry; the environment will, indeed, be destroyed—very efficiently so. Here's why: If the commons is, indeed, a commons, then A and B will not be the only ranchers with access to the commons. As a result, we can expect some third party, C, to look at the commons that has three hundred of A's cattle and three hundred of B's cattle on it as an invitation to enter the cattle business. By putting three hundred of her own cattle on the commons, she now makes six thousand dollars that she wasn't making before. Of course, C's profit is coming out of the hides of A and B; their profits have fallen from fifteen thousand dollars to six thousand dollars. But, as we see, the market is correcting itself. And the self-correction will continue. Even when the commons is right on the verge of collapse, some enterprising D, E, or F will realize that, even with 1098 cattle on the commons, he can put one more out there and make one dollar he wasn't making before.

Once again, it's important to see that the mechanism driving the tragedy of the commons is an integral part of the marketplace. It is not the dynamic of the prisoner's dilemma alone that keeps the marketplace free and competitively efficient. Even if two competitors do manage to collude in order to control a specific market, they will always have to watch out for the small-fry upstart who can crash the party because he or she is willing to operate on a thinner shoestring, accept less profit, and, thus, produce a better product for less than the established competitors. And, once again, if the market being crashed is one for something like pins (or computers), then everyone except the flabby and entrenched competitors will benefit. However, if the market involves a rapidly diminishing resource, then the invisible hand becomes the invisible backhand.

Once again, Callicott's theory adds a new and quite disturbing dimension to our understanding of these venerable tragedies. Smith (the father of the general sentiment theory) thought that a well-structured marketplace would turn egoistically motivated actions into ones that were altruistic in their results, and, thus, there would be a sort of harmony between egoistic and altruistic sentiments without making the dubious assumption that people can be made to regularly sacrifice their own self-interest and remain happy about it. What the above considerations show is that this is not the case, and it is not the case under fairly specific conditions, namely, those were scarce resources are involved. Strategies that are suboptimal from an egoistic point of view are also suboptimal from an altruistic point of view. Moreover, these doubly suboptimal strategies are also in collision with the bioempathetic sentiment as well. In short, what is rational in terms of equilibrium bargaining outcomes has come in direct conflict with *all* of our natural motivations.

CHAPTER 15

Postmodern Ecocentrism and Ecofeminism

Although postmodern environmental ethicists usually don't find much to like in either Hardin or Callicott, the idea that there is a broad class of important quandaries for which there are "no technical solutions" and, moreover, that are brought on and then aggravated by the exercise of ideal "rationality" certainly does add some fire to the rhetoric of the postmoderns. Regardless of the fact that it is impossible to pin postmodernism down as any specific position, it is not hard to characterize the general view that ties postmodernists together. At the core of the position is a familiar variety of relativism. Jim Cheney, an expositor of postmodernism generally and postmodern environmental ethics specifically, gives us this encapsulation:

> in the light of postmodernist deconstruction of modernist totalizing and foundationalist discourse, can we any longer make sense of the idea of privileged discourse, discourse which can lay claim to having access to the way things are? The dominant postmodernist view is that this is not possible, that language can be understood only as either a set of tools created for various human purposes or as a free creation of conscious persons or communities. This being so, it is argued, we should practice ontological abstinence in our beliefs about the relation between language and world. To the extent that the notion of objectivity enters into postmodern discourse at all it tends to take the form that "truth" is simply the result of social *negotiation*, agreement achieved by the participants in particular conversations.[1]

Here we see the first step of the postmodernists—deconstruction. But, as is the case with deconstructors going back to Nietzsche, deconstruction is usually merely a first step to something constructive. Of course, the position would be utterly boring without such a step; no one who has ever passed out of an introductory philosophy course should be surprised by the fact that there are powerful arguments for the position that everything is somehow relative. Relativism only becomes interesting when we are given some clarification on the range of "everything" (does it include the sentence "everything is relative"?), on the meaning of "relative" (relative to what?), and on the plans of the relativist to reconstruct discourse so that he or she can enlighten us with something more than permutations of the locution "everything is relative."

The *reconstructive* move that Cheney makes is a pretty standard one—Nietzsche's. Nietzsche's view was that the categories of God, the good, and truth had to be done away with not because they were utterly without a foundation but rather (as we saw in Chapter 11) because they had a *sick* foundation; they were all rooted in various forms of psychological disease that we needed to strip away in order to be *healthy*. Cheney gives us this rendition of the same point:

> Like the conscious ego which has turned its back on the id out of which it grew, such language [that which pretends to be true] becomes subject to bad dreams, neurosis, and psychosis—the return of the repressed.[2]

So here we have a partial explanation of what everything is supposed to be "relative" to; everything is relative to a certain kind of *psychological* background discourse. What turns out to be psychologically sick for postmodernists, like Cheney, is exactly what Nietzsche pinpointed as forms of "asceticism": Christianity, faith in scientific truth, and slave herd mentality generally. What turns out to be more healthy for Cheney and many other postmodern ecocentrists are the "storied residences" and the "bioregional narratives" we find in the "voices" of those struggling against "totalizing" and "colonizing" effects of modern ideology.

And so now we have the predictable indication of what the referent of "everything" is in the postmodern variant of the faith that everything is relative. What is importantly relative is precisely what modernity has taken to be not relative, namely, the scientific method along with the associated ideas of rationality and utility that support the contention that science is true and good. Moreover, it is important to note that the quarrel that the postmodernists have with science is not just a matter of how scientific information has been *applied*; their quarrel is with the method itself, which they find *inherently* colonizing and alienating. For this reason Cheney rejects (in his earlier work, anyhow) the idea that the science of ecology will be of much help in the construction of an appropriate idea of nature.

> A Western scientific description of the specifics of the ecosystem within which one lives is not adequate. It provides the wrong kind of myth. It can and ought to *inform* our construction of appropriate mythical images, but it cannot function as the centerpiece of a viable environmental ethic, much less a *mythos* for our times. . . . The integrity of the objective scientific model must, for the purposes I have been sketching (but not for all purposes), give way to the requirement of the health and well-being of the individual, community, and land . . .[3]

What *will* give us appropriate myths are the "privileged voices" of those typically found in groups with a history of exclusion from the channels of power, and thus "knowledge," in modern times. Aside from natives and other non-Westerners, women are generally in this privileged group as well since they do well under Cheney's criterion that "a voice is privileged to the extent that it is constructed from a position that enables it to spot distortions, mystifications, and colonizing and totalizing tendencies within other discourses."[4] The female voice is also "objective" given Cheney's definition of objectivity (for which he gives original credit to Sandra Harding): "Objectivity is defined negatively in relation to those views which oppositional consciousness deconstructs."[5] Thusly, Cheney's postmodernism (and postmodernism generally) supplements (often to the point of virtually replacing) its psychological foundation with an openly *political* one (showing that postmodernism is as influenced by Marx as it is by Nietzsche). Discourse is "privileged" and "objective" to the degree that it is "politically correct" (in the vague sense that this phrase has acquired).

The position that has come to be known as ecofeminism is almost exclusively to be found in the sort of intersection of politicized postmodern ecocentrism and postmodern (or at least antiliberal) feminism being suggested by Cheney. Karen Warren, perhaps the most widely read ecofeminist philosopher, finds that feminist and ecological issues are linked together inasmuch as both sexism and "naturism" grows out of an underlying "logic of domination," which props up "oppressive conceptual frameworks," which, in turn, sanction the "twin dominations of women and nature."[6]

From this general platform, Warren stakes out eight characteristics of an ecofeminist perspective. Ecofeminism

1. is antinaturist;
2. is contextualist; it "involves a shift *from* a conception of ethics as primarily a matter of rights, rules, or principles . . . *to* a conception of ethics as growing out of what Jim Cheney calls 'defining relationships'";
3. is pluralistic "in that it presupposes and maintains difference";
4. "focuses on patterns of meaning which emerge, for instance, from the storytelling and first-person narratives of women (and others) who deplore the twin dominations of women and nature";
5. is inclusivist; it listens to "the voices of indigenous peoples";
6. "makes no attempt to provide an 'objective' point of view";
7. "makes a central place for values of care, love, friendship, trust";
8. "denies abstract individualism" in favor of the view that humans are defined by their relationships with each other and with nonhumans.

Thus stated, Warren's position is a more moderate one than that held by other ecofeminists. Warren is really only claiming that there is some fundamental connection between sexism and environmental degradation (i.e., "naturism"), and surely there is such a connection. (Whether it is the underlying "logic of domination" that she describes or, rather, just greed, stupidity, ignorance, and short-sightedness is, of course, arguable.) Other ecofeminists have gone beyond Warren's position to claim that sexism is the *sole root cause* of environmental degradation and, thus, if sexism were ended, then so would our environmental crises. Such a position is held by Marti Kheel.[7] But this may be a difference without much substance to it because Warren believes that feminism will end only with the end of the logic of domination and that, in turn, would also end environmental destruction. So, for both Warren and Kheel, sexism (as understood by postmodern feminists) will end if and only if environmental deprecation does.

The connection between postmodern ecocentrism and postmodern feminism has, in fact, been bolted up so tightly by ecofeminists like Warren that many postmodern ecocentrists who shy away from the badge "ecofeminism" and many postmodern feminists who are, similarly, suspicious about what the "eco" adds to "feminism" wonder why there is any need for the redundancy entailed by the label "ecofeminism."[8] Indeed, I doubt that a single postmodern ecocentrist would not also describe him- or herself as a feminist or that a single postmodern feminist would not also describe him- or herself as an ecologist, environmentalist, or ecocentrist.

I will not attempt here, or hereafter, any sort of general critique of either postmodern ecocentrism, postmodern feminism, or ecofeminism. In fact, there is no way I (or anyone else) *can* mount a useful critique of anything postmodern. For those philosophically inclined to reject out of hand the openly psychologized and clearly politicized standpoint of the postmoderns, nothing enlightens except amusing laundry lists of quotes that only show the depth of the misology that postmoderns will shamelessly admit to. On the other hand, for those predisposed to adopt the postmodern perspective (though, trenchant deconstructors might deny that they have any perspective, or that they are "trenchant") any critique will be just so much more Western, patriarchal, sexist, racist, capitalist, Cartesian, linear, hierarchical, hegemonic, colonizing, totalizing asceticism.

Really, at a basic enough point in the argument, critique of postmodernism can only turn to insult. Callicott, for instance, notes that Cheney's "neologism, *totalizing,* seems to be a hybrid intended to evoke the political ogre of totalitarianism in the vocabulary of a Valley Girl, as in, 'I was *totally* totalized.'"[9] Sarcasm has turned to indignant threat among some as can be witnessed in a recent work by Paul Gross (a biologist) and Norman Levitt (a mathematician) who have more than tired of what they call "the academic left" and its attack on science and the concept of scientific rationality.

> If an aspiring scholar is to be judged on work affecting to make deep pronouncements on questions of science, scientific methodology, history of science, or the very legitimacy of science, it strikes us that scientists should have some say in evaluating it. This holds even if the candidate resides academically in the English department or the art department or the sociology department. . . . If an assistant professor of English is to stake his bid for tenure on work that, for example, purports to analyze quantum mechanics as an ideological construct, then he has no right to complain if a professor of physics is brought into the evaluation to say whether he evidences any real understanding of quantum mechanics.[10]

In threats like these there is a sad confirmation of the following assessment by Callicott of the debate between the postmoderns and their critics:

> it seems clear . . . [for postmoderns like Cheney] the ground rules for persuasion themselves are totalizing/colonizing. Our growing body of knowledge comes from science and [according to Cheney] "science has constructed itself in such a way that it has insulated itself from social negotiation." Never mind that science is an international activity, the hallmark of which is the falsifiable hypothesis and the repeatable experiment. Cheney even considers it to be politically suspect to suggest making *reason* an arbiter of what is worth believing and what isn't—since reason may be a colonizing device of patriarchy.
>
> Thus, in the new dark age of deconstructive *difference*, without even the minimum methodological agreements required for resolving differences of opinion by informed, reasoned argument, negotiation is our only recourse. Or is it? Mention of the Spanish Conquistadores' technique for securing consensus reminds us that a far more likely option for a *Realpolitik* of difference in a shattered and fragmented world is naked power—backed either by bullets or bucks. Why negotiate with someone with whom agreement is hopeless when you can have your own way—when the "other" can be bombed, terrorized, bought, pacified, or sweet-talked?[11]

It might be objected that the postmoderns' hatred of science and reason is being unfairly overstated here. After all, postmodernists from Derrida on have, on occasion, relied upon the findings of contemporary science to bolster their deconstructive moves. Even Cheney seems to have softened his position about the value of scientific ecology. In an article coauthored with Warren, there is a list of what they take to be ten important connections between a certain type of ecosystem ecology (generally known as "hierarchy theory") and ecofeminism.[12]

But such moves are usually disingenuous or, what only makes matters worse, silly. Derrida's meanderings about how Einstein's constant (i.e., c, the speed of light) "is not a constant, not a center . . . but the very concept of the game" receive this swat from Gross and Levitt:

> Fortunately for Derrida, few scientists trouble to read him, while those academics who do are, for the most part, so poorly versed in science that they have a hard time telling the real thing from sheer bluff.[13]

Of course, Derrida is not alone in the world of postmodern pseudo-scientific bluffing. The journals of postmodernism are full of dopey claims about how relativity theory shows that "everything is relative," how Gödel's Theorem shows that everything is uncertain, how the uncertainty principle (probably the most heavily confirmed theory in physics) shows that nothing can be confirmed, how chaos theory shows that everything is arbitrary, and so on. A lot of this nonsense is catalogued by Gross and Levitt and then proclaimed by them to be "wrongheaded, even fatuous, theories about matters in which their [the postmodernists'] knowledge ranges from shallow to nonexistent."[14] It is the work of "unfocused bores, and a certain deliberate, cheerful simple-mindedness is needed to hear them out . . ."[15]

Unfortunately, something just as harsh is in order with respect to the nod Cheney and Warren give to ecosystem ecology. They are willing to grant the legitimacy of at least a part of contemporary ecology but only after they have pushed it through their a priori political strainer until it is the correct kind of intellectual mush. First, the name "hierarchy theory" must be swapped for something less "toxic" like "observation set theory."[16] Then observation sets must be understood not (as ecologists now understand them) as specific measurements of specific phenomena according to specific analytic techniques but, rather, as "ways of thinking" and "world views."[17] Then something will have to be done about ecology's "inattention to issues of power," and there will need to be "an analysis of power and power-over relationships."[18] Then, in addition to collecting data from the field, "the perspectives of women and indigenous peoples with regard to the natural environment [must] also be recognized as relevant 'data.'"[19] Then, as soon as ecologists realize that there really aren't any "hard data" in the world because trees, rivers, and animals are largely "socially constructed," everything will be fine.

Such advise will, no doubt, be invaluable in shaping the research programs of field biologists and also, perhaps, in determining future orders of lab equipment. This sort of "analysis" of a scientific theory is as vacuous as it is useless; it borders on mere free association. By similar gyrations one could turn hierarchy theory into a mush that would bear at least ten points of resemblance to fascism, astrology, or diesel engine repair.

Sometimes, attacks on science are disguised as attacks on something called "scientism." Robin Eckersley, for example, tells us that

> ecocentric theories are not against science or technology per se; rather they are against scientism (i.e., the conviction that empiric-analytic science is the only valid way of knowing) and technocentrism (i.e., anthropocentric technological optimism).[20]

But this is obviously a set of distinctions utterly without substance. *Nobody* believes that empirical science is the only way of knowing *everything*. Who has ever claimed that the only way of knowing what *Hamlet* was about or that "P implies P" is true is through empirical lab work? Likewise, don't we all believe that there is at least one question about which only empirical research will enlighten us? What reasonable person believes that anything but "empiric-analytic science" would have led to a pharmaceutical cure for polio or an understanding of the mechanisms involved in atmospheric ozone depletion? Similarly, no reasonable person has ever said that there is a technological solution for every human problem and no reasonable person has ever said that no human problem has a technical solution. The most that any reasonable person can defend is the proposition that *some* problems are open to scientific and technological solutions and some other problems are *only* open to such solutions. Thus "scientism" and "technocentrism" are positions that *nobody* with any sense holds, and so what is it that Eckersley is out to get if it is not science and technology *per se*?

In the end, postmodern ecocentrism and variants of ecocentrism like Eckersley's that buzz around the flames of postmodernism's hatred of science, rationality, and technology are not motivated by any well-grounded analysis of science, rationality, or technology. These positions are balanced on an openly a priori set of politically correct assumptions and an insistence that facts and reason itself must conform in some undefined way to those unanalyzed and unargued assumptions. As such, Callicott, Gross, and Levitt are right. In the new dark age of academic postmodernism it is only threat, idle rhetoric, harassment, and embarrassment that count.[21] There can be no *reasons* produced for accepting postmodernism nor any for rejecting it that will be acceptable to the postmodernists; it can only be shouted down.

CHAPTER 16

Wrongness and Wilderness

The general thesis of this chapter can be stated fairly bluntly: as concerns issues of wrongness (i.e., questions of social policy), there is nothing in principle different between environmental regulation and other forms of social regulation. Social coercion will be justified when, and only when, the type of action to be proscribed is legitimately proscribed according to the harm principle as defined and defended in Part I of this book.

Even under a wholly anthropocentric assumption (which I will dispense with shortly) about what can and cannot be harmed, considerable common sense is entailed by this position. Everything from national (or international) legislation regarding atmospheric damage to local zoning ordinances can find easy prima facie justification under the harm principle. In fact, the sort of reasoning demanded by the harm principle seems to be exactly the kind customarily offered up in serious disputes about environmental regulation. At the global level, advocates of restrictions on emissions of carbon or CFCs are expected to give some pretty compelling evidence of the harmful consequences of not restricting such emissions. At the national level, the same standards will be applied to determine the legitimacy of various clean air and water standards. Even at the local level, zoning restrictions will be justified on the basis of real harms of various kinds that will ensue without proper restraints on population density, traffic congestion, waste disposal, and so on. Serious local disputes about environmental policy are most likely to arise either when alleged harms are highly arguable or when no real harms seem to be targeted as would be the case, for example, with purely aesthetic standards or growth restraints in areas not at all even likely to be threatened with the evils of urban blight.

Wilderness preservation, as opposed to pollution control, is a tougher issue, especially under a purely anthropocentric assumption about what can be said to be harmed. But even here, arguments are routinely made that preservation of rainforests, old-growth woods, and wetlands is necessary because such areas almost certainly warehouse an abundance of irreplaceable raw materials (e.g., plants of pharmaceutical use) and unique processes the investigation of which might lead to surprising human uses in the future. Under the harm principle, these kinds of arguments are, no doubt, on shakier ground than are ones concerning restrictions of pollutants but, then, preservation has always been tougher to defend than conservation and pollution control. My approach, then, can be seen as, at least, locating difficulty where it really exists. Even with respect to pollution control, my approach locates difficulty where it really exists, namely, with the practicalities of how serious various kinds of pollution are and how costly it is to control them.

There is, however, a philosophical quandary underlying all such practicalities, specifically, the one I have skirted above concerning what kinds of things can and cannot be reasonably said to be harmable. Although I have briefly assumed an anthropocentric solution to this quandary in the last few paragraphs, there is no reason I have to be committed to this solution. One might think that the general reliance on contractarianism in Part I does commit me to such a position, but I don't think it does. Indeed, other contractarians have used the position to exclude all but rational (generally human) contractors from moral considerability, but the logic of their arguments fails me.

Certainly it is the case that only humans (and perhaps some other mammals or some hypothesized extraterrestrials or robots) can be reasoned with and, thus, can be parties to any contractual agreement to be civilized, but the issue of whether of not an entity can have moral considerability has nothing to do with whether it is a contractor. It has, rather, to do with whether the contractors can agree to include that entity in the domain of the directly morally considerable. And I have already mentioned some of the arguments that have been given by animal liberationists, biocentrists, and ecocentrists for the proposition that *we* (i.e., human contractors) ought to concede the conclusion that nonhumans can have goods of their own that we are rationally compelled to respect.

To argue that we don't have to respect the ends of nonhumans because they can't make us is to reduce contractarianism to a power-based ethic rather than what it ought to be—a reason-based ethic. To turn it into a power-based ethic would, of course, be to turn it into a system that would exclude not just nonhumans but all humans except the most powerful and threatening among us. Such a system would not have a shred of the virtue I claimed for it in Part I, namely, the virtue of being a system predicated on the assumption that the whole point of moralizing is so that we may be led by reason and persuasion rather than by brute force. If we are to be led only by force, then morality is as irrelevant as Marxists and postmodernists have (without much consistency) said it is.

However, conceding that nonhumans can be included in the domain of the morally considerable does little to help us determine how, exactly, we are to consider them. What are the exact ends of the individual lemming or salmon? How much weight are we to give to the ends of ecoli or the AIDS virus (if viruses are to be counted as living things)? Things only get worse when we move up to the level of ecosystems. What are the ends of the Mojave desert? How much weight do we give to the ecosystem that has been established in the Los Angeles basin? What is the status of the Diablo Canyon nuclear power plant given that it is now a key component in an (altered) ecosystem off the San Luis Obispo coast that would change (for the worse for some entities) if the plant were shut down? Don't nuclear power plants have goods of their own that ought to be respected?

I am not raising these questions as a sneaky way of intoning that they have no decent answers and, thus, that the animal liberationist, biocentric, and ecocentric positions that attempt sensible nonanthropocentric answers to them are wrong. I would point out that there is a real danger of anthropomorphism in coming up with such answers. Specifically, there is a danger that, in coming up with the natural ends of certain organisms or ecosystems, we will paternalistically substitute ends familiar to us as common human ends or common ends of human artifacts. This is a problem Callicott has pointed out with respect to animal liberationism of the utilitarian stripe.

> The neo-Benthamites [like Singer] have in a sense taken the uncourageous approach. People have attempted to exempt themselves from the life/death reciprocities of natural processes and from ecological limitations in the name of a prophylactic ethic of maximizing rewards (pleasure) and minimizing unwelcome information (pain). To be fair, the humane moralists seem to suggest that we should attempt to project the same values into the nonhuman animal world and to widen the charmed circle—no matter that it would be biologically unrealistic to do so or biologically ruinous if, per impossible, such an environmental ethic were implemented.[1]

But the problem of anthropomorphism can be expected to get worse as we move from mammals, which are quite like us in many important respects, to nonmammalian animals to plants and, then, to ecosystems. In fact, Callicott himself (along with a lot of other ecocentrists) often gets very close to a cousin of the anthropomorphic fallacy. In claims like Callicott's that

> From an ecological point of view . . . the living natural world is much more fully integrated and systematically unified than it had habitually been represented. The biotic mantle of the earth, from an ecological point of view, is one because *its living components are reciprocally coevolved and mutually interdependent.*[2]

or Eckersley's claim that ecocentrism recognizes the "interrelatedness of all phenomena"[3] or McGlaughlin's claim that an "ecologically inclusive ideology" entails the image that "all of nature is . . . an interconnected network,"[4] we get dangerously close to a general picture of nature that makes it out to be a human artifact, namely, a machine. The image of an entity where there is a tight interdependence between the parts, where (to use an often repeated claim of ecocentrists) "everything is connected to everything else" is certainly not that of anything organic. In organisms (and, for that matter, in ecosystems) there is always redundancy, functional irrelevance, and disconnection of parts. As ecologists will always point out, uniform tight interrelation of parts would doom an ecosystem because the smallest disturbance within the system would threaten the whole.[5] The same would apply to individual organisms; the smallest injury would take the organism out of the evolutionary loop. Thus, we have no good reason to believe that the organisms and ecosystems that we see around us are tightly organized because they have made it through a few evolutionary hurdles.

The only kind of system where there *is* a genuinely tight interrelation of parts, where there is nothing redundant and nothing superfluous is a well-*designed* machine. And, as we all know, the idea that natural entities, or nature as a whole, is like a well-designed machine is a very old (and a distinctly religious) idea that was effectively pulled apart by Hume over two hundred years ago. It is especially odd that this mechanical metaphor would slip into the thinking of ecocentrists since most of them reject the idea that nature is designed (presumably by God), and they also, generally, like to talk about how contemporary science has dispensed with the "mechanical" science of Descartes, Galileo, and Newton.

Historical oddity aside, the disconnectedness of nature and the attendant clash between what ecocentrists claim that scientific ecology is telling us about the world and what ecology is really telling us has been pointed out as a significant problem for modernist ecocentrists like Callicott.[6] Perhaps the most careful and influential critique of ecocentrism's use of ecology is Harley Cahen's "Against the Moral Considerability of Ecosystems."[7] Cahen makes use of a substantial body of ecological and biological literature to make it clear that, for several decades now, mainstream life science has been pretty thoroughly *individualistic*. The few strands of holism that can be found in the early history of ecology, and even in the biology of Darwin, have been rather systematically purged. Even moves somewhat short of ecological holism, such as the theory of group selection, have been relegated to the margins of biology. In fact, in the hands of scientists like Richard Dawkins, individualism has been pushed to the level of *super*individualism, which has it that apparent attributes of individual organisms (and the goals that can be attributed to them) are mere byproducts of natural selection going on at the level of genes.[8]

The fact that contemporary mainstream science is not in synch with modernist ecocentrism does not, of course, mean that positions like Callicott's are false. Biology and ecology were much more holistic in their orientation sixty years ago than they are now, and they might well be much more holistic than they are now in sixty years. This is not an issue that philosophers should feel confident in speculating about. Nevertheless, modernists like Callicott must admit that the power of their position is tied to the standards of current science, and the status *and drift* of contemporary biological science does not make Callicott's holism look very attractive.[9] This is especially the case if ecocentric holism is going to be couched within my theory of social policy. The burden of *proving* that a harm to an ecosystem is a real harm will be on the holist, and, right now anyhow, it doesn't look like the ecocentrists can meet that burden.

This leads us back to the interim forms of "extensionist" individualism. As difficult as it may be to assign a precise measure to the exact amounts of harm that can be caused to various nonhuman animals or plants and as difficult as it may be to avoid anthropomorphism in the process, not just animal liberationism but also biocentrism must be viewed as compelling positions. The individualism of contemporary biological theory speaks as clearly *for* the proposition that all individual living things have definable ends of their own as it does *against* the holistic proposition, and there is no compelling argument that such ends should not be given some prima facie respect that will not also entail that the ends of most humans should not be given even prima facie respect.

As biocentrists like Taylor make clear, the granting of prima facie respect does not imply, for plants, animals, or humans, the granting of any simplistic right to life for all living things. Any right to life (even a human's) is always subject to compromise given the nature of what Schweitzer called "the ghastly drama" of life. Nevertheless, the idea that, eventually, the most trivial interests of any human always trump even the most vital interests of any nonhuman seems a completely unreasonable alternative to the view that we should never kill anything for any reason. The right to kill can (morally and legally) hinge on a claim of self-defense, the preservation of autonomy, or other vital interests; it cannot be legitimately hinged on a belief that the dead party was ugly or just plain fun to kill.

The idea that this sort of logic that is routinely applied (often with great difficulty and vagueness) to relations between humans should be extended (even if such entails difficulty and vagueness) as much as possible to relations between humans and nonhumans is, as we saw before, the central idea in Taylor. While I do not want to be committed to all of the details of Taylor's theory about how the interests of humans and nonhumans should be balanced, I have no problem with his general position that there should be some balancing. Moreover, I am not sure that the balancing can be done with much more precision than he does it. There must be some admittedly imprecise distinction drawn between "basic" and "nonbasic" interests of humans and nonhumans and, further, some earnest and principled attempt to insure that the interests of nonhumans are not trivialized out of existence. As imprecise as this proposal may be, the idea that nonhumans ought to count *at all* is a significant philosophical move—one that I am willing to make.

Previously, I had mentioned that preservationism would be a fairly tough position to hold under my theory. The move I am making now of admitting harms to nonhumans into calculations concerning social policy would certainly seem to allow a more charitable view toward preservationism. Moreover, a lot of the pesky questions mentioned before (e.g., How much weight are we to give to the interests of the AIDS virus? How much weight are we to give to the interests of a nuclear power plant?) have some sort of decent answer. AIDS poses a deadly threat to humans. A simple appeal to self-defense would seem to allow us to defend ourselves even if we were to grant prima facie respect to the virus's ends. Nuclear power plants have no real ends of their own. They are not naturally selected organisms. Thus there is nothing in contemporary science that would force one to admit that such artifacts have any ends of their own; they are explicitly designed (as organisms are not) to fulfill certain human ends and, so, any tendencies or functional patterns they exhibit are really just human ones.

CHAPTER 17

Wisdom and Wilderness

As irrelevant as ecocentrism may turn out to be as regards questions of social policy, there is still something compelling about the view (in both its modernist and postmodernist forms) at a different level of concern, namely, the level of individual wisdom. For all of the policy implications Callicott claims for the land ethic and all of the communitarian posturing of the postmodernists and ecofeminists, there is something right about Bryan Norton's observation that

> American and Australian deep ecologists are not political revolutionaries; they represent an individualistic and spiritualist movement, seeking an "inner" transformation of persons rather than a mere change in political forms—a new consciousness, not a new government.[1]

He goes on to note that the individualism of American environmentalists is regularly a cause of their being hooted off the stage at European environmental conferences where the business of cleaning up the world is almost universally seen in starkly political (usually Marxist) terms. As an outsider to the American environmental tradition, the Indian sociologist Ramachandra Guha has argued in a widely reprinted article[2] that the whole debate between anthropocentrists and ecocentrists (and everyone in between) is "at best irrelevant and at worst a dangerous obfuscation." The real roots of environmental destruction are overconsumption by the rich and militarization, which helps keep the rich rich. Moreover, the antianthropocentric wing of the American environmental movement is really itself as much a simple outgrowth of runaway capitalist consumerism as is the old-time American conservationism of Gifford Pinchot. Wilderness is just another commodity in a country where "it is perfectly consistent to drive a thousand miles to spend a holiday in a national park." Furthermore, the allegedly global perspective of the ecocentrists is nothing but the platform for a new kind of imperialism; American scientists and ecotourists want other countries to leave their wilderness areas undeveloped not so that the miserably impoverished citizens of those countries can vacation in a nice park but, rather, so that Americans can vacation (or do funded research) in a foreign park as a pleasant change of pace from Yellowstone and Yosemite.

No matter how much Callicott wants ecocentrism to be seen as a universal moral theory with an equally universal scientific undergirding and no matter how much Cheney and Warren want ecocentrism (and ecofeminism) to be seen as inclusivist, both modernist and postmodernist ecocentrism drips with individualism, *egocentrism, and Americanism.* The degree to which ecocentrism is at least as much about the search for self as it is about the search for any kind of theory about social policy is indicated in the following passages from ecocentrists, all of whom are quoted favorably by Callicott:[3]

From John Seed:

> As the implications of evolution and ecology are internalized . . . there is an identification with all life. . . . Alienation subsides. . . . "I am protecting the rain forest" develops to "I am part of the rain forest protecting myself. I am part of the rain forest recently emerged into thinking."

From Paul Shepard:

> in one respect the self is an arrangement of organs, feelings, and thoughts—a "me"—surrounded by a hard body boundary: skin, clothes, and insular habits. . . . The alternative [aspect] is a self as a center of organization, constantly drawing on and influencing the surroundings. . . . Ecological thinking . . . requires a kind of vision across boundaries. The epidermis of the skin is ecologically like a pond surface or a forest soil, not a shell so much as delicate interpenetration. It reveals the self ennobled and extended . . . as part of the landscape and the ecosystem.

From Holmes Rolston III:

> Does not my skin resemble this lake surface? Neither lake nor self has independent being. . . . Inlet waters have crossed this interface and are now embodied within me. . . . The waters of North Inlet are part of my circulatory system; and the more literally we take this truth the more nearly we understand it. I incarnate the solar energies that flow through this lake. No one is free living. . . . *Bios* is intrinsically symbiosis.

From Shepard again:

> Internal complexity, as the mind of a primate, is an extension of natural complexity measured by the variety of plants and animals and the variety of nerve cells—organic extensions of each other.
>
> The exuberance of kinds [is] the setting in which a good mind could evolve (to deal with a complex world). . . . The idea of natural complexity as a counterpart to human intricacy is essential to an ecology of man.

From Cheney we get an endorsement of the point of view of Edith Cobb who relates the story of a child named Alice who is "surrounded by empty psychological space" and is, in fact, "schizophrenic."

> In one situation only is Alice embedded in a geography larger than her own closed-in self. This occurs in yearly visits to the family summer home, when a "sea change" comes over her in the context of an immersion in the natural world. Alice's lyrical portrait of these summers poignantly illustrates the necessity of landscape for the coherent construction of the self.[4]

Thus we see, as Tom Jay did, that "psychology without ecology is lonely and vice versa."[5]

Regardless of all of the anti-Cartesian posturing of both Callicott and Cheney, there is soul searching afoot here, soul searching of a sort that is, as I said before, painfully (though, I'd say, happily) American. It is the search for what Holmes Rolston III has called "a storied residence," the search for a meaning to life that has nothing to do with semantics, truth conditions, and the circumstances under which *sentences* have content but everything to do with how a *life* can have content and richness. And, at this point, there is an important convergence of Callicott's modernism, Cheney's postmodernism, and a distinctively American understanding of the significance of the wilderness experience and wilderness narrative that is best not lost in the minutia of internecine theoretical squabbles. The wilderness experience has been revered by a long line of American thinkers (clearly including both Callicott and Cheney) for essentially the reasons being put forward by Cheney and the postmodernists. The wilderness can provide not just the sort of casual encounter through the windshield of a Winnebago that Guha derides but, rather, a deeply personal reconnection to things important, real, and meaningful. The wilderness experience is not a mere escape from the senselessness and fragmentation of modern life (although it is at least that); it is an opportunity, to use an unfortunately tired phrase, to "find oneself."

Among American writers, the works of Thoreau, Muir, Leopold, Abbey, and a host of contemporary writers attest to the centrality of the wilderness experience and its narrative recounting in American thinking about nature. What is characteristic, and characteristically American, of almost all of these narratives is their *individualism*. The degree to which it is useful to describe the writings of Thoreau, Muir, or Abbey as "antianthropocentric" is, as Callicott points out, the degree to which there is a clear scent of simple misanthropy in the air. The wilderness has always been a place to go to get away from other people and the shallowness of social life. From Thoreau, for example, we hear:

I wish to speak for Nature, for absolute freedom and wilderness, as con-
trasted with a freedom and culture merely civil—to regard man as an
inhabitant, or a part and parcel of Nature, rather than a member of society. . . . If you would go to the political world, follow the great road—follow that market-man, keep his dust in your eyes, and it will lead you
straight to it; for it, too, has its place merely, and does not occupy all
space. . . . I must walk toward Oregon, and not toward Europe.[6]

Misanthropy shows more clearly in Abbey's statement (mentioned previously) that he would rather shoot a man than a snake or Muir's wish
that alligators may "occasionally enjoy a mouthful of terror-stricken
man, by way of a dainty." Thoreau, Muir, and Abbey were decidedly not
trying to form a better community; they were trying to get away from it.

For all of his talk about "contextualizing narrative as the means for
locating oneself in a moral space out of which a whole and healthy self,
community, and earth can emerge,"[7] much of what Cheney denounces as
"colonizing," "totalizing" and "essentializing" cannot be seriously seen as
just "discourse." What is *really* colonizing, totalizing, and essentializing is
precisely what social life—life in the community—has become. What real
threat is posed by the *discourse* of poor old Rene Descartes compared to
the virtually inescapable tyranny, banality, and dreadful finality of a bad
job in a big city?

It is utterly unclear what sort of community Cheney and the postmodernists generally would like to see built on earth, and they are, of
course, by their own admissions, generally, not in the business of making
any serious suggestions about the structure of laws and institutions that
would be best. They seem mostly interested in simply "deconstructing"
what they see passing as civil society now. For the most part, I am
tempted to see the reconstructive communitarianism that runs through a
lot of postmodernism (including Cheney's) as an awkward attempt to
nail something politically correct onto an individualistic Nietzschean edi-
fice that will not support such politeness.

Be this as it may, the coupling of the idea that an "unstoried" life is
barely worth living and the idea that much of contemporary social life
lacks such a storied integration has some other roots—ones that grow out
of the most American of soils: the pragmatism of John Dewey. Although
I think it is hard to make Dewey out to be much of an environmentalist,[8]
the theory that emerges from his most philosophical works contains an
interesting position on the nature of experience and meaning that can,
without too much violence, be turned into a useful analysis of the wilderness experience and, moreover, that bears more than a superficial resemblance to the main drift of postmodern ecocentrism.

Although most of Dewey's writings deal with practical matters of
politics and, especially, matters of education, the two works that have

received the most attention from philosophers are *Experience and Nature* (1925) and *Art as Experience* (1934). The reason for this is pretty simple. At a time when linguistic analyses of meaning were at the center of almost all of the research projects going on in Anglo-American philosophy, Dewey proposed (as Nietzsche had before and as postmodernists do now) a radically different theory about how it was *experiences* (not *propositions*) that were importantly meaningful or meaningless but that still held (as Nietzsche and the postmodernists don't) scientific activity in as high a regard as did even the sternest of the logical positivists.

Briefly put, experiences were meaningful for Dewey to the degree that they were experienced as having a "consummatory" character. In the consummatory experience there is a structure, an integration, of all of the parts of the experience into a significant whole. It is marked off in the mind as *an* experience with an identity of its own. It has a clear beginning, middle, and a consummatory end. Whatever may develop as means in such an experience are tied in consciousness to the end, the successful resolution of the activity. To import some terminology used previously, it is precisely this unified and "storied" character of meaningful experience that makes it "esthetic."

Meaningless experience (the anesthetic, if you will) lacks this kind of experiential organization. It is slack, means are psychologically distanced from ends, or ends are mindlessly felt without any connection to means. An easy example of the sort of activity where means are endured without any clear connection to ends is what constitutes work for most people: the drudgery of performing the same task over and over without ever getting to finish anything, of putting lug nuts on car after car with as little a conception as is possible of actually taking part in the production of something that is of value to someone else. Better in such situations to not think of what you're doing at all, to perform it mindlessly until the whistle blows.

Mindlessness is, indeed, a reasonable strategy even after the whistle blows in a life where nothing is really connected to anything final, where money is made to buy things so they can break and be replaced and break and be replaced again. The antidote to this sort of fragmented existence—what will be expected of the "arts" in a disjointed society—is a parade of cheap consummations to impossibly simplified experiences received vicariously through phony TV characters. Fragmentation is met with more fragmentation; means and ends appear and disappear from consciousness and fade into a sort of psychic cubism.

Real art, for Dewey, does much more than to simply toss up disembodied consummations. Real art guides us through serious complications and on to interesting and truly satisfying resolutions. Insofar as it succeeds, it mirrors meaningful life. Art is not something that removes us from experience; it is not something to be pillaged for a Kantian "disinterested satisfaction." Meaningful experience *is* artistic, and real art should be met with all of the personal interest of the most deadly practical problem.

Dewey points out at some length the importance that myth and ritual has traditionally had in endowing the otherwise mundane with art. Work informed by myth is no longer mere labor; it is drama. "It was not conscience that kept men loyal to cults and rites, and faithful to tribal myths," he tells us, "it was the enjoyment of the drama of life . . . that kept piety from decay."[9] But it would be completely out of character for Dewey to suggest (as some postmoderns seem to) that a return tribalism is the cure for the fragmentation and alienation of contemporary social life. Rather, he saw the joy of scientific curiosity and problem solving and the genuine infusion of the experimental method into all aspects of our lives as providing the course to meaning in modern life. Science (both theoretical and applied) is, for Dewey, too enriching and too much fun to be left, as it largely has been, to a handful of geniuses in isolated laboratories. Hence, Dewey's intense desire to reform education so that it would build upon the natural desire of humans to experiment, to think for themselves, and to discover and solve increasingly intriguing mysteries in the natural world rather than to bore the general run of students sufficiently to leave only the most durable of minds to form the ranks of a technocratic elite.

Had Dewey much of a feel for the wilderness he might well have said a great deal about the value of the wilderness experience. What is typical of the wilderness experience is that it places upon us the same sort of demand to foresee, understand, and solve problems that true scientific investigation does. Moreover, there is an economy and a clear connection of means to ends about living in the wild that is usually lacking in life in the urban wastelands. Activities are not generally undertaken out of boredom or out of some distant and dimly perceived foreign end but, rather, out of a real need to solve real problems that are really *your* problems. Distances are walked to find suitable shelter. Fish are caught to eat. Firewood is gathered to cook. And attention is paid to everything, for there is little that is routine and predictable on turf controlled by bears, scorpions, or alligators rather than by bureaucrats.

In short, everything has a story in the wild, and one that makes sense and has meaning. These are not the stories of other times and other peoples fancifully burgled and fenced into the present. These are the stories of real living beings pursuing their own goods. The narratives of Thoreau, Muir, and Leopold are not those of long-gone tribal cultures but, rather, those of serious students of nature and of what science tells us about the interdependence as well as about the individuality of living things. These are also the stories of who the narrators are.

Similarly, our own stories will be stories about who we are. How we handle ourselves under the pressures that the wilderness can bring to bear on us has everything to do with this question of personal identity. Perhaps we don't just "find ourselves" in the wild the way we just find our lost pens in our clothes dryers. Perhaps, rather, we *make* ourselves under such conditions. We see who we are, who we can be, and even who we *ought* to be, free of the trappings of the artificial social positions that we, by and large, just luck into and out of.

The analysis of the wilderness experience I am suggesting here preserves much of what is insightful and right about what the postmodernists have to say about environmental matters. Meaning is a function of context, history, and aesthetic integration. But the analysis gets this result without alternating among misology, pseudoscience, and a patronizing political politeness that has it that just about every other culture that has gone before us has known more about nature than we do. It also preserves the spirit of that slightly misanthropic and anarchistic tradition of American narrative that includes Thoreau, Muir, Leopold, Abbey, and Callicott.

It is an account that can bring environmentalists—at least American environmentalists—of various camps together around a central theory of ecological *wisdom*. As important and as enduring as disputes about environmental *social policy* may be, a shared sense of why, exactly, the wilderness is important to us *as individuals*—a shared wisdom about the wild—is of no less significance. Perhaps the American love of nature must remain a mystery and an object of scorn for Guha and the Greens. But, there is no reason for it to be a point of divisiveness or embarrassment *for us*.

NOTES

INTRODUCTION

1. Gerald Marzorati, "Europe Recycles American Liberalism." *New York Times* (July 7, 1990).

2. Nozick, *Anarchy, State and Utopia* (New York: Basic Books, 1974).

3. By "descriptive adequacy" I mean, roughly, "in accordance with thoughtful common opinion." Aside from being vague, this kind of adequacy can hardly be seen as either necessary or sufficient for real adequacy. Common opinion often turns out to be absurd, and the apparently absurd often turns out to be true. Nevertheless, I take it that descriptive inadequacy is at least a prima facie reason to suspect that something is wrong with a theory.

4. The kinds of theories of the good I am concerned about here are those that would posit a notion of the good *for all*. As we shall see later, I am not at all opposed to the development of theories of the good, as these would be freely adopted *by individuals for themselves*. (Such theories are what Part II of this book is all about.) Also, I am not opposed to pyrrhic theories of the good that would define the good as the avoidance of wrongdoing and the protection of individuals' rights to do whatever is not wrong.

5. One might be inclined to think that I have, at this point, drastically overstepped both "the common moral sense of the liberal West" and Mill's position by ruling out any kind of social welfare mechanisms. Such mechanisms, it might be argued, will find their justification precisely in the fact that they will further the good, not just prevent harm. As we shall see (in Chapter 7), most of the welfare mechanisms (and the taxation necessary to support them) that would meet with wide support in the West *can* be justified under my view and, more importantly, can be justified without appealing to a conception of the good.

CHAPTER 1. SELF AND STATE: A HISTORICAL PERSPECTIVE

1. See especially section 462.

2. Sen and Runciman, "Games, Justice and the General Will," *Mind* 74 (1965): 554–562. For a criticism of this interpretation, see Jon Elster's "The Market and the Forum: Three Varieties of Political Theory," in J. Elster and A. Hylland (eds.), *Foundations of Social Choice Theory* (New York: Cambridge University Press, 1989), pp. 103–132.

3. *Principles of Morals and Legislation*, Chapter I, Sections IV–VIII. These passages also make it clear that, for Bentham, the *state* should be viewed as no

more than the agent of "the happiness of the *community*" (emphasis added). Thus, when Bentham speaks of the relationship between the individual and the community, he is also speaking of that between the individual and the state.

4. The idea that contractual agreements need to be *unanimous* is a complicated one. Obviously, the desired unanimity can be hypothesized only for individuals who are, to some degree, rational. Just how rational the individuals in a contractual situation must be will be a major concern of Chapter 8.

5. We can lay out the conflict here as follows:

		B	
		brutal	*civil*
A	*brutal*	2, 1	3, 0
	civil	1, 3	0, 2

This is based on the assumption that A's first preference is for the state of affairs where he is brutal and B is a willing victim. His second choice is for them both to be brutal, his third for him to be suffering for B's sake, and his last for them both to be peaceful. B's first choice is for her to benefit at the expense of A, her second for them both to be peaceful, her third for them both to be brutal, and her last for her to be the victim of B. The equilibrium outcome here is for them both to be brutal. Neither party is better served by any other outcome that would be mutually consented to.

6. The situation here can be laid out as follows:

		B	
		apples	*oranges*
A	*apples*	1, 0	1, 1
	oranges	0, 0	0, 1

The only outcome that is either optimal or in equilibrium is that in which both get what they want, that is, A gets apples and B gets oranges. No contract is needed to arrive at this outcome.

7. Moreover, the preceding discussion may account for the fact that careful nonlibertarian contract theorists like Rawls spend so much time being precise about a theory of basic human goods—even if they have been noticeably unsuccessful in securing any agreement (even among philosophers) about them.

8. These rights, once established, are entitled to protection. As Mill put it (in the fifth chapter of *Utilitarianism*), "When we call anything a person's right, we mean that he has a valid claim upon society to protect him in the possession of it, either by the force of law or by that of education and opinion." Accordingly, negative rights will have a tendency to turn into positive rights. For example, if it is determined that there is no good reason for the state to have an interest in the colors of my interior walls, then I will have a negative right to paint them whatever

color I want. If someone tried to interfere with this negative right, then I might be able to appeal to various positive rights (e.g., property rights, privacy rights, etc.) that the state could impose on my behalf simply because it has already determined that things like wall painting are things that the society should have no interest in. The distinction I am drawing here between negative and positive rights, then, has much less to do with the exact nature of the rights actually granted and protected by the state than it does with the rationale that the state may legitimately have in introducing rights for anyone to do anything. Positive rights theories (like Locke's) tend to justify rights in terms of their *sui generis* moral status; rights will be seen as things that all individuals have and thus as things that ought to be guaranteed by all societies. Negative rights theorists (like Mill) will tend to justify rights in terms of what societies *cannot prove* to be of legitimate social concern. The class of things that people have a right to do because there is some a priori claim that they do and the class of things that people have a right to do because there is no good societal claim to the contrary are hardly coextensive classes, however.

9. That both Hobbes and Rousseau go way beyond libertarianism in their specific legislative recommendations does not demonstrate that the points I have been trying to make are all wrong. The differences between either Hobbes or Rousseau and a libertarian may not be differences about fundamental principles concerning the legitimation of social coercion but, rather, differences about what is actually required under varying social conditions for the preservation of civility. There may also be differences with respect to what exactly "civility" amounts to. So, that Hobbes drifted off toward authoritarianism and Rousseau drifted off toward socialism may not imply a difference between either of them and the libertarian about principles and ends but, rather, only a difference about facts and means. In other words, the variances among the practical prescriptions of Hobbes, Rousseau, and the libertarian do not necessarily imply that either Hobbes or Rousseau did not see the contract as a mechanism for restricting the range of legitimate social coercion. Rather, all that may be implied is that they and the libertarian differ on the issue of just how much coercion is necessary to enforce civility (and, of course, they may have different ideas about what exactly "civility" requires).

CHAPTER 2. SELF AND STATE: A THEORETICAL PERSPECTIVE

1. *Principles of Morals and Legislation*, Chapter I, Section II.

2. "Bentham," in J. B. Schneewind (ed.), *Mill's Essays on Literature and Society* (New York: Macmillan Company, 1965), p. 266.

3. Sen, *Collective Choice and Social Welfare* (San Francisco: Holden-Day, 1970).

4. "Lady Chatterley's Lover and Doctor Fischer's Bomb Party: Liberalism, Pareto Optimality, and the Problem of Objectionable Preferences," in Elster and Hylland, pp. 11–43.

5. "The Purpose and Significance of Social Choice Theory: Some General Remarks and an Application to the 'Lady Chatterly Problem,'" in Elster and Hylland, pp. 45–74.

CHAPTER 3. UTILITY AND SOCIAL ETHICS

1. It is important to emphasize that I am only intent here on commenting on *general* strategies open to the utilitarian. Given the volumes upon volumes of objections that have been lodged against the theory, it would be folly to pretend that I could give detailed rebuttals to any substantial portion of them here.

2. Simple though it may be, the empirically verifiable claim that a dollar means more to a poor person than it does to a rich person (i.e., the poor person is willing to perform more labor for it than a rich person is) implies a resolution of a common complaint against utilitarianism (especially welfare utilitarianism). The complaint centers around the possibility of what Nozick calls "utility monsters" (see his *Anarchy, State and Utopia*, p. 41). Nozick's objection is based on the hypothesis of the existence of a being who is capable of absorbing so much pleasure that the suffering of a large number of other beings is of little hedonic importance. In other words, this being is so insatiable that, no matter how much of any kind of welfare others may receive from a distribution of a bundle of goods to them, the utility monster receives more. The resolution of this problem I have in mind follows from the simple denial of the existence of such a being; sentient beings on this planet just don't operate the way Nozick is supposing them to, and utilitarianism was never proposed to do more than work for all sentient beings on this planet.

3. "The H-Bomb Secret," *Progressive* 43 (November 1979): 6–8, 14–45.

4. Philip Agee, *Inside the Company: CIA Diary* (New York: Stonehill Publishing, 1975). In a subsequent work, *Dirty Work* (Secaucus: Lyle Stuart Inc., 1978), Agee gives over four hundred pages of biographies and two sections entitled "Who's Who" and "Who's Where" (see pp. 319–743).

5. See Rescher's *Distributive Justice: A Constructive Critique of the Utilitarian Theory of Distribution* (Indianapolis: Bobbs-Merrill, 1968).

6. See Parfit's "Overpopulation and the Quality of Life," in Jonathan Glover (ed.), in *Utilitarianism and Its Critics* (New York: Macmillan, 1990), pp. 134–150.

7. This (along with other considerations that will be discussed later) will avoid the possibility of an objection that my view would entail the rightness of a society of anesthetized morons.

8. The term is Jonathan Harrison's. See his "Utilitarianism, Universalization, and Our Duty to Be Just," *PAS* 53 (1952–53): 105–134.

9. This line of argument is at the core of David Lyons critique of rule utilitarianism in *Forms and Limits of Utilitarianism* (New York: Oxford University Press, 1965).

His conclusion was that, by the time we are done with all of the relevant specifications of all of the rules, any rule utilitarian theory will collapse into simple act utilitarianism.

10. A natural objection at this point would be that action is no more flimsy a target than social policy. Such policies can, after all, be either specific or general, applied to jurisdictions large or small, applied rigidly or loosely, and so on. These kinds of complications will be taken up in Chapters 4 and 5, but it is worth pointing out here that one consequence of these later arguments will be that, to

the degree that the effects of the enforcement of a policy are uncertain, the state will have more of a problem in justifying the enforcement. As we shall see, the burden of showing that any given policy will have certain costs and benefits falls to whatever social agency is seeking to enforce it. Thus, if any particular policy is too flimsy a target for utilitarianism then, perhaps, that is reason to think that the policy should not be enacted. Applying a parallel strategy in the case of individual action won't work, however, because, for the most part, no action will be sanctioned.

CHAPTER 4. UTILITY AND INDIVIDUAL ETHICS

1. The work of John Harsanyi has been especially influential in establishing the formal respectability of cardinal and interpersonal considerations. See his "Cardinal Welfare, Individualistic Ethics, and Interpersonal Comparisons of Utility," *Journal of Political Economy* 63 (1955): 309–321.

2. Scriven, "Plato's 'Democratic Man' and the Implausibility of Preference Utilitarianism," *Theory and Decision* 24 (1988): 43–55.

3. For an elaboration of this line of argument see my "Utility, Autonomy and Drug Regulation," *International Journal of Applied Philosophy* 2 (Fall 1984): 27–42.

4. See Harsanyi's "Rule Utilitarianism and Decision Theory," *Erkenntnis* 11 (1977): 25–53.

5. Elster, *Sour Grapes: Studies in the Subversion of Rationality* (New York: Cambridge University Press, 1983). See especially pages 1–15.

6. The kind of problem Elster is concerned with is different than the one I will bring up inasmuch as he is concerned with the problem of unicity (i.e., of generating a single best alternative) in terms of *given* preferences whereas I am concerned with unicity in terms of a hedonistic theory of utility. Moreover, he is concerned with unicity at the level where individuals try to optimize their own utility as well as the one where they try to maximize collective utility. I am, at this point, only concerned with the problem of judging individual alternatives from the collective point of view. My conclusion is as pessimistic as his: we can't get unicity or anything close enough to it to be at all practically useful.

7. There are many responses a utilitarian might make to this line of objection. One would be that there are often antecedent social conventions (which are, in turn, based on utility) that may be appealed to in order to decide between equally optimal alternatives. This is, no doubt, true. But this line of argument will not establish that utilitarianism has no problem at the individual level. The relevant conventions will be the result of various institutional arrangements that, in turn, are the products of various social policies to establish and maintain those institutions. That utilitarianism in some form, construed *as a social ethic*, could provide a satisfactory, albeit indirect, way of steering individuals away from certain courses of action and toward others is, of course, not a thesis I would want to deny. The important question is one about how indirect such utilitarian guidance ought to be. As we shall see, I think it ought to be *very* indirect; certainly it ought to be more indirect than anything that would count as "rule utilitarianism."

8. Mill, *Autobiography* in Max Lerner (ed.), *The Essential Works of John Stuart* (New York: Bantam Books, 1963), p. 83.

9. Taylor, *Good and Evil* (New York: Macmillan Company, 1970), pp. 93–94.

10. One might think that Feinberg should be included in this list since he, at one point defines "harm" as "setbacks to interests." See his *Harm to Others* (New York: Oxford University Press, 1984), p. 36. However, he is extremely careful about what should count as a *legitimate* interest, and, so, I would not include him with Mill or Harsanyi here.

CHAPTER 5. UTILITY, HARM, AND LIBERTY

1. This claim is in need of considerable clarification and some substantial modification. For example, severe psychological suffering and death would appear to be as universally loathed (among humans anyway) as is simple physical pain. The required clarifications and modifications will occur later.

2. This view is at variance with Bentham's (and others'). With his usual attention to detail, he lists almost as many kinds of "simple pains" (twelve) as he does "simple pleasures" (fourteen). However, most of the pains he talks about are just frustrations of the various pleasures he lists (see his *Principles of Morals and Legislation*, Chapter V). Moreover, the idea that pleasures can be so simply enumerated smacks of a philistinism that would be rejected by later utilitarians.

3. It is also central in Feinberg's work. See *Harm to Others*, p. 3, and the other passages referred to on page 3.

4. See his *Harm to Others*, Chapter 4.

5. Kant, *Perpetual Peace and Other Essays*, Ted Humphrey (ed. and trans.) (Indianapolis: Hackett Publishing, 1983), p. 135.

6. Marx, *The German Ideology*, C. J. Arthur (ed.) (New York: International Publishers, 1978), pp. 109–114.

CHAPTER 6. REFINEMENTS

1. It is important to note that I am aiming at a *stipulative* definition of harm here. That such a stipulation is at variance with any ordinary connotations of the word "harm" may be a prima facie reason to suspect that the stipulation is inadequate, depending upon the degree of the variance. Such a variance is not, however, in and of itself a reason to reject the stipulation.

2. I know of no one who claims that harm can be defined simply as the frustration of any desire.

3. I am aware that this "mostly verbal" difference opens my argument to a substantive charge. It can be argued that I am begging an important question against the offense principle and legal moralism (or, at least, what Feinberg calls "broad legal moralism") in that both principles are bound to be excluded from the range of the harm principle simply because the words "harm," "offense," and "moral harm" *mean* different things to begin with. However, I will eventually be

arguing that many kinds of activities that appear to be merely offensive or morally degenerate can, eventually, be the target of legitimate social control on the basis of their potential or indirect harmfulness. Thus, I may be begging the question against the offense *principle*, but I am not committed to the view that the routine *examples* of offensive behavior are immune from sanction.

4. Feinberg, *Harm to Others*, p. 3. Everyone understands that the law and informal public opinion are hardly disjoint. An overwhelming moral opinion is quite likely to, eventually, find its way into the law. (Although this is not always the case as demonstrated by the fact that prayer in public schools is not allowed in the United States although a firm majority of Americans think that it ought to be.) Likewise a liberalization of the law is likely to, eventually, result in a liberalizing of moral opinions. An example of this happening is to be found with respect to the laws and attitudes connected with divorce. As "no fault" divorce laws have been enacted in the United States, public opinion has drifted toward the view that divorce should carry no moral stigma; whether or not a marriage should have been dissolved is now generally thought to be a private matter about which others should hold their tongues (in public at any rate). A more troublesome example concerns abortion. Twenty years of legalized abortion has hardly settled all of the moral arguments on this topic. As we shall see later (especially in Chapter 8) my position will tend toward the view that whatever cannot be justified in the *ideal* law should not be subject to any other kind of sanction (other than internal prudential sanctions, like the feeling that one has acted stupidly or immaturely). Thus, my approach will tend to converge on Feinberg's inasmuch as he is also trying to establish the moral limits of the ideal law (although he is not attempting to claim that the demands of the ideal law will exhaust the demands of morality). Even so, there will remain one huge gulf between my view and his, namely, that the ideal law, for me, will have a quasi-utilitarian base whereas Feinberg is, ultimately, a rights theorist.

5. Feinberg, *Harm to Others*, p. 36.

6. Ibid., p. 105–106.

7. It should be noted that I am not the only person around making this claim that the realms of morality and harmfulness (as filtered through some harm principle) are coextensive. The position has also been defended by A. D. Woozley, "Law and the Legislation of Morality," in A. L. Caplan and D. Callahan (eds.), *Ethics in Hard Times* (New York: Plenum, 1981), pp. 143–174. (Mill, of course, is another person who defended the view, at least in *On Liberty*.) As Feinberg points out (*Harm to Others*, p. 165), such a move brings about a theory that is a bit of an anomaly under his analysis of what constitutes genuine liberalism. He lays out four liberty-limiting principles (the harm principle, the offense principle, legal paternalism, and legal moralism) and then insists that a genuine liberal will accept the harm principle, a limited version of the offense principle, but will reject legal paternalism and legal moralism. However, someone who accepts only the harm principle and then reduces the entire moral realm down to considerations of harmfulness becomes a legal moralist (even though the resulting theory is going to be even more liberal than Feinberg's). My theory is even more anomalous under Feinberg's analysis, for I accept the harm principle, reject the offense principle, accept some degree of paternalism as an inherent logical consequence of the harm principle, and (for the same reasons Mill and Woozley become committed to

the view) wind up committed to legal moralism as well. Still, my theory has consequences that are, in many important ways, more liberal (or, better yet, more libertarian) than Feinberg's. My views on offensiveness are, as we are about to see, certainly more libertarian than Feinberg's.

8. There is a small oddity in the claim that death is a harm. As Feinberg points out (*Harm to Others*, pp. 79–83), death, strictly speaking, is what occurs the split second one ceases to exist as a sentient being. As such, how can it count as a harm? There is, at the precise moment death occurs, nothing to be harmed. Feinberg gets around this problem by cashing out the harmfulness of death in terms of setbacks to interests the dead can have posthumously because of the existence of interests prior to death. For example, I might have an interest today that I get paid tomorrow that would be set back by my death tonight. Likewise, I might have an interest now in being remembered as a good person that would be set back by the spread of malicious and untrue rumors about me after my death. Feinberg thinks that I would be "posthumously harmed" by these rumors. I am inclined to take a more straightforward route out of the whole quagmire. I will simply refine my claim to one that has it that the immediate causes of death (i.e., the necessary and sufficient conditions of death as they are arranged just before death) constitute what is to be counted as harmful. This solves the "problem of the subject" Feinberg is worried about. Moreover, the undesirability of this state is just as unanimously agreed to as is the undesirability of the state of death. This also gets me around the general oddness of maintaining that there are "posthumous harms" at all. Frankly, I am inclined to the intuition that you can't harm anyone who is dead.

9. Derek Parfit, "On Doing the Best for Our Children," in M. D. Bayles (ed.), *Ethics and Population* (Cambridge, MA: Schenkman, 1976). The counterexample is discussed by Feinberg in his *Harm to Others*, pp. 100–104 and his *Harmless Wrongdoing* (New York: Oxford, 1988), pp. 27–28.

10. Mill, *On Liberty*, Chapter V (par. 7).

11. Although people who have lost all of their possessions because of some natural disaster commonly report that the experience has convinced them how little material possessions mean when they were, indeed, lucky to have just walked away alive and uninjured. Still, probably most such people would have gladly suffered broken arms in lieu of demolished houses.

12. How far such property rights should extend is being deliberately left open here. Whether or not one's holdings in a corporation should get the same protection as simple personal possessions is something I am not prepared to deal with directly, and the topic is extraneous to the issue at hand anyhow. Even if all possessions (including one's clothes and pens) are presumed under some radically communistic system to be the property of the state, there will still be the question of whether or not the state's property rights should be protected. Any political system must generate a set of entitlement rights or, at least, quasi-entitlement rights. Even where all of the underwear and socks in the land are, technically, state property, the state will have to delegate provisional custody to individuals and then delegate provisional custody rights to these individuals. My claim is that the basic kinds of larceny and vandalism that are protected everywhere (even where dental fillings are, technically, state property) will find easy justification under my theory even though it

restricts the basic set of harms to harms against persons, strictly speaking.

13. This example belongs to Feinberg, "'Harmless Immoralities' and Offensive Nuisances," in *Issues in Law and Morality* (Cleveland: Case Western Reserve University Press, 1973), pp. 99–134.

14. There has recently been a case where the connection between offensiveness and harm has been tested. In Portland, Oregon a leader of the White Aryan Resistance (WAR) was successfully sued for several million dollars. The grounds for the finding were not based on the offensiveness of the propaganda of WAR but, rather, on the fact that the leadership of WAR had gone far beyond the publications of outrageously racist material in that it systematically recruited, trained, and coordinated young men (skinheads) to carry out attacks on "nonaryans." The whole affair goes to the point that some kinds of indecent rhetoric, by virtue of their connection to ideologies that preach unjustifiable violence, may pose the threat of harm in their very expression in that such expression is almost invariably connected to organized harmful activities.

15. See Feinberg, *Offense to Others* (New York: Oxford, 1988), pp. 10–13.

16. Feinberg is aware that such questions can be raised against his offense principle, as can questions about whether or not interracial couples should have been prosecuted in the South a few decades ago because their mere presence (let alone their public appearance) was deeply offensive to rednecks. Feinberg covers himself by abandoning his earlier reliance on a strict universality criterion in favor of considerations involving the "magnitude" of the offense as it is determined by a weighing of the activity's "intensity," "duration," and "extent." I think there is a cleaner solution, namely, that the offensiveness of the handicapped person or of the African American cannot possibly be linked to any conceivable motive to disturb. No one changes his or her skin color or inflicts upon him or herself a disabling disorder in order to disgust or annoy. In such cases there is no reason to believe that one's skin color or physical condition is concocted out of some motive that, it is reasonable to suspect, might eventually move one to the infliction of harm in order to reach new heights of annoyance. It is, however, reasonable to believe that those who go out of their ways to annoy just for the sake of annoying will stop at nothing in their quest or, possibly, that they are victims of some psychosis over which they have no real control and that might well eventuate in harm to others. Again, the reason why we must endure some forms of offense but not others is that the latter pose some potential threat of harm whereas the former do not; the issue should, in the final analysis, be one about harm, not mere offense.

17. Those desiring more elaborate critiques of this variety of legal moralism can turn to Feinberg's *Harmless Wrongdoing* or H. L. A. Hart's *Law, Liberty and Morality* (Stanford: Stanford University Press, 1963).

CHAPTER 7. APPLICATIONS

1. See Lord Thomas Macaulay, "Notes on the Indian Penal Code," in *Works*, vol. 9 (New York: Houghton, Mifflin & Co., 1900, pp. 551–734.

2. Feinberg, *Harm to Others*, p. 158.

3. See Feinberg, ibid., pp. 138–143 for a discussion of the distinction.

4. See Chapter V (pars. 12–14) of Mill's *On Liberty*. It is important to note that Mill's proposal differs from many contemporary voucher proposals in that he does not advocate the distribution of vouchers to anyone except those who would otherwise not be able to afford to pay for the education of their children; he did not advocate that the rich should get the same benefits that the poor would. It should also be pointed out that there may be irresolvable pragmatic difficulties with any kind of voucher system. These might well force any Millian to abandon the idea and support a more-or-less state-run system. This issue, as all other concrete policy issues, cannot be settled purely at the level of principle.

5. It must be pointed out that leaving health care insurance to the private sector may not avoid the underlying problem here. Private insurers can effect infringements upon various risky activities just as easily as a state insurer can. By threatening termination of private policies unless the client ceases the risky activity or refusing to cover any damages that result from those activities, the private insurer can make the activity too risky for the individual to contemplate. (Of course, policyholders may find the restrictions of one company too restrictive and search for another, but this is not going to be possible if all insurers choose to settle on the same restrictions.) Moreover, it must be remembered that almost all American states have been able to publicly justify motorcycle helmet laws (largely by appealing to the harm principle), even though all of these states have basically privatized insurance systems.

6. *National Narcotics Intelligence Consumers Committee (NNICC) Report* (1987), pp. 27, 55. I am using an old report here because more recent studies indicate that heroin and cocaine use in the period between 1974 and 1993 peaked in the mid-1980s. See *National Household Survey on Drug Abuse: 1993* put out by the U.S. Substance Abuse and Mental Health Services Administration.

7. *1983 Annual Report* of the U.S. Consumer Product Safety Commission, Part II, p. 4. I am using an old report here just to provide a roughly contemporaneous basis of comparison for the 1987 NNICC figures.

8. Ibid., p. 5.

9. *NNICC Report* (1987), pp. 27, 55. These figures probably understate actual numbers and don't include statistics for New York City. However, the Consumer Product Safety Commission's report is based on figures that are incomplete for fifteen states (including New York).

10. Milton Friedman, "The Social Responsibility of Business Is to Increase Its Profits," *New York Times Magazine* (September 13, 1970): 32–33.

11. Mill, *On Liberty*, Chapter III, par. 16.

12. Adam Smith, *The Wealth of Nations* (New York: Random House, 1985), p. 388.

13. It is interesting to note that this argument cuts directly against one given by Ronald Reagan. He argued that the confusion about whether or not the fetus was a person should settle things in favor of the antiabortionist since the one and a half million abortions performed annually in this country *might* really be one and a half million murders. In other words, he was placing the burden of proof on the individual seeking an abortion, not on the state that might seek to outlaw the practice. See his *Abortion and the Conscience of the Nation* (Nashville: T. Nelson, 1984).

CHAPTER 8. POLITICAL CONSENT, INDIVIDUAL CHOICE, AND MORAL JUSTIFICATION

1. See Rawls's "Justice as Fairness: Political not Metaphysical," *Philosophy and Public Affairs* 14 (Summer 1985): 223–251.

2. Rawls, *A Theory of Justice* (Cambridge: Harvard University Press, 1971). See Chapter II, Sections 18 and 19.

3. See Rawls's "The Idea of an Overlapping Consensus," *Oxford Journal of Legal Studies* 7 (1987): 1–25.

4. In ibid.

5. For Mill it appears to be just a brute fact that there is agreement on the intrinsic value of happiness for individuals, and this, alone, is enough to secure the constructivist foundations. For me there is the added contractualist twist; the general will cannot be derived in a straightforward way from the will of all. I do not attribute the contractualist step to Mill.

6. For a small sampling of similar statements, see Carol Gilligan, *In a Different Voice* (Cambridge: Harvard University Press, 1982), pp. 64–69.

7. By "fact of the matter" I refer to the matter of *justification*. In other words I am making an epistemological, not a metaphysical, point. The issues of moral *truth* and *knowledge* are matters I care to say little about.

CHAPTER 9. EGOISM, ALTRUISM, VIRTUE

1. See Plato, *The Republic*, 441 d–e.

2. Ibid., 434 a–d.

3. I will be using the word "happiness" as though it were synonymous with "*eudaimonia*," even though the Greek conception of well-being is quite different from the concept of happiness as it has been developed by many modern philosophers.

4. Ibid., 359 b.

5. Stanley Milgram, *Obedience to Authority* (New York: Harper and Row Publishers, 1974).

6. See John Hospers, *Human Conduct*, shorter ed., (New York: Harcourt, Brace Jovanovich, Inc., 1972), p. 134.

7. Mill, *Autobiography*, p. 88.

8. Ibid.

9. See Aristotle, *Nichomachean Ethics*, Book X, 1179b31–1180a4.

10. David Hume, *A Treatise of Human Nature*, Book III, Part III, Section I.

CHAPTER 10. INDIVIDUALISM

1. Elster, *Sour Grapes: Studies in the Subversion of Rationality*, pp. 45–46.

2. This accounts for the wide gulf between the views of Plato (and Bentham as well), on the one hand, and Aristotle and Mill, on the other, with respect to art. All agreed that art inflames the emotions, but Plato and Bentham thought this was

bad whereas Aristotle and Mill both held that emotional maturity (which neither of them conceived of as the simple suppression of the emotions) was essential in the development of the good life.

CHAPTER 11. SUBLIMATION

1. Alexander Nehamas, *Nietzsche: Life as Literature* (Cambridge: Harvard University Press, 1985), p. 234.

2. Nietzsche, *Beyond Good and Evil*, Walter Kaufmann (trans.) (New York: Vintage Books, 1966), Section 12. See also Sections 481–492 in his *The Will to Power*, Walter Kaufmann (trans.) (New York: Vintage Books, 1968).

3. Sartre, for example, in *Existentialism as Humanism* (London: Methuen & Co., 1946) just drops a haphazard formulation of Kant's categorical imperative into his discussion without much explanation or any justification of the standard (see pp. 30–31).

4. See Nehamas, *Nietzsche: Life as Literature*, Chapter 7, as an example and for further references.

5. See Nietzsche, *The Will to Power*, Sections 508–544.

6. Hilary Putnam, *Reason, Truth and History* (New York: Cambridge University Press, 1981), p. 216.

7. Arthur Schopenhauer, *The World as Will and Idea*, R. B. Haldane and J. Kemp (trans.) (London: Trubner & Co., 1883), Volume I, Section 38.

8. Nietzsche, *On the Genealogy of Morals*, Walter Kaufmann (trans.) (New York: Vintage Books, 1967), Second Essay, Section 7.

9. Ibid., Second Essay, Sections 21–22.

10. Nietzsche, *The Will to Power*, Section 1021. This general line of argument comes from his Third Essay of *On the Genealogy of Morals*, Sections 24–28.

11. Nietzsche, *The Will to Power*, Section 1021.

12. Ibid., Section 78.

13. Ibid., Section 55.

14. Some of these occur in Ibid., Sections 1063, 1064, and 1066.

15. See Nehamas, *Nietzsche: Life as Literature*, Chapter 5.

16. Nietzsche, *Untimely Meditations*, R. J. Hollingdale (trans.) (New York: Cambridge University Press, 1983), Section III, 1.

17. Nietzsche, *Ecce Homo*, Walter Kaufmann (trans.) (New York: Vintage Books, 1968), Section II, 10.

18. *On the Genealogy of Morals*, First Essay, Section 13, emphasis added.

19. Ibid., emphasis added.

20. Nietzsche, *The Will to Power*, Section 517, emphasis added.

21. Ibid., Section 519.

22. See Parfit's *Reasons and Persons* (New York: Oxford University Press, 1984), pp. 209–217, for a discussion of this position.

23. Ibid., p. 216.

24. Nietzsche, *The Gay Science*, Walter Kaufmann (trans.) (New York: Vintage Books, 1974), Section 335.

25. Although the issue of identity at a time must, on Humean grounds, really be a species of the problem of identity over time, for, as Kant pointed out in the first *Critique*, impressions can only be apprehended in and over time.

26. Nietzsche, *On the Genealogy of Morals*, Preface, Section 5.

27. Ibid., emphasis on "sublimest" added.

28. Parfit, *Reasons and Persons*, p. 443.

29. Ibid., p. 329.

30. Nietzsche, *On the Genealogy of Morals*, Preface, Section 5.

CHAPTER 12. FRIENDSHIP, LOVE, MARRIAGE, AND GENDER

1. Perhaps, we are even capable of the sort of extreme altruism that Parfit (and Christ) endorses; perhaps we are really capable of loving our mere neighbors as ourselves. I am inclined to doubt this. Even Christians are careful to draw a distinction between *eros*, which is a feeling based on extreme *partiality* and prejudice in favor of the loved one, and *agape*, which is an *impartial* love of all humankind. We could love, in the sense of *eros*, all humankind only at the expense of turning it into *agape*. In this chapter I am going to be concerned only with *eros*.

2. See Aristotle's *Politics*, Book I, Chapter XIII.

3. John Stuart Mill, *The Subjection of Women* (Indianapolis: Hackett Publishing, 1988), p. 102.

4. Ibid., p. 98.

5. Ibid., p. 96.

6. Ibid., p. 100.

7. Ibid.

8. Ibid., p. 101.

9. Ibid., p. 103.

10. Ibid., p. 93.

11. See Carol Gilligan, *In a Different Voice*, and Annette Baier, "What Do Women Want in a Moral Theory?" *Nous* (March 1985): 53–63. Although this basic position has met with wide acceptance among feminist writers, it has also been met with considerable hostility from women who hold that what feminism ought to be is the position that there are no substantial *natural* differences between men that are at all relevant when it comes to aggressiveness, analytical hardheadedness, and other characteristics conducive to success in a competitive world. These women will argue that the idea that there is just something innately more kind and gentle about women than men is precisely the vehicle traditionally used by sexists to exclude women from various competitive domains. Similar paradoxes have occasionally arisen in other civil rights movements. For example, a certain segment of black activists (Malcolm X, at a certain point of his life, would be an example) have been intent on pointing out fundamental differences between blacks and whites that ought to be preserved even if that would require segregation and the creation of a separate black state. Other blacks would respond by pointing out that segregation was precisely the solution of the Ku Klux Klan.

12. However, it is not clear that things would be improved by falling into the converse error of resolving everything under some communitarian theory con-

structed out of feelings of partiality, familial love, care, or personal trust.

13. Nietzsche, *Ecce Homo*, Walter Kaufmann (trans.) (New York: Vintage Books, 1967), Section III, 5.

14. Nietzsche, *The Will to Power*, section 964.

15. Nietzsche, *Ecce Homo*, Section III, 5.

16. Nietzsche, *The Will to Power*, Section 296.

17. Ibid., Section 776.

18. Ibid., Section 808.

19. Ibid., Section 732.

20. At ibid., Section 732. See also his Section 39 of "Skirmishes of an Untimely Man" from *Twilight of the Idols* in *The Portable Nietzsche*, Walter Kaufmann (ed.) (New York: Viking Press, 1968) p. 544.

21. Nietzsche, "Skirmishes of an Untimely Man," Section 39.

22. In Bloom, *The Closing of the American Mind* (New York: Simon and Schuster, 1987), pp. 97–108.

23. Nietzsche, *The Will to Power*, Section 453.

24. This axiom is obvious in the writings of postmodern feminists. Perhaps the clearest case of the move to sort science into the realm of narrative is Donna Haraway. See her *Primate Visions* (New York: Routledge, 1989).

25. Jaggar's examination of "radical feminism" appears in her *Feminist Politics and Human Nature* (Totowa, N.J.: Rowman and Allanhled, 1983). The core of disagreement between radical feminists and Marxist feminists concerns whether sexist oppression is (as Marxists have held) an outgrowth of economic class oppression or, rather, a more basic form of oppression tied directly to male control of women's fertility and sexuality. What Jaggar calls "socialist feminism" attempts to be an integration of Marxist and radical feminism. Marxist, radical, and social feminism along with liberal feminism constitute the four forms of feminism delineated by Jaggar.

26. Haraway, *Primate Visions*, pp. 256–257. The reference to Harding concerns Harding's "Why Has the Sex/Gender System Become Visible Only Now?" in S. Harding and M. Hintikka, *Discovering Reality* (Dordrecht: Reidel, 1983).

CHAPTER 13. ANTHROPOCENTRISM AND ECOCENTRISM

1. Passmore, *Man's Responsibility for Nature* (London: Gerald Duckworth & Co., 1980).

2. Callicott, *In Defense of the Land Ethic* (Albany: SUNY Press, 1989).

3. Naess, *Ecology, Community and Lifestyle*, D. Rothenberg (trans.) (New York: Cambridge, 1989).

4. Rodman, "Ecological Sensibility," in Susan Armstrong and Richard Botzler (eds.), *Environmental Ethics* (New York: McGraw-Hill, 1993), pp. 383, 384.

5. Rolston, "Values in Nature," *Environmental Ethics* 3 (1981): 113–128.

6. Stone, *Should Trees Have Standing? Toward Legal Rights for Natural Objects* (Los Altos: William Kaufmann, Inc., 1974).

7. Leopold, *A Sand County Almanac* (New York: Oxford University Press, 1981).

8. For a discussion of the terms "extensionism," "first-stage extensionism," and "second-stage extensionism," see Callicott's "The Search for an Environmental Ethic," in Tom Regan (ed.), *Matters of Life and Death* (New York: Random House, 1986), pp. 381–424.

9. See Bentham, *Principles of Morals and Legislation*, Chapter XVII, Section 1.

10. Feinberg, "The Rights of Animals and Unborn Generations," in W. T. Blackstone (ed.), *Philosophy and Environmental Crisis* (Athens: University of Georgia Press, 1974) pp. 43–68.

11. Regan, *The Case for Animal Rights* (Berkeley: University of California Press, 1983).

12. Singer, *Animal Liberation* (New York: Avon Books, 1977).

13. Schweitzer, *Philosophy of Civilization: Civilization and Ethics*, John Naish (trans.) (London: A. & C. Black Co., 1923).

14. Taylor, *Respect for Nature* (Princeton: Princeton University Press, 1986).

15. This line of argument has been made by Kenneth Goodpaster in "On Being Morally Considerable," *Journal of Philosophy* LXXV (1978): 308–325.

16. See Myers, *The Sinking Ark* (Oxford: Pergamon Press, 1980), pp. 3–31.

17. Regan, *The Case for Animal Rights*, p. 362.

18. This suggestion is made (argumentatively) by William Aiken, "Ethical Issues in Agriculture," in Tom Regan (ed.), *Earthbound: New Introductory Essays in Environmental Ethics* (New York: Random House, 1984), p. 269.

19. In Callicott, *In Defense of the Land Ethic*, pp. 15–38.

20. In *Osgood Hall Law Journal* (1984): 297–307.

CHAPTER 14. MODERNIST BIOCENTRISM
AND ECOCENTRISM

1. The tag "animal rights" is to be separated from Singer's "animal liberationism" because Singer, being a utilitarian, is suspicious about any theory that takes rights as fundamental, whether it be a theory that is supposed to apply to animals or just humans. In the previous chapter, I lumped Regan in with the animal liberationists because this term seems to cover both Singer and Regan, whereas the "animal rights" tag would not include Singer even though both he and Regan are primarily concerned with the extension of direct moral considerability to animals.

2. John Rodman, "Ecological Sensibility."

3. Ibid., p. 384.

4. Callicott, *In Defense of the Land Ethic*, p. 27. The article anthologized is "Animal Liberation: A Triangular Affair" (originally published in *Environmental Ethics* in 1980). Callicott is using the word "biocentric" as an equivalent of "ecocentric"; this is before biocentrism came to be standardly associated with the *individualistic* position of Schweitzer and Taylor.

5. Tom Regan, "The Case for Animal Rights," in S. Armstrong and R. Botzler (eds.), *Environmental Ethics*, p. 327.

6. Darwin, *Descent of Man*, 2nd ed. (New York: J. A. Hill, 1904), p. 107.

7. See Hardin's "The Tragedy of the Commons," *Science* 162 (1968): 1243–1248, and his "Living in a Lifeboat," *BioScience* 24 (1974): 561–568.

8. Adam Smith, *The Wealth of Nations*, p. 225.

CHAPTER 15. POSTMODERN ECOCENTRISM
AND ECOFEMINISM

1. Jim Cheney, "Postmodern Environmental Ethics: Ethics as Bioregional Narrative," *Environmental Ethics* 11 (Summer 1989): 117–118.

2. Ibid., pp. 119–120.

3. Ibid., p. 132.

4. Ibid., p. 118.

5. Ibid.

6. Karen Warren, "The Power and Promise of Ecological Feminism," *Environmental Ethics* 12 (Summer 1990): 125–146.

7. Marti Kheel, "Ecofeminism and Deep Ecology: Reflections on Identity and Difference," in I. Diamond and G. Orenstein (eds.), *Reweaving the World: The Emergence of Ecofeminism* (San Francisco: Sierra Club Books, 1990).

8. Warwick Fox, in particular has wondered, "Why doesn't she [Warren] just call it [her ecofeminist position] deep ecology? Why specifically attach the label *feminist* to it . . . ?" (Fox, "The Deep Ecology—Ecofeminism Debate and Its Parallels," *Environmental Ethics* 11 [Winter 1989]: 5–25). Without going into a serious analysis of the deep ecology of Fox or others (like Sessions, Devall, and Naess), let me just assert that, generally, deep ecology is close enough to what I am calling postmodern ecocentrism to make the point I am making, even though the positions of Sessions, Devall, and Naess strain to make use of distinctly modern philosophers like Spinoza.

9. Callicott, "The Case Against Moral Pluralism," *Environmental Ethics* 12 (Summer 1990): 117n.

10. Paul Gross and Norman Levitt, *Higher Superstition: The Academic Left and Its Quarrels with Science* (Baltimore: Johns Hopkins, 1994) pp. 255–256.

11. Callicott, "The Case Against Moral Pluralism," pp. 119–120.

12. Warren and Cheney, "Ecological Feminism and Ecosystem Ecology," *Hypatia* 6 (Spring 1991): 179–197.

13. Gross and Levitt, *Higher Superstition*, p. 79.

14. Ibid., p. 254

15. Ibid., p. 255

16. Warren and Cheney, "Ecological Feminism and Ecosystem Ecology," p. 182 (and p. 194, n. 8).

17. Ibid., p. 183.

18. Ibid., p. 193, n. 4.

19. Ibid., p. 190.

20. Eckersley, *Environmentalism and Political Theory* (Albany: SUNY Press, 1992), p. 51.

21. It is interesting to note that the challenges that postmoderns have become most agitated about have had nothing at all to do with anything relating to the content or sensibility of their position. Rather they are concerned about the political incorrectness of the leaders of postmodernism. Specifically, they are concerned about the fact that Paul de Man and Heidegger (Derrida's hero) were Nazis. Derrida, quite embarrassingly, attempted to defend both of his cohorts in the pages of the *New York Review of Books* (February 11, 1993, and March 23, 1993).

CHAPTER 16. WRONGNESS AND WILDERNESS

1. Callicott, "Animal Liberation: A Triangular Affair," in his *In Defense of the Land Ethic* (Albany: SUNY Press, 1989), p. 33.

2. Callicott, "The Search for an Environmental Ethic," in *Matters of Life and Death*, Tom Regan (ed.) (New York: McGraw-Hill, 1993), p. 359.

3. Eckersley, *Environmentalism and Political Theory*, p. 52.

4. McLaughlin, *Regarding Nature* (Albany: SUNY Press, 1993) p. 144.

5. See, for example, R. V. O'Neill et. al., *A Hierarchical Concept of Ecosystems* (Princeton: Princeton University Press, 1886), p. 94.

6. Postmodernists, of course, don't have to worry about whether or not their theories are compatible with anything scientific unless, for some reason, science becomes politically correct or some of its results can be of use to attack something modernist. The latter seems to be behind the use made of ecosystem ecology by Warren and Cheney to attack Callicott in their "Ecosystem Ecology and Metaphysical Ecology: A Case Study," *Environmental Ethics* 15 (Summer 1993): 99–116.

7. Cahen, *Environmental Ethics* 10 (Fall 1988): 195–216.

8. See Dawkins, *The Selfish Gene* (New York: Oxford, 1976). Superindividualism is, of course, as much a threat to individualism as it is to holism. Cahen responds to this threat as follows: "Cells [or genes] do have their own goals, but these goals are largely subordinated to the organism's goals, because natural selection selects *bodies*, not cells. If the cells do not cooperate for the body's sake, the body dies and the cells die, too. That, very roughly, is how natural selection coordinates the body's activities" (p. 211). A similar position is taken by Elliot Sober in *The Nature of Selection: Evolutionary Theory in Philosophical Focus* (Cambridge: MIT Press, 1984) and Stephen Jay Gould in *The Panda's Thumb* (New York: Norton & Co., 1980), Chapter 8.

9. Callicott could try to dodge the bullets fired by current ecological science by moving in the way he does in his "Metaphysical Implications of Ecology," in his *In Defense of the Land Ethic*, pp. 101–114. There he claims that he is not interested in arguing that his holism is *logically* entailed by contemporary science but, rather, that holism is "complemented" by and "consistent" with the "new ecology" (and the "new physics") as well. Critics like Cahen would argue that complementarity and consistency aren't even in the cards for Callicott's holism.

CHAPTER 17. WISDOM AND WILDERNESS

1. Norton, *Toward Unity Among Environmentalists* (New York: Oxford University Press, 1991), p. 227. It does no damage to Norton's point to substitute "ecocentrists" for "deep ecologists."

2. Guha, "Radical American Environmentalism and Wilderness Preservation: A Third World Critique," *Environmental Ethics* 11 (Spring 1989): 71–83.

3. Callicott, "The Metaphysical Implications of Ecology," in his *In Defense of the Land Ethic*, pp. 112–114.

4. Cheney, "Postmodern Environmental Ethics: Ethics as Bioregional Narrative," p. 127.

5. Ibid., p. 126.

6. Thoreau, "Walking," in S. Armstrong and R. Botzler (eds.), *Environmental Ethics*, pp. 108, 110.

7. Cheney, "Postmodern Environmental Ethics: Ethics as Bioregional Narrative," p. 127, emphasis added.

8. Such an attempt is made by William Chaloupka in "John Dewey's Social Aesthetics as a Precedent for Environmental Thought," *Environmental Ethics* 9 (Fall 1987): 243–259, and critiqued by Bob Pepperman Taylor in "John Dewey and Environmental Thought: A Response to Chaloupka," *Environmental Ethics* 12 (Summer 1990): 173–184. Section III of Taylor's paper seems, to me, quite telling against Chaloupka. There Taylor points out what is pretty obvious about Dewey's general system, namely, that Dewey was an instrumentalist who held some fairly standard anthropocentric views about how the progress of humanity could be measured by the degree to which it had subdued and manipulated the environment to its own ends.

9. Dewey, *Experience and Nature* (New York: Dover, 1958), p. 79.

BIBLIOGRAPHY

Agee, Philip. *Inside the Company: CIA Diary*. New York: Stonehill Publishing, 1975.

———. *Dirty Work*. Secaucus: Lyle Stuart Inc., 1978.

Aiken, William. "Ethical Issues in Agriculture." In *Earthbound: New Introductory Essays in Environmental Ethics*. Ed. Tom Regan. New York: Random House, 1984, pp. 247–288.

Armstrong, Susan, and Botzler, Richard, eds. *Environmental Ethics*. New York: McGraw-Hill, 1993.

Aristotle. *Nichomachean Ethics*. Trans. David Ross. New York: Oxford University Press, 1925.

———. *Politics*. Trans. Ernest Barker. New York: Oxford University Press, 1946.

Baier, Annette. "What Do Women Want in a Moral Theory?" *Nous* (March 1985): 53–63.

Barry, Brian. "Lady Chatterley's Lover and Doctor Fischer's Bomb Party: Liberalism, Pareto Optimality, and the Problem of Objectionable Preferences." In Elster and Hylland, 1989, pp. 11–43.

Bentham, Jeremy. *Principles of Morals and Legislation*. Oxford: 1789.

Bloom, Allan. *The Closing of the American Mind*. New York: Simon and Schuster, 1987.

Cahen, Harley. "Against the Moral Considerability of Ecosystems." *Environmental Ethics* 10 (Fall 1988): 195–216.

Callicott, J. Baird. "The Search for an Environmental Ethic." In *Matters of Life and Death*. Ed. Tom Regan. New York: Random House, 1986, pp. 381–424.

———. *In Defense of the Land Ethic*. Albany: SUNY Press, 1989.

———. "The Case Against Moral Pluralism." *Environmental Ethics* 12 (Summer 1990): 99–124.

Chaloupka, William. "John Dewey's Social Aesthetics as a Precedent for Environmental Thought." *Environmental Ethics* 9 (Fall 1987): 243–259.

Cheney, Jim. "Postmodern Environmental Ethics: Ethics as Bioregional Narrative." *Environmental Ethics* 11 (Summer 1989): 117–118.

Darwin, Charles. *Descent of Man*. 2nd ed. New York: J. A. Hill, 1904.

Dawkins, Richard. *The Selfish Gene*. New York: Oxford University Press, 1976.

Dewey, John. *Art as Experience*. New York: Minton, Balch, 1934.

———. *Experience and Nature*. New York: Dover, 1958.

Eckersley, Robyn. *Environmentalism and Political Theory*. Albany: SUNY Press, 1992.

Elster, Jon. "The Market and the Forum: Three Varieties of Political Theory." In Elster and Hylland, 1989, pp. 103–132.

———. *Sour Grapes: Studies in the Subversion of Rationality*. New York: Cambridge University Press, 1983.

Elster, Jon, and Hylland, A., eds. *Foundations of Social Choice Theory*. New York: Cambridge University Press, 1989.

Feinberg, Joel. "'Harmless Immoralities' and Offensive Nuisances." In *Issues in Law and Morality*. Cleveland: Case Western Reserve University Press, 1973, pp. 99–134.

———. "The Rights of Animals and Unborn Generations." In *Philosophy and Environmental Crisis*. Ed. W. T. Blackstone. Athens: University of Georgia Press, 1974, pp. 43–68.

———. *Harmless Wrongdoing*. New York: Oxford, 1988.

———. *Harm to Others*. New York: Oxford, 1984.

———. *Offense to Others*. New York: Oxford, 1988.

Fox, Warwick. "The Deep Ecology—Ecofeminism Debate and Its Parallels." *Environmental Ethics* 11 (Winter 1989): 5–25.

Friedman, Milton. "The Social Responsibility of Business Is to Increase Its Profits." *New York Times Magazine* (September 13, 1970): 32–33.

Gilligan, Carol. *In a Different Voice*. Cambridge: Harvard University Press, 1982.

Goodpaster, Kenneth. "On Being Morally Considerable." *Journal of Philosophy* LXXV (1978): 308–325.

Gould, Stephen Jay. *The Panda's Thumb*. New York: Norton & Co., 1980.

Gross, Paul, and Levitt, Norman. *Higher Superstition: The Academic Left and Its Quarrels with Science*. Baltimore: Johns Hopkins, 1994.

Guha, Ramachandra. "Radical American Environmentalism and Wilderness Preservation: A Third World Critique." *Environmental Ethics* 11 (Spring 1989): 71–83.

Haraway, Donna. *Primate Visions*. New York: Routledge, 1989.

Hardin, Garrett. "The Tragedy of the Commons." *Science* 162 (1968): 1243–1248.

———. "Living in a Lifeboat." *BioScience* 24 (1974): 561–568.

Harding, Sandra. "Why Has the Sex/Gender System Become Visible Only Now?" In *Discovering Reality*. Eds. Sandra Harding and Merrill Hintikka. Dordrecht: Reidel, 1983, pp. 311–324.

Harrison, Jonathan. "Utilitarianism, Universalization, and Our Duty to Be Just." *PAS* 53 (1952–53): 105–134.

Harsanyi, John. "Rule Utilitarianism and Decision Theory." *Erkenntnis* 11 (1977): 25–53.

———. "Cardinal Welfare, Individualistic Ethics, and Interpersonal Comparisons of Utility." *Journal of Political Economy* 63 (1955): 309–321.

Hart, H. L. A. *Law, Liberty and Morality*. Stanford: Stanford University Press, 1963.

"The H-Bomb Secret." *Progressive* 43 (November, 1979): 6–8, 14–45.

Hospers, John. *Human Conduct*. Shorter ed. New York: Harcourt, Brace Jovanovich, Inc., 1972.

Hume, David. *A Treatise of Human Nature*. London: 1740.

Hylland, Aanund. "The Purpose and Significance of Social Choice Theory: Some General Remarks and an Application to the 'Lady Chatterly Problem.'" In Elster and Hylland, 1989, pp. 45–74.

Jaggar, Alison. *Feminist Politics and Human Nature.* Totowa, N.J.: Rowman and Allanhled, 1983.

Kant, Immanuel. *Perpetual Peace and Other Essays.* Ed. and trans. Ted Humphrey. Indianapolis: Hackett Publishing, 1983.

Kheel, Marti. "Ecofeminism and Deep Ecology: Reflections on Identity and Difference." In *Reweaving the World: The Emergence of Ecofeminism.* Eds. Irene Diamond and Gloria Orenstein. San Francisco: Sierra Club Books, 1990, pp. 128–137.

Leopold, Aldo. *A Sand County Almanac.* New York: Oxford University Press, 1981.

Lyons, David. *Forms and Limits of Utilitarianism.* New York: Oxford University Press, 1965.

Macaulay, Lord Thomas. "Notes on the Indian Penal Code." In *Works,* vol. 9. New York: Houghton, Mifflin & Co., 1900, pp. 551–734.

Marx, Karl. *The German Ideology.* Ed. C. J. Arthur. New York: International Publishers, 1978.

Marzorati, Gerald. "Europe Recycles American Liberalism." *New York Times* (July 7, 1990): I, 23.

McLaughlin, Andrew. *Regarding Nature.* Albany: SUNY Press, 1993.

Milgram, Stanley. *Obedience to Authority.* New York: Harper and Row Publishers, 1974.

Mill, John Stuart. *On Liberty.* London: 1859.

———. *Autobiography.* In *The Essential Works of John Stuart.* Ed. Max Lerner. New York: Bantam Books, 1963, pp. 1–182.

———. "Bentham." In *Mill's Essays on Literature and Society.* Ed. J. B. Schneewind. New York: Macmillan Company, 1965, pp. 240–289.

———. *The Subjection of Women.* Indianapolis: Hackett Publishing, 1988.

———. *Utilitarianism.* London: 1863.

Myers, Norman. *The Sinking Ark.* Oxford: Pergamon Press, 1980.

Naess, Arne. *Ecology, Community and Lifestyle.* Trans. D. Rothenberg. New York: Cambridge, 1989.

National Narcotics Intelligence Consumers Committee (NNICC) Report. Washington: NNICC, 1987.

Nehamas, Alexander. *Nietzsche: Life as Literature.* Cambridge: Harvard University Press, 1985.

Nietzsche, Friedrich. *Beyond Good and Evil.* Trans. Walter Kaufmann. New York: Vintage Books, 1966.

———. *On the Genealogy of Morals.* Trans. Walter Kaufmann. New York: Vintage Books, 1967.

———. *Ecce Homo.* Trans. Walter Kaufmann. New York: Vintage Books, 1968.

———. "Skirmishes of an Untimely Man" from *Twilight of the Idols.* In *The Portable Nietzsche.* Ed. and trans. Walter Kauffmann. New York: Viking Press, 1968, pp. 463–564.

———. *The Will to Power.* Trans. Walter Kaufmann. New York: Vintage Books, 1968.

———. *The Gay Science.* Trans. Walter Kaufmann. New York: Vintage Books, 1974.

————. *Untimely Meditations.* Trans. R. J. Hollingdale. New York: Cambridge University Press, 1983.

Norton, Bryan. *Toward Unity Among Environmentalists.* New York: Oxford, 1991.

Nozick, Robert. *Anarchy, State and Utopia.* New York: Basic Books, 1974.

O'Neill, R. V., et al. *A Hierarchical Concept of Ecosystems.* Princeton: Princeton University Press, 1886.

Parfit, Derek. "On Doing the Best for Our Children." In *Ethics and Population.* Ed. M. D. Bayles. Cambridge, MA: Schenkman, 1976, pp. 100–115.

————. *Reasons and Persons.* New York: Oxford University Press, 1984.

————. "Overpopulation and the Quality of Life." *Utilitarianism and Its Critics.* Ed. Jonathan Glover. New York: Macmillan, 1990, pp. 134–150.

Passmore, John. *Man's Responsibility for Nature.* London: Gerald Duckworth & Co., 1980.

Plato. *The Republic.* Trans. G. M. A. Grube and C. D. C. Reeve. Indianapolis: Hackett, 1992.

Putnam, Hilary. *Reason, Truth and History.* New York: Cambridge University Press, 1981.

Rawls, John. *A Theory of Justice.* Cambridge: Harvard University Press, 1971.

————. "Justice as Fairness: Political not Metaphysical." *Philosophy and Public Affairs* 14 (Summer 1985): 223–251.

————. "The Idea of an Overlapping Consensus." *Oxford Journal of Legal Studies* 7 (1987): 1–25.

Reagan, Ronald. *Abortion and the Conscience of the Nation.* Nashville: T. Nelson, 1984.

Regan, Tom. *The Case for Animal Rights.* Berkeley: University of California Press, 1983.

Rescher, Nicholas. *Distributive Justice: A Constructive Critique of the Utilitarian Theory of Distribution.* Indianapolis: Bobbs-Merrill, 1968.

Rodman, John. "Ecological Sensibility." In Armstrong and Botzler, 1993, pp. 382–386.

Rolston III, Holmes. "Values in Nature." *Environmental Ethics* 3 (1981): 113–128.

Sagoff, Mark. "Animal Liberation and Environmental Ethics: Bad Marriage, Quick Divorce." *Osgood Hall Law Journal* (1984): 297–307.

Sartre, Jean Paul. *Existentialism as Humanism.* London: Methuen & Co., 1946.

Schopenhauer, Arthur. *The World as Will and Idea.* Trans. R. B. Haldane and J. Kemp. London: Trubner & Co., 1883.

Schweitzer, Albert. *Philosophy of Civilization: Civilization and Ethics.* Trans. John Naish. London: A. & C. Black Co., 1923).

Scriven, Tal. "Utility, Autonomy and Drug Regulation." *International Journal of Applied Philosophy* 2 (Fall 1984): 27–42.

————. "Plato's 'Democratic Man' and the Implausibility of Preference Utilitarianism." *Theory and Decision* 24 (1988): 43–55.

Sen, A. K. *Collective Choice and Social Welfare.* San Francisco: Holden-Day, 1970.

Sen, A. K., and Runciman, W. G. "Games, Justice and the General Will." *Mind* 74 (1965): 554–562.

Singer, Peter. *Animal Liberation*. New York: Avon Books, 1977.

Smith, Adam. *The Wealth of Nations*. New York: Random House, 1985.

Sober, Elliot. *The Nature of Selection: Evolutionary Theory in Philosophical Focus*. Cambridge: MIT Press, 1984.

Stone, Christopher. *Should Trees Have Standing? Toward Legal Rights for Natural Objects*. Los Altos: William Kaufmann, Inc., 1974.

Taylor, Bob Pepperman. "John Dewey and Environmental Thought: A Response to Chaloupka." *Environmental Ethics* 12 (Summer 1990): 173–184.

Taylor, Paul. *Respect for Nature*. Princeton: Princeton University Press, 1986.

Taylor, Richard. *Good and Evil*. New York: Macmillan Company, 1970.

Thoreau, Henry David. "Walking." In Armstrong and Botzler, 1993, pp. 108–118.

U.S. Consumer Product Safety Commission. *1983 Annual Report*. Washington: U.S. Consumer Product Safety Commission, 1983.

Warren, Karen. "The Power and Promise of Ecological Feminism." *Environmental Ethics* 12 (Summer 1990): 125–146.

Warren, Karren, and Cheney, Jim. "Ecological Feminism and Ecosystem Ecology." *Hypatia* 6 (Spring 1991): 179–197.

———. "Ecosystem Ecology and Metaphysical Ecology: A Case Study." *Environmental Ethics* 15 (Summer 1993): 99–116.

Woozley, A. D. "Law and the Legislation of Morality." In *Ethics in Hard Times*. Eds. A. L. Caplan and D. Callahan. New York: Plenum, 1981, pp. 143–174.

INDEX